D1370011

THE
BUSINESS
OF
PHYSICAL
EDUCATION

Michael J. Ellis, PhD
University of Oregon

Human Kinetics Books
Champaign, Illinois

Library of Congress Cataloging-in-Publication Data

Ellis, Michael J., 1936-
  The business of physical education.

  Bibliography: p.
  Includes index.
  1. Physical education and training—United States.
  2. Physical education teachers—United States.
  I. Title.
  GV223.E44   1988   613.7'07'073   87-17344
  ISBN 0-87322-127-3

Senior Editor: Gwen Steigelman, PhD
Production Director: Ernie Noa
Projects Manager: Lezli Harris
Copy Editor: Lise Rodgers
Assistant Editor: Julie Anderson
Typesetter: Yvonne Winsor
Text Design: Keith Blomberg
Text Layout: Denise Mueller
Cover Design: C.J. Petlick, Hunter Graphics
Printed By: Braun-Brumfield

Data for Figures 6.2, 6.3a, and 6.3b are from Teacher Supply/Demand
1985, James N. Akin, Kansas State University

ISBN: 0-87322-127-3

Printed in the United States of America

10 9 8 7 6 5 4 3 2 1

Human Kinetics Books
A Division of Human Kinetics Publishers, Inc.
Box 5076, Champaign, IL 61820

1-800-DIAL-HKP
1-800-334-3665 (in Illinois)

To Jack and Cath who went before,
To David and Stephanie who will follow,
And especially to Margaret with whom I have traveled so far

Acknowledgments————

While the ideas herein are my responsibility, no book occurs without the help of others. I would like to acknowledge and thank Shirl Hoffman, University of North Carolina at Greensboro, and Hal Lawson, Miami University, for their insightful reviews and helpful suggestions. I acknowledge also the contributions of past colleagues at Loughborough University, University of Illinois, and Dalhousie University with whom I struggled to learn about physical education. My current colleagues at the University of Oregon have been especially influential because together we have worked through the first wave of the major disturbances to influence physical education that are discussed in the book. Kris Nickerson, of Kinko's, used his compliant Macintosh to prepare the diagrams; Diane Baxter, a faculty colleague, did the photography; and Tom Rowney, a doctoral student in physical education at Oregon at the time, read the early drafts and suggested many helpful revisions. Margaret Ellis was most helpful in the proofreading and indexing process. Finally, I would like to acknowledge the effort and insight of Gwen Steigelman, the senior editor behind this book. This book is much the better for her interest and skill. By a wonderful twist of fate, I had served on Gwen's doctoral committee years ago and for this project the roles were reversed. On both occasions it was a pleasure to work with Gwen.

I thank you all.

Acknowledgments

*Contents*_____

*Preface*_____

This book is about the business of physical education, and the word *business* in the title has two meanings. The first meaning implies the proper goals, missions, and activities of the field—what physical education does. The second meaning suggests *how* physical education will meet these goals and carry out these missions. During the next two decades physical education will make the transformation from a social service supported almost exclusively by public sector taxation to a service industry that earns its way largely by selling personal services as part of the broad retail market. Physical education will be increasingly driven by the forces of the marketplace to become more of a business.

The goal of this book is to survey the socioeconomic context of physical education. It presents a sketch of the roots of the field, and by relating the field to the changing nature of the society in which it exists, seeks to predict the nature of the profession, its content, and its relation to society in the future. It assembles in one place a large body of facts and projections. It presents scenarios, or pictures of conditions, that are likely to work upon us as we shape our professional future.

The likelihoods and prognoses presented here are the product of a set of selected data filtered through my specific experiences. I entered physical education in the 1950s, and then taught health and physical education in schools and leisure studies and physical education in universities. I entered graduate school in the fall of 1964. This occurred just after a major challenge to the field made by Franklin Henry (1964) in a speech to the national convention that winter. Henry, a distinguished curmudgeon from Berkeley, challenged the field to respond to the allegations made by Conant (1963), then President of Harvard, that physical education had no substance and should be curtailed. Henry argued that physical education was capable of being a discipline, but that it would have to come out of isolation and behave like other disciplines, that is, build a body of unique knowledge about human movement to support the profession. The original allegations and the recommendations made by Henry captured the field's attention. They became the focus for the redirection of the field as people all over the nation responded. University physical education is what it is today in part because of Henry's visions for its development.

My experiences in graduate school and my early career were influenced dramatically by the responses made by the field as a whole to Henry's challenge. As was expected at the time, I went on to do the research for which my degree prepared me. I conducted research full-time through the affluent 1960s and early 1970s. I then entered administration in time to learn the special skills required to manage during times of declining resources.

Thus, in a sense, the view of the health, activity, and leisure industry I present in this book is that of an entrant to the field during the early sixties. I am one of the early post-Henry physical educators who was accorded the opportunity of diverging from the traditional role of physical educator as schoolteacher or teacher educator. Also be warned of a further bias. I am an optimist with a firm belief in the creativity and imagination of people stretched by circumstance.

The specificity of my experiences is a major threat to the validity of the scenarios, opinions, and prognoses threaded throughout the text. The reader should be cautious. However, rejection of a scenario should carry with it the responsibility for recombining the objective data provided here with the reader's subjective experiences into new scenarios, which are more likely to explain things for them. My scenarios can be considered examples. Readers should substitute their own personal expectations if they are uncomfortable with mine.

The book is organized conventionally into chapters that can stand by themselves. Each is in a sense an essay. However, the essays relate to each other because they are explorations of the future of different but complementary aspects of the field. Taken together, they form a prescription for the reintegration of physical education with allied fields on the one hand and clients on the other, so that the field may thrive despite the turmoil of change that besets it.

The first two chapters set the scene by showing that physical education is embedded in the wider society and is changed by it. They indicate that the problems for contemporary physical education are rooted in massive forces that have developed in society at large. Chapters 3 and 4 deal with specifics. Chapter 3 discusses the changing demography and geography of the U.S.A. as sources of influence on the field. Then, chapter 4 charts the effects that the reorganization of the health care industry is likely to have on physical education and its neighboring fields. Chapters 5 through 7 discuss the changes occurring within physical education itself. The effects of an aging America and an increasing concern for marketing the technologies of physical education to adults as part of the emerging service economy are dissected here. Chapter 8 proposes models for physical education that will carry it though its next phase of development. The last chapter closes the book with a summary of the major challenges and opportunities just ahead.

What, then, does the future hold for physical education? Join forces with me and look for answers among the ideas in this book.

Michael J. Ellis

Introduction

This book is a commentary on the future contribution of physical education to the enhancement of health and the enjoyment of life in North America. It is about the partnership between the clients who make myriad lifestyle decisions affecting their health and their enjoyment of it and the physical educators who use sport, dance, exercise, and play to facilitate the process.

Physical education is the cluster of public and private sector enterprises that attempt to use structured physical activity to aid in the development and conservation of people and to improve their quality of life. This book projects the future for physical education and is a manifesto for change in the field. It offers advice to professionals already working in all aspects of the industry that uses physical activity in all its forms to enhance the experience of its clients. The book will also assist students who are about to enter physical education to understand the forces at work to change the field.

Individual lifestyle decisions made by the people of North America in the interests of both their personal health and the enjoyment of their lives are changing. These changes will alter the jobs of those who serve the public by providing activity and leisure services. For those professionals engaged in the activity and leisure service industry, these changes will play a large role in the near future.

Lawson (1984) argues that problem-*setting*, rather than problem-*solving*, is a major determinant of a profession's functioning. Professionals are expected to monitor the circumstances troubling society and frame those problems in such a way that solutions can be sought. This is a critical reflective activity, which requires an ability to edit and select; in other words, problem-setting requires wisdom and guidance. Physical education finds itself in an era of change. Its old problems and solutions are no longer so clear. The old imperatives that sustained physical education are changing as society races toward new formats. The principal problem facing physical education today lies not in finding solutions—we have an armamentarium of recipes, techniques, and tools—but in framing the problems that society would have us solve. For example, physical educators have been concerned with questions about how much physical activity was possible (i.e., elite performance), yet it is now important to determine how little activity is enough. The field would have been different today if the second question had guided the field rather than the first.

In this connection Lawson warns,

> The maintenance of professional status depends on a profession's ability to address problems that are important, complex, and uncertain in the eyes of laypersons, and whose solutions cannot be reduced to a recipe-like routine anyone can master. If these preconditions for professionalization change, then deprofessionalization begins. . . . Consequently, a profession's failure to engage in problem setting and to respond to social change brings serious consequences. Aside from decreased effectiveness, the profession runs the risk of deprofessionalization, bringing declining opportunities for employment. (1984, p. 51)

This book is a concerted effort to set problems for physical education and to assist the profession in finding the important, complex, and uncertain problems that exist in our society and that we can help solve. It is targeted at one set of professionals, physical educators, working in the two major divisions of the activity and leisure industry. One group of physical educators is interested in the effects of physical activity on life quality and on health. The second major group is interested in making provision for leisure, recognizing that physical activity makes up much of its content. The interests of these two major groups overlap in that leisure has major effects on health, both mental and physical. Both groups attempt to change people's understanding of the relationships between their lifestyle and their health. Furthermore, they overlap with the neighboring professional specialities of recreation and health education.

Because of the overlapping of interests this book often raises issues and concerns that some health educators and recreators would argue are not the business of physical education. Yet, as the issues unfold, it will become clear that larger forces in the society will force a rethinking of the current boundaries between the three neighboring professional groups: physical education, health education, and recreation.

Health educators, physical educators, and recreators are practicing today much as they have done for decades, yet dramatic changes are underway in our society. These established occupations will have to take rapid action to avoid being caught flat-footed by new professions and businesses springing up in response to change.

The text presents data, examples, and opinions about the changing circumstances in the wider society. Its goal is to produce a compendium of insights that will provide a platform from which professionals, aspiring and established, may prepare for their futures. It raises questions about schools, the public and private sectors, competing industries, paraprofessionals, the content of the field, and the future of sport. All are debated against a backdrop of the many bewildering social and economic changes that are emerging from our rapid evolution into a postindustrial society. It presents starkly the notion that physical education is a service industry engaged in retailing activity and leisure services to individuals and that, without markets for its professional expertise, physical education will cease to exist.

The next two decades will see massive changes as North America accelerates toward a service-dominated economy. Each physical educator concerned about being effective and valued—about surviving in the activity and leisure service industry—needs to prepare for the changes that are breaking over us all. Each professional needs a personal, long-term plan that is based on the projected state of the industry during the next two decades. This book attempts to tell professionals what is needed. It is intended to challenge readers to take the actions necessary for survival either by following the author's prescriptions or by creating their own.

Readers may not like all the advice offered. Assumptions that may have worked for decades will be questioned during the decades ahead, resulting in a call for professional practices to change. The call for changes will polarize the groups involved. Some will try even harder to make established practices work. They will run into rival programs and professionals eager to show that the old must be given up. These clashes will be part of professional life in the industry for the rest of the century. The ideas in this book will likely contribute to the furor.

Analyses are projected into the future as often as possible because preparation for future agility is part of today's professionalism. The stimulation of an effort to plan for future professional agility is the goal of this book. Uncertainties inherent to predicting the future lead directly to the question, "Why bother?" The answer is simple. The future can, to a significant extent, be determined. A frequent source of countertrends that dampen, accelerate, reverse, or change existing trends is that people, recognizing problems, take action to alter the outcomes. We must accept that we are largely responsible for our own future.

*Physical Education: Youth Service or Adult Business?*_____

Many facets of our lives together are changing. Although all periods in the history of humankind have brought change, there is now widespread belief that the rate of social change is accelerating. World population is growing, and the pressures upon us to apply technological advances to the unique problems of our time are intensifying. We all too often find that earlier solutions were applied simplistically, or that what were once considered to be solutions instead have become new problems. The sheer magnitude of the change we are faced with has become a problem in itself as people are forced to adjust rapidly within their lifetimes rather than across the generations. The memories of people in nearly every North American family encompass some of the most startling changes that have occurred in the history of humankind. There are those who can remember both the first airplane flight and the first landing on the moon. The rate of change now frequently requires redesign of occupations, systems, and habits within a lifetime. The changes become a challenge in themselves.

These forces that will change the face of society as we know it will also change the nature of physical education, which attempts to bring the benefits of structured physical activity to all members of a society. Physical education involves the conscious use of sport, dance, exercise, and play within an existing culture. It is a part of our North American culture and is buffeted by the same turbulence of change that is buffeting North American society in general. Attempting to understand the nature of the changes that beset us and their potential effects on the field of physical education is an important task for all physical educators, both as professionals and as participants in society.

Many problems derive from forces for change that are truly beyond our control. For example, the exportation of extractive and manufacturing jobs and the aspirations of third world countries are influencing our economy drastically; we physical educators have little control over these processes. However, there are forces for change that we can influence. In the field of physical education, for example, the "New Games" movement has sought to develop non-zero-sum games to substitute for competitive activity. If non-zero-sum games become important, they will make many of our existing facilities obsolete, which were originally designed to support competitive team games, once the centerpiece of physical education. We need to recognize such implications and make the effort to shape our emerging future.

Each problem facing physical education presents new opportunities, as the Carnegie Commission Report, *Three Thousand Futures*, makes clear:

> Our version of the future is, instead, that problems, even severe problems lie ahead, but that there are reasonable solutions to most if not all of them; that it is better to plan to meet the future effectively than just to fear it as a new dark age. The performance of higher education becomes ever more important to the welfare of the nation and thus it becomes ever more important for the nation to ensure the continuing welfare of higher education. (Carnegie Council on Policy Studies in Higher Education, 1981, p. 8)

If "physical education" is substituted for "higher education" in the above quotation, then what results is a forthright statement that future-gazing is important for physical education. Our capacity to serve the people of the nation, to have them thrive, and to thrive ourselves, demands it.

The notion of attempting to predict the nature of future change is a relatively new concept. Until the idea of progress entered our collective experience, the safest bet to make about the future in general, and in one's own life, was that it would be just like the present because the changes were slow. But change now occurs so quickly that we must prepare for it. We cannot read the future, however, without understanding the influence of the past. Extrapolating into the future is an activity inextricably linked to its mirror image activity, the study of history.

Studying the Future

The case for the formal study of the future has been made persuasively by Platt (1975). His argument is succinctly presented in the following statement.

> It is worth remembering that three different kinds of problem-solving were needed in evolution. The first is problem-solving by survival: the creatures

that didn't solve the problems died off. That kind is encoded in the DNA. The second is problem-solving by learning, with the nervous system. That kind is encoded in the neurons: you don't have to fall over the cliff before you draw back. The third is problem-solving by anticipation; this can only come with science, with the knowledge of laws and regularities, so that one can predict things that have never happened. The Sputnik is a good example of these differences. The first Sputnik was not one of ten thousand that were shot at random and only one survived; nor was it something that flew too high and then too low until it learned the right orbit. No, it was designed by anticipation—programmed with a feedback-stabilization program to go right into orbit first time. In the same way the human race collectively is now encountering families of hard problems that have never been encountered before. We cannot solve them by learning because it would require living through them; and we cannot solve them by survival, because we have in a sense only one world for one trip. We must therefore solve them by anticipation. This requires us to understand the laws of social dynamics so that we can anticipate all sorts of things that have never happened before. (pp. 155-156)

The virtue of studying the future lies in the way that it prepares us for the various eventualities that may happen upon us—contingency plans reduce the reaction time to change. The goal of studying the future, then, is not to reduce or eliminate uncertainty but to absorb it and, subsequently, to reduce the dangers inherent to change (Dror, 1975). It is clearly in our interest, then, as physical educators, to study the future.[1]

There are two schools of thought about the future that set thinkers on the subject apart. One school holds that the future is already determined—fixed by the will of God or by the fine grain of past events and the laws of the universe, thus rendering all actions, including our own, predetermined. This thinking allows no scope for independent or collective action to change the emerging future. If the future is fixed, there is no point in contemplating either what it will be like or how it might be changed. The other belief about the future is that, to some extent, our actions can affect what lies ahead. In other words, we continually stand at forks in the road, and our present choices define what path the future will take. This belief assumes a fixable rather than a fixed future. The former places responsibility, in part, upon our own actions and the accuracy of our map of the various possibilities. The belief that physical educators can fix the future of physical education, at least to some extent, sustains this book.

---

[1] A short essay on the processes used to study the future is provided in the Appendix, "The Nature of Prediction."

Activity and Leisure Industry Defined

If we accept the idea that physical education and physical educators must engage in making prognoses about the field, then it becomes important to define the context of physical education, or where and how it fits into society, so that prognoses of value can be made. People are the source of change and are in turn challenged by the changes they induce. Healthy people are a fundamental resource in any society, for they determine the vigor of their society. Thus both the state and the individual have an interest in the individual's health. The health and efficiency of the nation is determined by the health, morale, and skill of its people.

Human resource development, or health enhancement, is a central concern for us all. Lifestyle decisions concerning nutrition, drugs, safety, activity, stress management, and other related areas have been clearly identified as major influences on health and disease. The people's health needs are met by a complex web of service delivery systems—hospitals, clinics, health centers, counseling centers, fitness programs, advertising, health clubs—designed to enhance health as well as to eliminate disease. These systems exist in both the public and private sectors of our economy. They are created by individual action, by businesses for profit, by philanthropic organizations, and by the government. They employ a very large number of people and consume an enormous proportion of the nation's wealth even as they contribute to it. Together, they are known as the *health enhancement industry*, and they share a simple, common goal: improving people's health.

But people also seek leisure—a sense of joy through self-directed, self-paced behaviors. This desire, too, is strongly motivated. It is as if we wished to use our health and our time for our own good. The behaviors that result, our leisured behaviors, are as varied as our individual differences and circumstances. The resulting vast demand for leisure opportunities has been met by a huge and complex array of service delivery systems best described as the *leisure industry*. The systems within this industry are distinguished by a common concern: improving the quality of life.

The activities of the two industries are not discrete; rather, they overlap. For example, a particular activity, say a sport, can simultaneously serve an individual's needs for health enhancement, status, activity, social interaction, relaxation, and, if the activity is perceived as voluntary and enjoyable, leisure. There is no clear differentiation between the health enhancement and leisure-seeking goals of many activities. Where the health enhancement industry and the leisure industry overlap, they produce what is known as the *activity and leisure industry*. This industry is set apart by the conscious effort to enhance personal health and promote personal leisure simultaneously.

Despite this common ground between them, however, the health enhancement industry and the leisure industry often compete for resources, clients, and profits. Although they may share activities, personnel, and facilities as they seek to serve their clients, there is often confusion, and sometimes even acrimony, as different occupational groups and different enterprises seek to reach the same goals in competition with one another.

Physical Education, Health Education, and Recreation

Physical education can claim that it plays a part in both the health enhancement and the leisure industries. However, the physical education profession does in fact dominate the activity and leisure industry as it uses structured physical activity both to enhance healthy lifestyles and to achieve joyful leisure. The activity and leisure industry also includes professionals from health education, recreation, and many other areas (see Figure 1.1). So in the course of trying to gaze into the future of physical education, we must frequently look into the neighboring fields of recreation and health education.

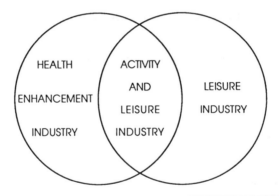

Figure 1.1 The relationship between the health enhancement, leisure, and activity and leisure industries.

Over the last half-century or so, the academic fields of health education, physical education, and recreation have become refined and distinct from one another; that is, they have evolved into specialized fields that concentrate on separate aspects of the same general concern—that of improving people's health and increasing their ability to enjoy life. Because of this evolution, we are learning more and more about specific aspects of a large and complex concern.

The professions of health education, physical education, and recreation, however, remain inextricably linked. All of them develop and deliver services that are part of the total health care package. All contribute to the constructive use of leisure. If the boundaries between them are difficult for the professionals themselves to draw, they are impossible for the client. The client's body has multiple needs and possibilities, but the client lives and experiences these needs, and the connections between them, as a whole. Because the client is rapidly becoming the driving force behind the industries that health, physical education, and recreation serve, the boundaries are likely to become more, rather than less, obscure as time passes. Hence, although this book is primarily about physical education and its future, the processes of physical education cannot be discussed apart from those of health education and recreation.

Larger social forces are creating a clientele that grows more sophisticated and more demanding, as our society places ever more power in the hands of the individual. As a result, the consumers of health, activity, and leisure services are demanding higher quality integrated services from their professionals; they want one-stop shopping. Efforts to maintain a completely separate physical education will undoubtedly put the profession onto a collision course with the forces changing North American society.

Relationships Between Client and Professional

A client is a person who receives the benefit of the activity and leisure programs designed and operated by physical educators. While in the past the clients were primarily schoolchildren and students, in the future they will increasingly include adults. The partnership between adult client and professional physical educator has evolved because of the need for an organization, or an infrastructure, to make possible a healthy and enjoyable lifestyle in a contemporary industrial—even postindustrial—society. The simplest physical activity—jogging—requires rules of the road and, in some cases, jogging trails to separate joggers from the traffic. More complex activities often require elaborate preparation and facilities—consider the infrastructure necessary to support a ski resort or a health maintenance organization. Preparing the infrastructure and managing the client have given rise to a massive and multifaceted activity and leisure industry—a loosely woven set of businesses, government enterprises, and professional activities that are united only by a common goal: They all seek to improve the quality of an individual's life by influencing people's voluntary decisions about the use of their own bodies at work and at play.

Most physical education professionals work face-to-face with their clients, either individually or in small groups. They may counsel or teach or lead as first among equals, and their success depends substantially upon their leadership abilities and their example. However, other professionals may be distantly involved in servicing the client. For example, one may have negotiated the rights of way to the firebreak for skiing or hiking; another may have made all the arrangements for a 10k run. In both kinds of involvement—face-to-face or indirect—the physical educator uses his or her special skills or knowledge to increase the likelihood that clients will reach their personal goals.

The goals of this partnership need not be altruistic. The professional physical educators may work for a salary, for a profit, or as volunteers contributing for emotional rewards. And, of course, they may be people driven by an amalgam of these motives. The particular motive of the physical educator, however, does not drive the system. The prime driver of the system is the client, because in most cases, particularly in the private sector, the adult client chooses to participate, pays a fee, and then chooses to become, or not to become, a repeat user. Thus as the center of gravity of the activity and leisure industry shifts from child to adult clients, so the clients gain increasing control of the industry.

Because a healthy lifestyle requires establishing healthy habits that are practiced regularly over a long period of time, attracting the clients initially and then converting them into repeat users (and payers) is the central challenge of the industry. The activity and leisure industry is thus faced with both creating and marketing activity and leisure services for individuals who can choose whether or not to participate. The basic function of the industry, then, is retailing—delivering services directly to the consumer—and retailing involves myriad successful face-to-face encounters. The lessons learned in other retail services can be of service in this regard to the activity and leisure industry.

Activity and Leisure as a Secondary Industry

The activity and leisure industry contributes to the self-actualization as well as to the health of individuals and populations. Despite this, self-actualization and health are not among people's most basic needs, and therefore do not receive a great deal of attention. Though there are convincing arguments that people have strong needs for activity, leisure, and good health, these needs are contingent on the meeting of other preemptive basic needs (Lawhorn et al., 1970). In other words, people will not be interested in the self-actualization found in sport, the joy found in leisure, or even their future health if they are hungry, fatigued, or their lives are in danger. The demand for the industry's services, then, are somewhat elastic simply because people may choose whether or not to participate.

Any model for the demand for the industry's services must therefore take into account the fact that hunger, chronic and acute disease, absence of shelter, social disruption, and depression reduce the urgency of the demand for the services of the activity and leisure industry. The demand shrinks as more of the creativity and energy of a people are expended on achieving basic needs. If this is a reasonable assumption, we may conclude that such axioms as "sport for all" are figments of the social imagination of successful and stable industrial nations. While the jogging phenomenon in the Western nations may be an essential contribution to health enhancement, it cannot be so in those societies where the per capita share of the GNP does not permit adequate calories, protein, clean water, or other basic needs. The activity and leisure industry can exist as a service to the general population only when there are surplus resources and social stability. If the industry's activities depend on surpluses at the individual and national levels, then its members should be deeply concerned about the processes that determine both the generation and the distribution of those discretionary resources and funds. Without them our industry cannot exist.

Production Plus Consumption Equals "Prosumption"

No matter how sophisticated our predictions of economic trends, in the Western world we must recognize that the activity and leisure industry can only be of secondary importance in fashioning our predictions, because the businesses and activities of leisure are in the main consumptive rather than productive. That is, surpluses generated elsewhere are consumed by the activities that individuals may choose. Thus the first critical factors to study are those factors that influence the generation of surpluses, and only then those that influence the individual's choice about how those surpluses are to be allocated.

An important exception to the generalization that leisure activities are by nature consumptive is the ability of the industry to produce health and vigor. To the extent that an activity generates an increased capacity to function, or extends the duration of effective functioning, it adds to the productive potential of the people and, through them, the society. Productivity might be increased, then, directly—people could work harder, longer, or faster—or indirectly by reducing health maintenance costs. Businesses are increasingly inclined to invest in health enhancement at the worksite not only for the benefit of their employees, but also for the sake of improved production and profit.

The notion that the activity and leisure industry is a productive industry is closely allied to the notion of "prosumption" advanced by Toffler (1980). He argues that, increasingly, we will seek to generate goods and services for our own consumption outside the market. In other words, the producer is also the consumer, hence the word "prosumer." Toffler cites do-it-yourself schemes and gardening as examples of a multitude of activities that will become increasingly popular as prosumption grows. Health-inducing activities that increase fitness, reduce stress, and create satisfaction are also prosumptive: The loop of production and consumption is closed within the individual.

Prosumptive activity will grow to immense proportions as nonwork time is filled with barter and generative activity on the edges of the regular capitalist economy. Retired people, vacationers, and the unemployed or partially employed will engage in extensive prosumption, one part of which will be the self-maintenance activities that are at the core of health education, physical education, and recreation.

Sources of Support for the Industry

What, then, are the sources of the industry's support? At root, the nature of these sources depends upon how successful other sectors of the economy are in generating new resources by extraction, growing crops, and exporting products to reap the benefits of others' work abroad. The amount of income over expenditure that is generated by a society depends, of course, upon the extent that the volume of sales or productivity grows. These surpluses are then distributed in complex ways: Some are redistributed by the political process via taxation, the source of most of the funds for physical education in the public sector. The rest is shared by the members of the society and expended in the private sector. In the final analysis, the future of the industry, both public and private, depends upon the size of the surplus.

The proportion of the national earnings that are spent in the industry comes from two sources: taxes and discretionary personal income. Available funds from the first are dependent upon the size of the tax burden acceptable to the people, and the political process that allocates those funds; the second, discretionary spending, is determined by the size of the surplus and the people who share it. Neither people nor discretionary income are evenly distributed across the nation, and the distribution of both will have considerable effect on any industry that must persuade people to buy its goods or services.

In general, both the population and the personal discretionary income have been growing in our lifetime. Although there have been peaks and troughs in the growth curves, we have nevertheless shared in an expanding market. For example, total recreational expenditures (including both the participation in, and the viewing of, sports) have grown from $49 billion in 1972 to $140 billion in 1983. More people with more money to spend have dramatically expanded our horizons as an industry. That growth represents a compound annual growth rate of 10 percent, exceeding the average inflation rate and therefore signifying real growth in the industry. Further and more detailed analysis of the roots of the industry, population, and income is included in chapter 3, "The Changing Activity and Leisure Market."

Despite the fact that our professional interests are clearly and intimately linked to economic circumstances, we rarely seem to show much concern for the wider economic realities. The next program, the next game, capture our attention. Furthermore, the assumption that the circumstances of the past will continue, or that those resources supporting our interests will always be there, seduce us into complacency. Failure to heed the future is especially bad for those who offer activities that are virtually dispensable. Services that have an elastic demand, that is, that are discretionary in nature, are highly vulnerable to the possibility of needed resources drying up and disappearing. This can easily happen, because those activities that are not elastic, for example the search for food, shelter, and love, will always outweigh elastic activities. To the extent that the industry lies toward the inelastic end of the spectrum, we are not vulnerable. If the demand is elastic, however, we can expect trouble during times of falling population and/or diminishing discretionary income.

However, the activity and leisure industry's professionals are like other people. Few of us can transcend the immediate or the near. A 1972 report by the Club of Rome (Meadows, Meadows, Randers, & Behrens) demonstrates how we expend our efforts when coping with the future (see Figure 1.2). If this analysis is correct, most people, including physical educators, do not worry about much more than their immediate families and the next week. Yet it is clear that the activity and leisure industry needs to plan far beyond these things.

Thus far, our lack of interest in the future has done us no real harm. With the exception of the last few years, the activity and leisure industry in the

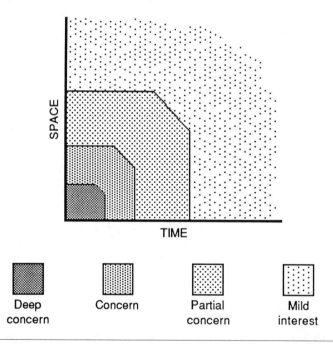

Figure 1.2 Human perspective: The propensity for immediate concerns to be the focus our attention.

United States has experienced substantial growth over a long period of time. Until recently, there was work for all. Professionals in the industry knew where most of the work was needed, and they entered the field either through the teaching profession or through public agency recreation. However, the last decade has demonstrated that the old systems are undergoing change. Population growth has slowed because of a diminishing birthrate. At the same time, as longevity has increased, there has been a rapid increase in the numbers of older people in our society. The demographic structure of our society has thus become heavy at the top, and is getting heavier still. The aging of America is beginning to upset our comfortable school system of delivering services to a school-, youth-, and sport-oriented public.

Physical educators must change their youth-oriented approach if they are to participate in the rapidly developing health enhancement and leisure service industries. Our capacity to make these changes will depend upon our collective attitude toward change itself, which is to some extent determined by our professional roots. Our history is a long one: The alliance of professionals serving the industry was one hundred years old in 1985. Although a certain amount of inertia exists in any profession, any group that is capable of surviving for a century should be able to respond to new challenges successfully. The question, then, becomes one of changing fast enough to thrive in our new environment.

Physical Education's Recent Roots

While the changes that we must deal with have their roots in relatively recent developments associated with the maturation of our industrial society, our own capacity to change is rooted in the personal professional histories of those people currently in the profession. The nature of that collective experience will determine whether or not we are agile enough, as a profession, to adapt to new circumstances. Because the entire career history of all practicing physical educators encompasses only fifty years, I am going to assert, for simplicity's sake, that the roots of the changes affecting us, plus our capacity to respond to those changes, reach back approximately to the Great Depression, or perhaps to the end of World War II.

The Baby Boom

World War II, ending as it did with the onset of the nuclear age, established U.S. economic and military supremacy. It presaged a short, troubled period of recovery and then a period of optimism, calm, and growth which set the scene for many of the patterns that many of us think of now as normal. The population was growing, money was available for education, and the opportunities for teaching at all levels were good. For physical education and health education, the baby boom created a wealth of opportunity, and for two decades, the fifties and the sixties, the bulk of our attention was quite correctly focused on teaching and teacher preparation.

The Babies Grow Up

Then the babies began to graduate and a variety of processes depressed the nation and the birthrate. In the late seventies and early eighties, schools lost students, people lost confidence, Vietnam divided the nation, and the economy ran out of steam. The tax revolt left the public sector starved for money.

The impact of all this on the teaching profession was profound. Education came under attack. The familiar cry of "back to the basics" was aimed at the way many subjects were taught, and even resulted in public questioning of the role of health and physical education. Education did not have the money it needed, and worse, it did not seem to have the same support that it had enjoyed earlier. The general reaction for some time was to try hard to restore the old systems. Teachers unionized in an attempt to force the economy and protect their numbers. As a result, people began to question how their taxes were being used and insist on changes normally resisted by the teaching profession. These changes rendered the profession less attractive, less secure, and more difficult to enter. Physical educators and health educators thus became dramatically disinclined to commit themselves to teaching. They forced a rethinking of the profession as many of them created new opportunities for themselves in the private sector. They participated in the creation of an activity industry.

The Leisure Industry in the Public and Private Sectors

The leisure industry followed a slightly different path. It began as a movement to correct the ill effects of urban impaction on poor children living in the rapidly growing industrial cities of the Northeast. The "playground movement" became the kernel around which grew a social service that took upon itself the task of providing recreation services to all members of the community. At first the target clients were those who could not afford to purchase leisure services and products. As industrialism became more effective and surpluses distributed more democratically, the discretionary income and time enjoyed by most of the people spawned rival leisure service retailers in the private sector.

As the economy grew through the postwar decades, those services that catered to the leisure demand thrived in both the private and the public sectors. Communities were wealthy and could afford to tax themselves to provide for extensive and sophisticated recreation and park programs. Citizens' real income was increasing, and demand for services was great. The two decades between 1955 and 1975 saw unprecedented growth in the industry. There was little overt or acrimonious competition between the public and the private sectors, for there seemed to be demand and money enough to satisfy both.

In the last decade, however, circumstances have changed. Not only have people become unwilling to provide discretionary social services through self-imposed taxes, but there have been intensified efforts from the private sector to capture the discretionary dollar. These efforts are fueled by the manner in which public sector agencies have compensated for their loss of tax dollars: Behaving like private sector businesses, they have begun to charge user fees to augment their falling income, thereby causing the business community to cry foul as the agencies collect income from both the tax rolls and the citizens they serve, offering services at below true cost. This practice, plus the expensive facilities that the agencies acquired in earlier times at the taxpayers' expense, offers them very real advantages in the competition.

Such unfair business practice has been prevented by legislatures in the past. State prisons and universities have been prohibited from competing openly on the market. Unions have managed to prevent prisoners and students from working in such a way that private sector businesses could be placed at a disadvantage. This pressure to discourage unfair competition by handicapping the public sector will undoubtedly increase. The next decade will force a reevaluation of the role of activity and leisure professions.

Both health and physical education and the leisure industry have experienced the same tendency to begin as public services supported by taxation, and then to come under attack from the private sector as tax income has decreased. Shifting emphasis from the public to the private sector in providing activity and leisure services has induced great stress on the traditional structures of the professions serving the industry.

University Influences

There have also been great changes in the way employees entering the profession have been prepared by the universities. While the industry will find its employees where it can, the universities have successfully arranged for new professionals to be channeled into the public sector. A university degree is necessary if one wishes to teach health and physical education, and has become the standard means of entry into recreation as well. As a result, the universities exert enormous influence on the character of the industry. Their prescriptions determine both skills and attitudes of newcomers to the professions that the industry employs, and so the recent history of the universities is also important.

To begin understanding the university, one must understand that university departments are essentially fiefdoms struggling independently of one another to attract students and resources and to support contributions to scholarship that their faculty members consider valuable. Departments are set up to offer their own degrees, albeit under the supervision of the university faculty at large. Cooperation among departments is not necessary for success, and the very nature of the process of studying smaller and smaller areas in more and more detail may splinter a discipline. This separation into small fiefdoms, however, is rewarded by the freedom it brings. Faculty are driven by the imperatives of academe, including the search for unpopular truths, and the academy protects their independence by encouraging specialization and granting tenure.

Disintegration

University departments were permitted to splinter off in their search for academic and disciplinary freedom throughout the period of growth following World War II. As a result, the original department of health, physical education, recreation, and dance at most universities was allowed, and even encouraged, to divide itself into separate, specialized departments. The old conception of a unified concern for the enhancement of health and the quality of life was lost. Agendas, curricula, attitudes, behaviors, loyalties, and tools drifted apart, and new, separate departments became the principal suppliers of highly specialized professionals to the industry. These professionals had been prepared by their departments to be either physical educators, health educators, or recreators, and were not able to work comfortably where these programs were integrated. In fact, integrated programs withered and became the exception.

For several reasons, professional organizations over the past half-century have been shaped in this compartmentalized image of the university. University faculty members were, and still are, rewarded for attempting to exert influence on their professional worlds. They are expected to conduct and communicate research; they are expected to be of wider service beyond their research and teaching. Consequently, faculty members who survive tend to be assertive and to influence the profession from their base of operation in academe. By virtue of this and their energy, professional organizations over the years have splintered into narrow affinity groups competing for scarce resources to advance their own narrow agendas. As a result, the two prime professional organizations—The American Alliance for Health, Physical Education, Recreation and Dance, and The National Recreation and Park Association—are in effect loose umbrellas under which shelter a large number of smaller organizations of like-minded professionals each pursuing specialized interests. The umbrella organizations are often like universities in that it is difficult to engineer cooperation among their constituent parts.

Because the faculty of the universities prepare new professionals to enter the industry, and because they have accumulated enormous influence within the professional associations, they have found it relatively easy to fashion the industry. The result has been the splintering of what was essentially one profession catering to the enhancement of health and the quality of life in general. The three separate areas of academic preparation and professional practice—health education, physical education, and recreation—now behave as if they were pursuing three separate endeavors.

Reintegration Necessary

These three areas continue to develop separately, independent of the pressures for integration that are mounting among the clients. Clients cannot understand why they have to consult with, and pay for advice from, three different people when they wish to plan and implement a revision of their lifestyle. They want to be able to ask the same person questions about such diverse, but fundamentally related, topics as smoking, release of stress, exercise, buying cross-country skis, and choosing a good skiing group. Ideally, the client should not be charged with the responsibility of reintegrating the professions, and health educators, physical educators, and recreators who ignore this pressure for integration do so at great risk. Some can quite capably assemble the technologies into new combinations desirable to clients; the threats to those who cannot, however, will come from the other health professions at the edges of the activity and leisure industry. The disciplines of health education, physical education, and recreation are actually well placed to reintegrate and to create new combinations of knowledge, information, and services required by the retailing of health enhancement and leisure services to people of all ages. The question is whether they can respond quickly enough to capture the market.

From Prescriber to Listener, Counselor, and Friend

As our clients age and seek our services as adults who are used to purchasing services, it will become clear that the old system of prescribing to large numbers of captive youths will no longer work. We will have to become less dictatorial and more adept at persuasion and counseling as we become counselors to people of our own age and older. We will therefore need to cultivate skills very different from those that are currently well developed in our profession—a profession that has built its methods and traditions on the objective of delivering services to youths in school.

Our professional roles will likely change in response to two major pressures. The first will be that of our need to respond to the "graying of America," or to the needs of an older clientele. Demand for our services will reflect the preferences and capacities of an adult market; the first baby-boomers have already had their fortieth birthdays. The second will be the pressure upon us to shift from curative to preventive health care. Together, these two pressures will force physical education to focus on the entire life span. Our clients will no longer be young; our emphasis will no longer be on competitive sport. As a result, the former mainstays of the profession—teaching and teacher preparation—while remaining important concerns, will nevertheless become only two concerns among many as other areas of the field grow and diversify in response to underlying economic pressures.

The changes that are already upon us will affect the kinds of people we recruit into the profession, the methods we use to attract and prepare them, the content of our curriculum and programs, and the nature of our delivery systems. They will also affect the way we relate to our clients.

Summary

The center of gravity of our field is changing rapidly. Old assumptions have broken down—including the assumption that physical educators necessarily work with sport skills and with youth in educational settings. Increasingly, professionals in our field are working with adults in the private and semiprivate sectors of the economy. Changes taking place outside the field will drive physical education into new niches, and force it to take on new forms. The challenges will be many, but each will present a new opportunity for us to be of service. Delivering prized services will create a larger place for physical education and physical educators in the economy; failure to recognize and accommodate to the changes will mean the extinction of our field.

■■■■ **Chapter 2** ■■■■■■■■■■■■■■■■■■■■■■■■■■■■■■■■■■■■■■

*Major Trends in Society*_____

In the preceding chapter, we reviewed some of the recent history of the activity and leisure industry. Now it is time to turn our understanding of the past into prognoses for the future. This chapter looks into the future. It begins by surveying briefly eleven trends that are now at work in our society, and that together will change society. Because physical education exists within and is influenced by that society, each will in turn influence physical education.

Survey of Multiple Changes

Naisbitt, in his widely read book *Megatrends* (1983), identified ten major trends that seem to be affecting our society. Although some have criticized his conclusions and the fact that they were derived from the extended analysis of the way the column inches of newsprint were distributed, they are included here because they have been widely read and quickly sensitize the reader to at least ten of the major trends that seem to be affecting us now. Thumbnail sketches of each and the effects they will have on the activity and leisure industry follow.

From Industry to Information

Since World War II there has been an accelerating shift away from manufacturing toward service- and information-based business. This shift is the twentieth century analog of the industrial revolution, when the dramatic economic shift from agriculture to manufacturing took place over the course of a century. The current revolution, however, is moving at a much greater pace. Jobs have been lost by the millions in the smokestack industries, and the vast majority of jobs replacing them have been in the service- and information-rich industries.

The growing number of lawyers, preachers, vacation workers, fast-food workers, researchers, and computer operators and programmers have replaced those who used to labor in manufacturing and extractive jobs. The problem has been that the older, displaced workers have not had the skills, opportunity, or sometimes even the inclination to retrain and compete for postindustrial jobs. Two obstacles stand in their way: The new jobs either require extensive education and training or they are probably service jobs that pay poorly.

This new revolution will produce startling gains in efficiency and wealth on the leading edge. But on the back side we will find that many have been driven out of the megawage manufacturing businesses, by competition from low-wage earners abroad, into a vast number of low-wage service jobs. Fast-food and other personal service occupations will subject many to mindless, unsatisfying jobs. There are now vast numbers of young people, for example, trapped in minimum-wage food service occupations.

On the positive side, however, information is power, and information will be generated, moved, and consumed in quantities never before dreamed of. The exportation of technology, ideas, licenses, programs, and cultural and entertainment products will grow into a vast market. Many people will earn their keep with their information-processing skills; even political alignments of the world will be influenced by the commercial flow of information. Those professions that are information-rich will grow, and the growth of the profession of physical education is one example of the effects of the service/information revolution.

High Tech/High Touch

As our environment becomes increasingly high tech, and a massive proportion of our decision making automated, there will also emerge a greater need for social interaction of an ever higher quality. Humankind came into being as a species that made a specialty of cooperation. We evolved in small groups, working and playing together: *Family, village, tribe, gang, friend, conversation* are just some of the words that suggest our essentially social nature. Belonging to a group, nurturing and being nurtured by others, are at the center of our lives. The high tech revolution will not impair our sociability; it will enhance it.

As sophisticated machines begin to handle much of our information, and to control the information that is distributed, people will tend to interact with each other less often and with machines, in isolation, more often. Cooperating with a computer-driven machine, no matter how "friendly," is no substitute for the interaction with another, truly friendly, human being who has interesting and enlightening experiences to share.

One result of the high tech revolution will be an increasing need for social interactions that are rewarding to people—people who are designed by nature for continuous and close cooperation with one another. If this need is denied in one part of our lives, it will have to be satisfied somewhere else—a countertrend that offers increased opportunities for those of us in the activity and leisure industry. The demand for social interaction of high quality will be great, and we will benefit by designing our services accordingly.

From National to World Economy

Interdependence is the watchword of this trend. The regional and national economies of the world will become increasingly dependent upon one another. Construction of modern products will require sophisticated coordination of materials and cooperation among workers. Both construction and marketing patterns have already been revolutionized. The information revolution has made it possible to coordinate action over vast distances in the twinkling of an eye.

Earlier systems of coordination profoundly affected the nature of developing regions and nations. The smallest geographical unit had to be an area whose furthest points could be traversed on horseback within an optimum response time. Nowadays information can travel around the world at the speed of light. The realities of communication make a mockery of the old, economic necessities for national and ethnic boundaries. The result will be that our economies will rapidly become one world economy. Nevertheless, political boundaries, as markers of social and ethnic structure, will remain, creating tension between economic and political realities. This trend, though far removed from the activity and leisure industry, will affect the industry indirectly in that the economy that supports the industry will be affected.

From Short Term to Long Term

The system of capitalism practiced in the United States rewards managers and planners for short-term performance. The single strongest influence on this system is the expectation of stockholders that the value of their stock will increase and pay dividends each quarter. Because of this, there is enormous pressure on those in management within publicly held companies to maximize immediate gains, sometimes at the expense of the long-term health of the organization. Compounding the problems that result from such a system is the system of electing politicians for short terms. Politicians are nearly always running for election and are thus inordinately sensitive to short-term concerns. Long-term concerns for the future of resources, environment, and the quality of life are often sacrificed.

Fortunately, citizens have become increasingly aware of this shortcoming in our system and have shown signs that they, by their power as voters and as consumers, will insist that long-term issues be addressed. The recent debacle in the auto industry is a case in point: Despite efforts by the unions to persuade management to build small, high-quality cars, the industry continued to produce behemoths. As the fuel crisis, pollution crisis, and recession overtook us, Detroit was caught off guard. Consumers began to insist on efficient, longer lasting vehicles. Short-term concern for next quarter's sales had distracted the industry's attention from an obvious, though more distant, crisis.

The Japanese system is an example of a system that is tuned in to problems of a long-term nature. The Japanese will sacrifice immediate benefits in the interest of more distant gains. The nature of their economy, which is relatively centralized, encourages this. Because Japan is our principal economic competitor, we will need to learn to do the same.

In the face of these powerful political and economic forces, we must reorient our management strategies and achieve consensus that the future will not necessarily be like the present and that anticipation and long-range planning are imperative. Clearly, the focus on long-range trends in this book is a call for physical educators to look to the future.

From Centralization to Decentralization

In response to the difficulties involved in coordinating and communicating over long distances, the need for a strong central government evolved. Worthy citizens representing their constituencies were called together in one place to weigh concerns and to seek coordinated and effective responses to important, shared problems. Democracy was shaped by patterns of communication that existed during the agrarian era, and worked well, or at least better than any other system.

The fundamental reasons, however, for this form of a government have been called into question by modern communications technology. We now have conference phones, microwave hookups, computer billboards, on-line information searches and electronic libraries, and Zap Mail. We also have a citizenry that is by far better educated than its forebears. The wisdom and technical expertise necessary to solve a given problem is now likely to be available locally. Information is no longer a scarce resource, and coordination is no longer a function reserved solely for central government, but can be adequately undertaken from any location via extended electronic communications networks.

These features of a society with a waning necessity to centralize apply equally well to today's large, commercial organizations. There is a strong tendency for the very large organizations in our society to split up and to decentralize as power shifts to the states, the towns, the branch plant managers, the franchisees, and the local operators. The proper role of central authority is being redefined as strategist, leader, motivator, evaluator, facilitator, and mediator.

Physical education is already decentralized. It takes place in small groups and authority of organizations rarely exceeds that of people. Even so it is clear that as society is decentralized, the organizations designed by physical educators should also be decentralized. To fail to do so will be to create organizations out of synchrony with the society at large.

Self-Help

During the last two decades people have begun to lose confidence in larger social institutions such as the government, the military, large corporations, and the professions. It seems that as our trusted institutions moved to solve large problems, they often merely created more intractable problems that in turn needed to be solved. Such challenges as achieving racial balance in the schools, maintaining the viability of the inner city, disposing of toxic and radioactive waste—challenges that are still unmet—have all demonstrated that our institutions, formerly so effective and so deserving of trust and respect, have often failed us.

As people lost confidence in larger institutions, they began to take action themselves as they gained confidence in their own ability to solve problems. Local governments and organizations began to implement their own unique solutions. State and local government, branch plants, universities, school districts, utility districts, local organizations of all kinds have clashed with larger, central organizations and have aggressively wrested power away from them. People have become active consumers, insisting that the services they desire are in fact delivered as claimed. Efforts to obtain redress are growing: Lawsuits have increased and the cost of errors and omissions insurance has risen. As power has shifted, large institutions and the professions have entered a new era in their relations with their clients. Authorities now have to practice the fine art of persuasion and justify their proposed solutions to problems. The citizenry are quite likely to oppose the experts and to win—not solely by political clout, but by sheer force of argument.

As the cost of professional expertise rises, and its perceived value falls, citizens are more and more likely to decide that they can fend just as well for themselves. This trend can offer a major opportunity for those of us in physical education if we have the foresight to form supportive alliances with our clients in helping them to achieve their own goals. The notion that each person can best manage his or her own lifestyle plays right into our hands; we can offer to help.

Networks Versus Hierarchies

Organizations are finding that the old "inverted tree" management system does not necessarily produce the best results. This system, where a limited group of people report to one boss, and more people report to lesser bosses down the chain of command, was designed when limited wisdom was available. The jobs of underlings could be defined and refined so that the boss's job was essentially one of monitor, exhorter, and punisher. This system worked well as long as individual initiative was not a prime consideration, or an integral part of operation.

We have understood and acknowledged only recently that people like to feel instrumental in seeking imaginative solutions to everyday problems that are of common concern to themselves and to the organization they work for. We have also grown to understand that the people most able to solve a problem are those people directly in touch with it. The question becomes one of creating organizations that encourage underlings to participate directly in deciding how to get the job done better and more efficiently, to use their energies and talents in activities formerly thought of as the preserve of bosses. The more people *thinking* like bosses on the job, we have discovered, the better. As a result, more people are now involved in the process of identifying and solving local problems.

More effective organizations grew away from their inverted tree structures and developed networks of influence. Today people are likely to have multiple roles in an organization, to report to several others and to have several responsible to them. This kind of interlocking network permits information and influence to flow in many directions at once. More people feel instrumental and involved *as humans* rather than as mere tools of management. As a result, networks of cooperating individuals in the workplace and in the leisureplace will increasingly become the norm.

Increased Democratization

Society is drifting towards increased democratic participation by its citizenry in affairs that once were centralized. This tendency is closely related to the tendency to decentralize, to do for oneself, and to build networks. Hearings, open meetings, citizens' initiatives, neighborhood organizations, oversight committees, write-in campaigns, political action committees, protests—even sit-ins and riots—are all evidence that people believe they have a right to influence events, and that they can do so competently. Citizens in all walks of life no longer see their role as passive. This increased sense of involvement and responsibility weakens the authority of those nominally in power, who are being held publicly responsible by citizens exerting their democratic right to wield influence.

This increased democratization also changes the way citizens think about authority. Those in authority must persuade people first before making pronouncements and finalizing decisions. As a result, concerted action becomes more difficult, dependent upon the success of persuading a group of citizens, all of whom espouse differing views even among themselves. On the other hand, democratization forces decision makers to justify their proposed actions, which can only be good in the long run for everyone involved.

Given the complexity of our world and the fact that many problems can be solved only by convincing many people to change their behavior, the democratization of all facets of contemporary life will inevitably prove beneficial. It will also alter the way that the activity and leisure industry delivers its services. Each client will become important as he or she makes the decision to participate or to drop out.

From North to South

Like a fairy ring, our society has spread outward from the original colonies on the eastern seaboard. New lands and new opportunities seemed to lie to the west. It was easier to start again in a new place. A similar movement continues today, only now we are moving from the "Rustbelt" states, which flourished during the era of heavy extractive industry and manufacturing, to the Sunbelt states of the South and Southwest. The old creaking infrastructures of the industrial revolution are costly to modernize, and old social attitudes toward management-labor relations are proving difficult to alter. For many, it is simply easier to move south and southwest, avoiding the hassles and enjoying better weather. The results of this movement will inevitably affect all the industries that are sensitive to population shifts. The activity and leisure industry serves people, and as people move, so will opportunity.

Increased Diversity

Old mainline divisions that once broke American society into major segments—black/white, male/female, Catholic/Protestant—are now splintering. In their place has arisen a multiplicity of diverse ethnic groups, lifestyles, preferences, and religions; options and diversity have become the new rule. It is now acceptable to pursue a lifestyle uniquely suited to the individual, and to exhibit options and preferences of one's own. The result is an increasingly heterogeneous society, in which categorizing people has become much more difficult and much less appropriate. No longer can sweeping generalizations be made about the "Democratic vote" and "the Protestants." Block voting is less likely, split tickets more likely. Mass marketing will become less effective in this kind of a society, and small special interest markets will increase.

Industry must necessarily follow this trend. Retailers will have to regard the needs and wishes of their clients with greater sensitivity. Professionals— including those in the activity and leisure industry—will need to pay closer attention to the preferences of their clients.

Masculine/Feminine Merger

To these ten trends, *Time* added an eleventh (Leo, 1984). A July 1984 issue of the magazine carried a satirical treatment of a heterosexual couple's conversation in which they discuss their own confusion about their sex roles. This article, openly lampooning its subject, is an indication in itself that traditional sex-role stereotypes are being rapidly dismantled. Men no longer predominate in the work force. Women have entered the work force in increasing numbers since World War II, and they have entered the growing service and information sectors of the economy, while the old male-dominated industries have been shrinking. In the United States about 70 percent of the 20 million jobs created since 1970 have been in the service sector (Williams, 1984). Women have become an economic force to be reckoned with.

However, the changes we have seen in sex roles have not been just economic. During the last two decades women have insisted upon, and have been granted, a fuller participation in all facets of American life. In sport, politics, and management particularly, and to a lesser degree in the male-dominated areas of trucking, maintenance, and construction, women have joined in and demonstrated clearly that they are equally capable. The process has not run its course, but it is clear that our society will continue to evolve in the direction that welcomes women into all areas of endeavor and achievement and breaks down sex-role stereotyping.

The *Time* article addresses itself to an area of life in which change has created major social confusion—and that is the area of sex-role differentiation. There are obvious differences between the sexes that are welcomed by most and that will undoubtedly be maintained. In the eighties, however, there is confusion about separating the necessary differentiations from the unnecessary. But society is plastic, and its members will learn by the end of the century to deal comfortably with this problem. *Time's* article, in 1994, will be an anachronism.

The activity and leisure industry requires very few, if any, sex-role differentiations. It is essentially a service and information industry, and it will be one of the first industries in which sex-role stereotyping will be functionally eliminated. None of the professional roles in the activity and leisure industry requires an incumbent to be male or female. Some tasks might be performed differently in response to local preferences and expectations, but the growing presence of women truckers and steel-erectors in our society strongly suggests that women strength coaches are an equally plausible idea whose time has come. The merger of what used to be men's and women's physical education programs has created a management structure that virtually ignores gender. This process will continue in the profession, even though there may remain activities that are generally preferred by one gender or the other.

Three Macrotrends

The activity and leisure industry will be influenced by all eleven trends. Some of Naisbitt's megatrends, however, act in combination on the activity and leisure industry. These combinations, or clusters, of megatrends have great importance for the industry. Because they are larger in scope than Naisbitt's megatrends, they will be called here *macrotrends*. While Naisbitt's megatrends are still worth understanding separately, when they are grouped into three macrotrends—demystification of the professions, segmentation of markets, and personalization—they suggest concrete actions that the activity and leisure industry may take.

The megatrends previously discussed that act in combination with one another are those trends from industry to information, from centralization to decentralization, from hierarchies to networks, toward self-help, toward increased democratization, toward growing individualism, and toward the merger of masculine and feminine roles in society. These trends have been growing for decades, but there is one critical development that is bringing about their rapid coalescence: the computer and telecommunications revolution. Our collective capacity to assemble and distribute information throughout our society in easily understandable form will increase to levels we are only just beginning to comprehend.

Information

The information revolution is occurring now because of three related and simultaneous developments: first, the incredible reduction in price of relatively powerful computers to the point that many people have access to them at work and/or at home; second, the dramatic increase in power of easy-to-understand software packages for managing information; and third, an impending telecommunications revolution that will hook those computers and their software packages together interactively. The advances in fiber-optics, digital coding, and new processes that will be formed by the heat of competition now possible in a deregulated telecommunications industry will put the finishing touches to our information revolution. Information will be available as never before.

Self-Help or Do-It-Yourself

Coincident with, or perhaps because of, the information revolution, there has been a growing tendency among us to use available information ourselves rather than to seek the assistance of a professional. The do-it-yourself movement was perhaps the first example. However, this tendency has created ripples that have spread outward to include aspects of health care (self-testing for cancer, pregnancy, home birthing, redesign of the diet, self-treatment of injury, etc.). It has created a mini-industry of courses, offered in the private sector as well as in educational institutions, which teach us how to become independent of a host of authorities and "do it ourselves." As a result, clients' attitudes towards professionals are changing.

Decentralization, Networking, and Democratization

Decentralization has become a guiding force. We have learned that a larger organization becomes less and less efficient as the span of control grows so large that the organization begins to creak with its own weight. Smaller, leaner organizations have come to be seen as more efficient. Head offices have delegated more control, and large companies deliberately set up divisions, sometimes to compete with each other, in their emulation of smaller organizations (Peters & Waterman, 1984; DeMott, 1985).

This tendency is also reflected in the public sector. Naisbitt (1983) has analyzed the causes of the shift in power from the large, central institutions of finance and government to the individual, the city, the political action committee, and the consumer group. This "new regionalism" has inspired a new do-it-yourself politics of citizens' initiatives. Local organizations of concerned citizens are organizing people and information to achieve their own goals. These developments have wrested power away from the center; smaller groups have acquired influence, and it shows in our governance and in our marketing.

Our social organizations are rapidly becoming less hierarchical. They are creating networks, often with multiple supervisors, to produce situations in which the motives and creativity of individuals most intimately connected to a given task or process are recruited. Organizations are seeking to avoid being either "top-down" or "bottom-up" and more "horizontal," or networked, in their organization.

Individualism and Role Merger

The result of these forces has been to distribute authority and empower the individual. People are now more willing to pioneer their own paths. They seek to influence outcomes for themselves and to accept more responsibility for their own lives. Roles are not so clear-cut; in a sense there has been an increase in the search for existential authenticity of many people's lives.

Workers and "little people" in all walks of life have asked for, and taken on, more responsibility. This has changed the relationship between the worker and the supervisor, and between the client and the authority. Many more people entertain the notion that their ideas in the workplace and in the serviceplace are potentially as good as anyone else's.

All of these influences felt together to change the fabric of the society within which the activity and leisure industry functions. An analysis of the three macrotrends that will have the greatest effect on the activity and leisure industry follows.

Macrotrend 1—Demystification

The first major coalescence of trends that will influence the activity and leisure industry, along with all other professions, is demystification. Demystification means that the arcane knowledge considered the private preserve of authoritarian professionals, which earns them power, respect, and profit, will become increasingly available to laypeople. The private knowledge bases of the professionals will be less closely held. Would-be clients will often have access to this knowledge and be able to exercise judgments formerly reserved for professionals "owning" that knowledge. The professions will thus become demystified as their knowledge becomes more public.

Attitude Change

Demystification of the esoterica of our profession, along with many other professions, will result in changes in the attitudes of our clients towards us. Questioning, second opinions, the demand for informed participation in the decision-making process, rejection, lawsuits alleging malpractice, and doing it oneself without the professional authority are all growing indications that the professions are becoming demystified. Now, though there are still vast realms of esoterica beyond the reach of even educated citizens, citizens' attitudes have changed. There is an increasing willingness to question and to disregard the expert. The notion grows that, with effort, one could master the technicalities oneself, as the information base of the professions becomes increasingly available. The mystery is waning, and to some extent it can be said that the tendency to deprofessionalization currently affects all professions (Lawson, 1984).

As a result of this demystification process, the relations between the professional authorities and their clients will change. Increasingly the clients and the professionals will function as a team with the clients participating in the collection of information, analysis, and decision making as informed partners. It will become an increasing part of the professional's role to educate—to lead clients to a situation where they can understand the processes, and join in the actions, undertaken on their behalf.

Professionals will increasingly become listeners, counselors, and friends. Their function will be to support the decision making of the client rather than to prescribe. For those of us in the activity and leisure industry, accommodating to these trends may prove difficult. As a field, we have shared in the objectives of education in general—to provide the knowledge and the skills needed to make informed choices. Paradoxically, physical education itself has usually not striven to encourage choice, but more often uniformity and subjugation of self.

Authoritarianism in Education

There are two problem areas for us in our striving to become listeners, counselors, and friends rather than prescribers. In many cases the methods and expectations of the industry have been shaped by two specific learning environments in which our clients were, to a significant extent, captive, and the organization hierarchical: in athletics and in the schools.

In schools, colleges, and other learning institutions it is obvious that at some point we must prescribe. Students too young to appreciate the ultimate goals of an activity may need eventually to be told, for their own good, what to do. In fact, at the beginning of the process of education, they may need to be told frequently. One problem here lies not so much in deciding what will be desirable as in inspiring the students' motivation so that they themselves will perceive the benefits of the prescription and become willing to work for it.

Another problem lies in balancing the direction given by the teacher or prescriber with the students' need for self-directed activity and exploration. Playful activity permits self-learning and, more importantly, "creative leaps." Balancing prescription with self-directed behavior and unique responding is difficult under the best of circumstances—especially when the clients are captive.

There is no question, however, that in the last two decades educators have learned much about this balance. In the sixties we saw educators responding to the need for choice with individual agendas. Requirements were liberalized or dropped altogether, and the individual's opinions and motives became of great concern. By the midseventies, however, we saw the development of resistance to the new, freer educational patterns. "Back to basics" was simply a response to the results of the balance being tipped to the point that too few of society's agenda items for an educated person were being addressed. As a result, there has been a redrawing of the balance between prescription of content and levels of performance, and the creative needs of individuals.

Nevertheless, as physical educators and health educators, we "know" essentialistically the content of our field, and so have a propensity to know exactly how things should be done and organized. To the extent that we can get away with our prescriptions with captive audiences our authoritarian propensities are reinforced. Authoritarianism is not going to serve us well in the future, however, because our clients will not often be captive.

Authoritarianism in Sport

Now let us examine another source of authoritarianism—athletics. The structure of elite sport is authoritarian. The competitive leagues and conferences, procedures for establishing the winners and the losers beyond doubt, the coach-centeredness, and, in many team games, the very strategies and plays themselves, all reinforce the fact that the client must subordinate the self to the goals of the collective and the will of the coach. Clearly this mirrors many other activities in business, in the military, and in our social world. Physical educators often find themselves as the people controlling the process. A full-time coach, like others cast in authoritarian roles, does not experience the mixture of role expectations commonly experienced by people who sometimes lead, sometimes prescribe, and sometimes follow. To the extent that physical educators are socialized by their experiences as athletes, following the rules from the top, or by prescribing the rules from the top as coaches or organizers of athletics, then their authoritarian propensities will be enhanced.

Resisting Authoritarianism

The pulls toward authoritarianism are often successfully resisted. New methods have been created that permit a successful balance and a recognition of the individual. However, the pulls are still there, and essentialism is alive and well in some teaching (learning) institutions. Many authoritarian physical and health educators will be able to survive in protected environments with captive audiences. To the extent that authoritarian actions are necessary and desirable, that is good. However, many more are going to find themselves in settings where the audience is anything but captive.

Adults are increasingly convinced that health enhancement is desirable. Being active and healthy, learning and enjoying the process and the social interaction that usually accompanies being active and healthy, are an increasing part of people's lifestyles. Satisfying the adult's needs for this learning, doing, and enjoying is increasingly the field of opportunity for professionals in the industry (Drowatsky & Armstrong, 1984). However, those opportunities will come from persuading the adult client to choose, to participate, to bear the financial costs, and then to remain a participant and become a repeat customer. This will require new strategies for meeting the multiple motives involved in participation. The relationship between client and professional will be under the control of the client. For many, this new trend will be difficult to accept.

Absence of Authoritarianism in the Leisure Industry

The characterization of those in the activity industry as having a propensity to authoritarianism by virtue of the settings in which many of them work does not apply to those in the leisure industry. Since the beginning of the playground movement, the leisure industry has grown and flourished to the extent that it could serve the voluntary participation of its children and adult clients. The absence of a captive audience and the definition of the product as a leisured and joyful state of mind has insulated the vast majority of the leisure industry from authoritarianism. With only minor exceptions, the leisure industry has had to fight for its resources and earn the interest and participation of its clients.

Because of the fundamentally different relationship between clients and professionals in the leisure industry as compared to education and sport, its methods, content, and curricula have been biased in favor of the client. In the same way, the recruitment and retention patterns of the industry have selected those people who work comfortably and successfully in client-centered settings. The leisure industry will have less to learn in order to deal with its clients successfully and survive.

Summary of Demystification

Trends in our society have been moving for some time towards the empowerment of the individual. It was the goal of the founding fathers to move in this direction. We first established a secure nation and built an extractive and manufacturing industrial base to assure us of our basic needs. In fact, we were so successful that there were surplus resources to invest in education, leisure, and research. Progress accelerated and productivity rose. The result was that we are now on the threshold of another step. We are moving beyond industrialism to a new economic order where information will become a principal force behind the economy. While extraction and manufacturing become relatively less important, creating and offering services will become more so.

In such an environment, individuals will have readier access to the information that was formerly the preserve of an educated professional elite and, moreover, will have the confidence to use it. The tendency to demystify the professions will be accelerated by increasing competition between professions and members of professions who share information bases. As a result, the professions will be caught between confident clients willing to do for themselves and rival professions vying to deliver the same service. Those who can recruit and maintain the confidence of their clients will survive.

These pressures will work their effects on the activity and leisure industry. There will be less mystery; there will be fewer guarantees. All kinds of health-enhancing services and delivery systems will vie for clients. Health, activity, and leisure professionals will have less of an advantage because the knowledge they possess will become increasingly available to the public. To survive, they will have to generate high-quality experiences for their clients. They will have to create superior settings and superior social interactions and do those things more efficiently than ever before. Above all, they will have to become listeners, counselors, and friends.

Macrotrend 2—Market Segmentation

The marketplace has become progressively differentiated since World War II as a result of the empowerment of individuals and their rising confidence in their own judgment. More efficient production technology, when allied to more sophisticated marketing, has permitted the business community to create products that target small segments of the market. The outcome has been an acceleration in the number of products sharing a market niche. Each product varies in nature to satisfy preferences due to locality, social class, income, ethnic background, and so forth. For example, our gasoline is "localized for you," and Detroit wants "to build a car for you." The supermarket presents a bewildering choice of breads, detergents, wines. There are choices of name brands, house brands, and the generic no brand at all. Our professional organizations offer a smorgasbord of options to members in affinity groups within the umbrella organization, and the magazine market has splintered from a few national magazines to a myriad of titles targeted to more and more specialized markets. The choice is bewildering and people are beginning to develop retail counseling services to help others make wise choices.

Two clusters of trends seem to interact here to encourage market segmentation. The movement towards an information-driven society and decentralization have made profitable small production runs of items with customized elements. These tendencies are affecting the production of goods and services. The cluster has affected the customers, who because of the trends towards increased social diversity and democratization, now demand more personalized goods and services. As a result, the market for all goods and services has become increasingly segmented.

Retailing Choice

The root of the process seems to be improved marketing, which has resulted from the information revolution. Sales personnel recognized that while people wanted the benefits of mass production, they were uneasy about the effect that mass production had on their personal identities. Henry Ford's early cars could be bought in any color, so long as they were black. Owning exactly the same car as millions of other people raised questions of personal sovereignty, and soon competition created choices. One can now, for a price, order a car with so many options that there is a reasonable chance it is unique—built for you. Furthermore, with the help of auto-detailing companies, the basic vehicle can be further decorated and customized so that it is truly an expression of the owner's individuality.

Added to this pressure from consumers for the exercise of options, the "seeking of authenticity" if you will, is the massive development of data-handling systems. The amount of data that has to be managed to support this level of consumer choice is enormous. Naturally, the development of computers permitted the process to accelerate, but there were intermediate systems for remembering, like addressographs, that started the process.

Along with these changes in production technology came changes in systems for developing markets via advertising and direct mail marketing campaigns. The development and sale of sophisticated directories of consumers coded by demographic characteristics and preferences bring us to the present where there are a large variety of relatively cheap systems for developing contacts with likely customers. Marketing is carefully targeted towards small segments of the overall market. It is now possible to search for clients in much the same way that one can search a computerized library catalog for particular titles or topics.

This segmentation of the marketplace has served both the consumer and the producer. The consumer gains real or apparent choice and the producer is able to compete across a larger series of markets. It has also permitted smaller organizations to find small, specialized niches and compete successfully. Ma and Pa granola companies and family magazines are able to compete in segments of the market and to survive and expand. There are more windows of opportunity, and the costs of meeting the demand for a very special product or service in a local market are small.

Activity and Leisure Retailing

This segmentation process has affected the activity and leisure industry similarly. The industry is in fact substantially a retail distribution system. It delivers services in a face-to-face setting. There are few economies of scale; consequently, small systems are at an advantage in designing products and services for tiny market segments. At the top end of the scale are the tour wholesalers and cruise line companies. Here the companies have to work hard to combat the impression that they cannot serve individuals exercising choices and doing their own thing. In fact, these large leisure suppliers create matrices of options to maximize their chances of making a sale. At the bottom of the scale

there are tiny organizations that serve just a few clients with highly specialized services—fishing guides and expedition leaders, coaches of small teams,
golf pros, athletic trainers.

Between the extremes falls the majority of the industry organized into aggregates of between a few and a few hundred professional employees. These
organizations are about the same size as small firms, and with the same characteristics, as they compete to develop their markets. These middle-sized organizations are the ones that we are most familiar with. They are school
districts, recreation and park districts, universities, prison systems, health spas,
nutrition and weight control centers, health maintenance and promotion systems, boys' clubs, and YMCAs.

Franchising

In addition to the increased number of opportunities to start small businesses
offering health-enhancing services, a new strategy has entered the industry—
franchising. Franchising is a centralized system for helping people set up small
businesses that target local needs. "Jazzercize," one of the first franchising
systems, offers franchisees a way to develop and market activity classes for
a fee. Jazzercise has spread nationwide and has been so successful that there
are now imitators. Franchising supports a new business for a fee or percentage. It produces many of the benefits of economies of scale available to a
larger organization. It can purchase centrally on behalf of all franchisees, develop advertising and marketing strategies for use locally, and provide
managerial expertise and services. It usually uses local capital and owner-
ship so that the local motivation and creativity needed to succeed are assured.

Franchising as a method of providing opportunities for professionals to create
their own businesses will increasingly capture the markets formerly served
by public sector organizations. The small private sector organizations, whether
franchised or not, will become more aggressive and more agile than the public sector agencies. The result of the increased competition will be that the
consumer will be presented with more choices, and standards of quality will
rise.

Private Sector Businesses

As a result of market segmentation, the number of opportunities for professionals in the activity and leisure industry has expanded and will expand much
more. New systems of franchising and marketing will result from the interaction between the new information technologies and people's desire for services tailored to their individual needs. The result will be a shift of the industry's
center of gravity from the older agencies founded with public funds towards
private sector initiatives.

As the private sector organizations increase in number, they will compete with each other and with the public sector agencies. Pressure will develop to close the public agencies due to unfair competition. Because the public sector agencies were originally created to serve those who were excluded from the private sector, a variety of mechanisms will be created whereby persons unable to purchase the services will be assisted directly by the public purse. The argument will be that the private sector organizations, driven by the need to be highly competitive, will be able to deliver these services to the taxpayer at lower cost. It will be politically more expedient to subsidize the disadvantaged client's use of private sector services than to maintain an expensive publicly supported service delivery system.

Summary of Market Segmentation

The old markets for competitive sport forms primarily serving youth will continue to exist. However, the major new opportunity for physical education will come from the shift in emphasis from youth and sport to lifetime development. This will bring about a massive shift of physical education's market from children to adults. Adults are more heterogeneous and assertive. Their numbers and their distribution across multiple market segments will create many new opportunities in the retailing of physical education services. The effect will be the segmentation of physical education to match the segmentation of the market.

Activity and leisure services will shift substantially from the public to the private sector. Competition will be strong as other professions and businesses attempt to exploit the same opportunities. Clearly, the skills needed by physical educators working with adults in the private sector will be vastly different from those customarily taught to entrants into the teaching profession. This set of circumstances will present both a challenge and an opportunity to those in the universities who are responsible for educating new physical educators and for continuing the education of the existing cadre.

Macrotrend 3—Personalization

The United States of America was, from the beginning, a social experiment. Since its founding, our society has proclaimed that it exists to serve the individual's harmonious development and enjoyment of time on earth. The Constitution and the Bill of Rights elegantly proclaim this goal. Two centuries of hard work, and some strife, have produced much progress. Many in the U.S. feel well served, yet there are still many left to be included in the kind of life defined by the founding fathers. However, our society is accelerating towards the time when it is possible to strike a balance between the unique needs of the individual and the strictures of society itself.

Although we have been successful creating wealth, only recently have we created the technology to revolutionize its distribution. People have had to be treated as massive aggregates served by mass production techniques because it was not possible to manage the data necessary to do anything else.

Serving Individuals

Now, we have not only the will to treat people as individuals, we also are developing the capacity very rapidly. The methods and skills developed in the business sector that permitted the segmentation of the market will also permit us to realize the social expectations of the people. Major classifications useful in earlier times are breaking down. The demands of people to be treated as individuals are causing a restructuring of society. The old contrasts that have been used to give form and order to society are becoming decreasingly useful. Consider the following polarities that used to carry clear signals about how to behave in society:

> male - female
>
> management - worker
>
> homosexual - heterosexual
>
> ethnic - white

Each of these categories are now subject to questioning; which characteristics associated with any of the above categories are relevant to the situation at hand? We are beginning to realize that very few of the characteristics make substantive differences. We are also learning that the stereotyping, when used as a kind of convenient social shorthand for avoiding individual differences, debases social intercourse.

Our ability as a society to respect individuals for what they are has come a long way. This change will rapidly and deeply affect the activity and leisure industry. The industry is currently in danger of losing touch with individual Americans. Physical education was established at a time when it had to deal with people as aggregates. The technology to do otherwise was not available, and the clients of the time had actually been socialized to expect such treatment. We assembled clients into classes and taught using norms and standard progressions. Individual differences were classified as errors, or at least as irritations. We organized sports and games into teams, gathered the teams into leagues, and used standings to select and reject. These, and a host of other procedures, were all designed to classify and select groups so that we could deal with individuals as members of aggregates. Our problem now is that our adult clients will no longer stand for this.

Because our clients will not be captive and have been socialized to expect individual treatment, we will have to recognize that the old strategies will not satisfy them. We can already see the drift away from the old core activities of team sports and games. People, at least adults with the opportunity to choose freely, are choosing to receive their physical education via activities that do not (a) force them into aggregates, and then (b) identify them within a hierarchy that selects some and rejects others. People are choosing activities in which they can function as individuals following their own paths towards their own goals. They are decreasingly interested in their standings relative to others, and more interested in their standings relative to their own goals. Personal development and personal experience guide their choices.

Zero-Sum Activities Wane

Sports and games that are necessarily zero-sum activities are waning in importance for the industry. The growth of the industry is occurring, rather, in self-developmental, experiential, "everyone-can-win" activities. While the clients interested in sport and competition remain loyal, new clients that were formerly excluded, weeded out by competitive activities, are becoming increasingly insistent on being served. This clientele is larger and more broadly based and will become increasingly heterogeneous. It represents a major opportunity, but to exploit that opportunity will require the industry to shift its emphasis from competitive activities. Too few people can win under those rules. New rules, activities, and practices that focus on the individual are being developed.

Physical education is going to become more personal as a result. More of the field's content and structure will be designed to service individuals in such a way that there are no odious comparisons among them. Rather, comparison, the servant of goal-seeking, will occur within individuals.

Summary of Personalization

People will seek activities that bring them into contact with new experiences, conceptions, and groups. Physical activities will be incorporated into learning activities in high-quality surroundings. The clients themselves will insist on the reintegration of the cognitive, affective, and motoric aspects of their being. *Cooperation* will describe the nature of the field better than *competition*. As a result of the new clients and their unique expectations, the field will undergo a revolution.

Summary

The three great trends—demystification, segmentation, and personalization— will act together to alter the relationships that physical educators will have with their clients. The first two, demystification and segmentation, will alter the way that physical educators are selected and then educated. In the future physical educators will need to be selected more on the basis of their personalities, their bedside manners as it were, rather than for their accomplishments in sports skills. Their education will have to include identifying, finding, and keeping markets for their services—something that at the moment is not included in the professional preparation curriculum.

The third great trend will influence what the profession will do with its clients. Physical education will become less of a public service delivered because the state believes it worthy. It will instead become part of the enormous service sector of the economy. Clients will more likely be adult and will purchase services because they wish to advance their health and their self-identities. The physical educator will have to learn how to retail activity and leisure services and how to become listener, counselor, and friend to the client. The content of the field will become more personalized, avoiding odious comparison among clients of differing abilities.

The next twenty years will require physical educators to deal with these three great trends.

Chapter 3

The Changing Activity and Leisure Market

The activity and leisure industry is a service industry. It arranges activities and experiences for its clients in the service of their goals. The service itself involves arranging people, programs, and facilities, and using knowledge about them to produce desired effects and affects. The vast majority of the industry's clients avail themselves of the service by choice, and so to a substantial extent the industry must persuade them to do so. As in all other service industries, marketing goods and services is a crucial ingredient of success.

In a capitalistic system people are rewarded for creating services, and there develops intense competition for the opportunity to deliver these profitable services to clients. It is no different in the activity and leisure industry. The industry must compete for its clients because many other service providers are also competing vigorously for the same discretionary income of the people. The size of the market that is open for competition is determined by three factors. The simplest factor is the absolute size of the population. The more people there are, the more potential clients there are to serve. The next factor involves the capacity of those people to buy the service or support it through taxes. If the people have little discretionary or taxable income the surpluses to purchase the services will not be available either in their private purses or in the public purse. The final factor is the people's desire to fill the time they have available with activity and leisure services. This factor can be directly influenced by professionals in the activity and leisure industry, in that it involves persuasion that the services are beneficial and worth the investment.

Thus the size of the market is determined by three factors: the number of people, the amount of their discretionary income, and the time they have available. The success of physical educators as a group will be determined by the share of the total activity and leisure market that they are able to capture. This chapter discusses in detail these three determinants of the market.

Effects of Population

In any location the size of the population determines the absolute number that it is possible to attract into activity and leisure programs; but in impacted urban settings the sheer number of people seems to enhance the need for services to ameliorate the effects of crowding. The more people there are in a given location, the greater the chances of creating a profitable clientele. The activity and leisure industry is therefore very greatly influenced by the raw numbers of people present in the nation, the region, and the locale.

Predicting the size of the population at any time is a very complex task. The nation expends much effort once every decade to conduct the national census. In brief, this census involves the use of additive model of the forces at play. Figure 3.1 presents a simple view of these forces as an introduction to the process of predicting population.

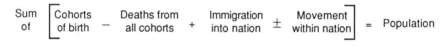

Figure 3.1   Simple model of the sources of population.

There are three main forces at work that influence the population: the birthrate, the deathrate, and the immigration rate of the nation as a whole. The population can also be defined as the number of people in a region, state, county, or other geographic area of interest within a nation, in which case the model must also account for a fourth force—the number of people entering or leaving the cohorts in the area. This part of this chapter looks at these four influences on the population, identified in Figure 3.1, in order to provide a general picture of future population by age in the major regions of the nation. Once the nation's demography is presented, we can then turn to predictions and prognoses for the activity and leisure industry based on these population trends.

Changes in the Cohorts

A cohort comprises all the people born in the same period, often within a year. Thus a cohort shares a common cross section of experiences in a sociological sense. A cohort can take on characteristics that may influence the way the entire cohort behaves as it ages. For example, the adults of young families struggling to enter the work force and rear their young children in the late 1920s and early 1930s were changed by the Great Depression. Attitudes and behaviors formed then have remained with them as they have aged.

Characteristic attitudes towards employment, thrift, food, and education can be traced to the common traumas of the depression. These traumas have changed the behavior of an entire cohort.

Cohorts are not all the same size. Each cohort's size is a reflection of the conditions working on its parents' cohort at the time of conception. This fact is dramatically represented when the number of annual births throughout the nation (i.e., the national cohort) is plotted against year of birth as in Figure 3.2.

The size of the cohorts since 1940 show dramatically the effect of the optimism created by the end of World War II. One year after the cessation of hostilities, the number of children born rose steeply. The postwar period of relative calm permitted the cohort, denied opportunities for building families during the war, to have children. When the cohort that was forced to delay having children was added to the cohorts coming naturally to childbearing age, a massive upswing in births resulted. That upswing, the baby boom, peaked fifteen years after the war. Compared to the preceding boom, which occurred with the previous generation just after World War I, the baby boom of the 1950s and 1960s was enormous.

The disproportionate numbers of children in the 1946-66 cohorts disturbed the equilibrium of the population at large. What is more, these cohorts will grow along the same life cycle and come to childbearing age at essentially the same time. Thus the first baby boom will reverberate, producing another baby boom in the years 1980 to 1990.

Such perturbations of the steady state move like waves through the population, producing dramatic changes in many sectors of the society and economy. For an industry that is so sensitive to changing numbers of clients and their ages, the population profile and the way the age distribution varies with year will have great influence. The dramatic shifts in the kinds of people living in the population at any one time will influence the kinds of provision that must be made for their activity and leisure. Thus Figure 3.2 demonstrates convincingly why the industry has been youth-oriented since the baby boom and why it is changing to a more adult orientation as that cohort matures.

Longevity and Immigration

If no other factors were at work, this oscillation would continue to smooth out gradually over the generations and eventually reach a steady state. However, our life expectancy has changed due to a variety of improvements in medicine and health promotion. The deathrate has declined and large numbers of people are living longer than was normally the case prior to 1900. The result has been that, despite the reduced birthrate during the late 1960s and 1970s, the population has increased.

To this must be added the effect of immigration. The Department of Commerce (Spencer, 1984) projects the immigration rate quite tentatively. It makes

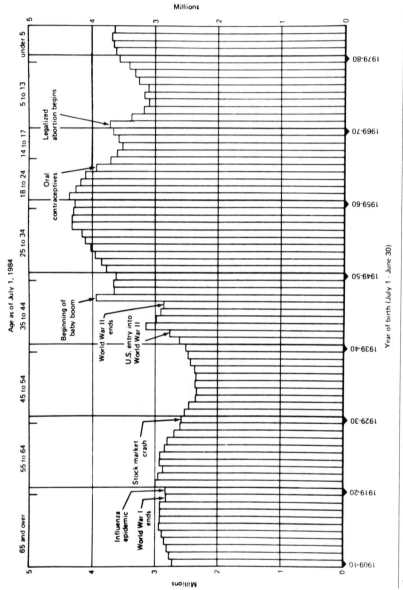

Figure 3.2   Number of births by year, 1983 age groups, and critical events affecting the population (Miller, 1984).

estimates for a low immigration rate at about 250,000 per year, a high immigration rate of 750,000, and finally chooses the middle road with a final estimated rate of 450,000 immigrants per year. These different estimates can only result in dramatically different projections.

If all the presumed changes are computed—that is, high, low, and intermediate estimated rates of change—then projections for the total population of the United States can be plotted along three curves (see Figure 3.3). The lowest curve requires all influences to act at the lowest intensity, and the highest curve at the highest intensity. The middle curve assumes that all influences will, on the average, work at the intermediate rate. The resulting differences are startling. By the end of the projections, the year 2030, the range is from 250 million to 370 million people. This graphic example indicates the ease with which it is possible to accumulate error by simple extrapolation of assumptions.

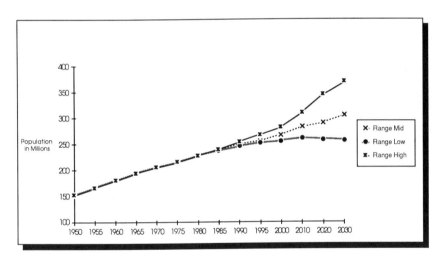

Figure 3.3   Estimates and projections of total population—1950 to 2030 (Miller, 1984).

The most probable projection is of course that which assumes that not all forces will work at their greatest intensity for the duration of the projection. While some forces are temporarily stronger, others will weaken and work in the opposite direction; the result will lie somewhere in the middle. The middle series of assumptions result in an estimated population of 249 million by 1990 and 267 million by the year 2000. The population as measured by the 1980 census was 226 million.

The population is expected to increase from 1980 to 1990 by 9.7 percent. This is reassuring. About 10 percent more people needing our various services will join the market in the current decade. However, very few people in the industry are involved in an undifferentiated market on a national scale. The question of interest to the industry now becomes, Who and where are the people comprising our potential markets?

Age and Place of the Market

The population projections shown in Figure 3.3 are larger than can be explained by changes in the birthrate. The population is growing because life expectancy is also growing. Improved living conditions, the control of germ disease, and the increasing control of cardiovascular disease is permitting more people to live out longer life spans. Furthermore, the old idea that the average life span is three score years and ten is also outdated. The number of people living beyond one hundred years is climbing fast, as can be seen in Figure 3.4.

This figure presents each five-year cohort of men and women in the population as percentages, and then projects to the year 2080. These charts reveal three things of interest. First, the stacks are not bilaterally symmetrical. There are more women than men in the upper half of the population stack, and the imbalance increases with age. This of course means that leisure activities will be called upon to serve many people who would now be considered very old, disproportionately female, and, by current standards, unusually healthy and vigorous.

By the year 2000 the baby-boomers who were about twenty-five years old in 1982 will be about forty-five. The people in this group will be at the midpoint in their various careers, and because there are so many of them, competition for a place in the sun will be intense. In fact, occupational failure is actuarially guaranteed for many, presenting important opportunities to the activity and leisure industry to provide compensatory leisure activities that will bring meaning to people's lives.

The grown-up baby-boomers will also carry the burden of educating those just below them in the stack, their own children, and supporting an increasing number of older persons above them, their parents and grandparents. The strains resulting from such a situation are only just beginning to be felt, and will intensify until the cohorts come into balance sometime in the first half of the next century.

Examination of the stacks for 2030 and 2080, too far into the future to influence our planning, show that the disproportionate nature of the cohorts that now exists will even out. The cohorts are similar in size and the stacks do not bulge as they do in the 1982 and 2000 samples. Furthermore, the stacks tend more slowly to a higher peak fifty years from now.

Nearly all of this information can be summarized in the median age of the population in the coming years. Figure 3.5 shows how the median age reached its low point in about 1970. Since then it has been on the rise and we are now in the period when, for half a century, the median age will rise steeply.

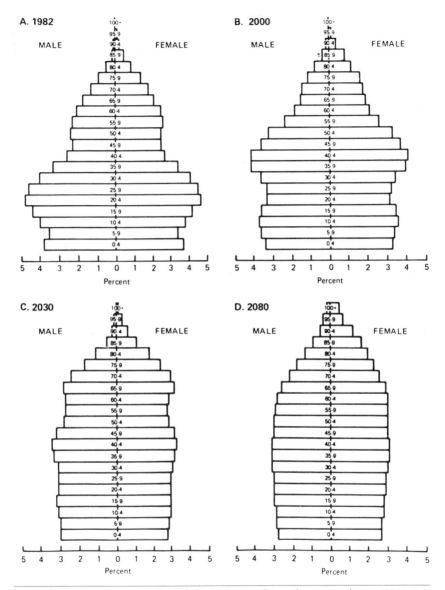

Figure 3.4 Percent distribution of the U.S. population by age and sex—1982 to 2080 (Spencer, 1984). (In 1982 there were 32,000 centenarians in the U.S. By 2000 they are projected to number 108,000 using the middle series of alternatives. A century from now there will be nearly 2 million.)

All our current planning needs to reflect this major social upheaval. The population is aging rapidly, and this will affect every aspect of the industry. Our industry's personnel, our attitudes, and our clients will be substantially different during the next evolutionary cycle.

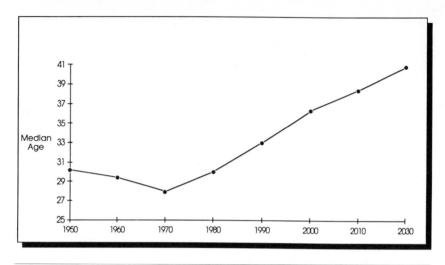

Figure 3.5   Estimates and projections of median age (from Spencer 1984).

All of the above data can be summarized in just a few ideas. By the end of the century we can project that there will be nearly 270 million people in the nation. We know that they will be older, disproportionately female, and by current norms healthy and vigorous. We also know that by then the baby-boomers will be middle-aged and their children will be leaving home. By 2000 the median age of the population will be thirty-seven years.

Characteristics of the Aging Population

Older people have not, until now, been a major target population for the activity and leisure industry. It is worthwhile at this point to characterize briefly the older adults who will become a major market for our services in the future.

Living Arrangements

The percentage of men who are married will be twice that for women (80 percent to 40 percent). Two-thirds of the population that is not institutionalized will live in family settings, and one-third will live alone. Married people will usually live with their spouses, and because fewer women will be married due to the fewer numbers of older men, more women will have to make other living arrangements. Three times as many women as men now live with relatives (18 percent to 6 percent) and about 2½ times as many women live alone or with nonrelatives (43 percent to 18 percent). These arrangements are unlikely to change much, and mean that noninstitutionalized older Americans are distributed in small living groups just like other Americans. Marketing aimed toward them will pose the same distribution problems of identification, access, and transportation as with any other group.

Income

Delivering high-cost services to older Americans will prove difficult. The income picture in 1983 revealed important differences between older Americans living in family units and older Americans living alone. The median family income was $16,862 while that for singletons was only $6,938. This disparity stems from the fact that older males have, and will continue to have for some time, greater income protection after their retirement, and their death often leaves the longer lived females as poor or nearly poor. This situation is exaggerated among black and Hispanic women and in cities. To the extent that the recent trends towards the economic emancipation of women continue, increasing numbers of women will retire with retirement income assured. However, it will be many decades before the picture is altered materially.

Presence in the Work Force

About 12 percent of older Americans are considered to be in the labor force, and comprise about 3 percent of the total labor force of the U.S. Of those seeking work, only 3 percent were unemployed. This percentage can be expected to increase to the advantage of the economy as the health of older Americans continues to improve. However, competition from the younger workers will mean that only those with highly competitive skills will remain in the labor force. This selection process will improve the general quality of the nation's work capacity.

Educational Level

The two remaining characteristics of import to the industry are education and health status. The educational level of older Americans has been rising quickly, reflecting the improving educational climate during their childhood. Between 1970 and 1983 the median level of education rose from 8.7 years to 11.0 years of schooling. That increase can be expected to continue because completion of high school and college became commonplace after World War II. This means that the older American market will be increasingly well educated and sophisticated. Unfortunately, educational advantages have not been equally distributed, and black and Hispanic older Americans will be markedly less educated. Median years of schooling for whites was 11.6 years in 1983, yet blacks had 8.0 years and Hispanics had only 6.4 years.

Health Status

Health status presents both opportunities and limitations for the activity and leisure industry. The opportunities to be of service will come from the impaired health of older Americans. These clients will have a dramatically increased need for habilitation. On the other hand, services requiring high levels of vigor and unimpaired health will be limited because most older Americans report some identifiable health limitation. For example, older Americans report that the number of days in which activity is restricted because of illness is about double the rate for younger Americans (about forty days compared to seventeen days per year). Of course, these limitations increase with age until people need functional assistance with their lives. About 12 percent of noninstitutionalized older Americans need assistance in some form[1].

Although the size of the aging population will continue to grow, it is important to realize that the opportunities associated with an aging population will not be equally distributed across the U.S. Because older people are now able to retire from their occupations, many are free to contemplate moving to a place they consider more salubrious. The result is that some parts of the U.S. receive an increasing number of retirees, pushing the median age of those regions far higher than the rest of the nation. The migration of the older members of the population from the Northeast and North Central regions to the South is demonstrated in Figures 3.6a and 3.6b.

The loss of older people from the Northeast and the North Central regions and their concentration in the South makes for more homogeneous populations in those regions. The older people take with them their income and the service work they can purchase. The areas they leave behind also lose the older people's stabilizing influences, their contributions to the rearing of grandchildren, and their capacity to volunteer their efforts and wisdom to the community. The geography of the situation and the mobility of the retirees will confront the regions with the imbalances that will have to be addressed now and for the next generation.

The dramatic reductions in cardiovascular disease in the last two decades and the incredible rise in concern for physical fitness and a healthy lifestyle presage a continued rise in health and longevity. These expectations are reflected in the data. However, it is suspected that the gains in vigor, health, and longevity have been underestimated. The nation is achieving its goals for wise personal lifestyle decisions that prevent disease (Richmond, 1979). Health promotion will accelerate the process and create more and healthier people than expected.

While there are problems with being old, just as there are with any age, the older Americans will be more vigorous, more numerous, wealthier, more

---

[1]The data presented in the last four paragraphs were extracted from a report of the American Association of Retired Persons (see Fowles, 1985).

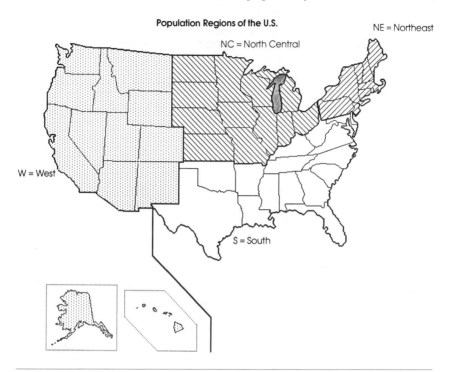

Figure 3.6a Map of the U.S. showing regions identified in Figures 3.6b, 3.8, and 3.9.

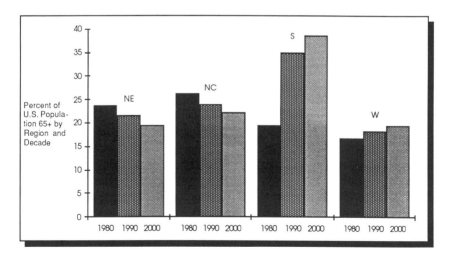

Figure 3.6b Percentage of the U.S. population 65 years and older by region (Miller, 1984).

sophisticated, and healthier than the stereotypes we have of them. The industry must address the needs of this very large and growing segment of the nation's people.

Ethnicity

Having digressed to cover what is probably the major social influence that the industry will face—the aging of the population—we can now attend to the distribution of the population by ethnicity. While it is possible to break down the population into its ethnic constituents using very fine-grain analysis of ethnic type and location (see the census tracts and their analyses), we will follow the lead of the Department of Commerce, which makes only one major division: "white" and "black and other races." The effects of race and ethnicity, although extremely powerful influences on attitudes and behavior, require careful local study in order to bring out useful guidelines for planners in the activity and leisure industry. Our purpose here is to discuss national trends.

Despite the fact that data are presented for only two major ethnic groups—black and other races, and white—they still present an important picture of the kind of nation we are in process of becoming. Figure 3.7 shows the percent of the total population that is of races other than white and their growth rates. Although the growth rates of all races are declining, the current growth rate of nonwhites is about three times that of whites. As a result, the percent

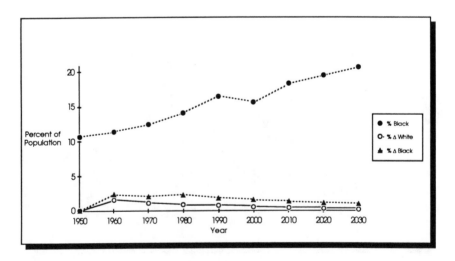

Figure 3.7 Estimates of the percent of total population that is black and other races and growth rates for whites (o) and black and other races (▲) (Miller, 1984).

of the total population represented by people of "black and other races" is rising. This group represents 14.5 percent of the nation now and this figure will rise to 16.9 percent by the end of the century when there will be 223 million people of the white race and 45 million people of black and other races.

The trend is clear. The United States is in the process of becoming less homogeneous. The complexities of this heterogeneity will require more sensitivity to local and ethnic wishes and preferences on the part of the activity and leisure industry. In fact, this very heterogeneity is contributing to the increasing segmentation and differentiation of people's preferences and ways of receiving service, which is one of the major trends (i.e., market segmentation) discussed in chapter 2.

Population Shifts—People and Place

That the population is not equally distributed across the territory of the United States is a well-known fact. The natives of the land were displaced by a massive colonization originating in Europe and starting from the East Coast. The status of Europe and the power of its markets and culture rewarded proximity to the Atlantic; thus opportunities were centered on the East Coast for most of the history of the U.S., and the population still clusters there. There are two concerns for physical educators planning the long-term development of their own careers. The absolute number of people in a region will be one determinant of the size of the activity and leisure market. Large, stable populations with well-developed social infrastructures exist in some parts of America; thus people wishing to serve in these kinds of settings should look there for opportunities. However, population is growing in some regions and the social infrastructure is still being shaped. Those who want the increased turbulence of growing, relatively unstable populations should pursue their careers where the populations are in greatest flux. The question becomes, Where is the population shifting from and to in America?

Together, the Northeast and North Central regions are currently the home of about 45 percent of the nation. The South, a region of approximately the same size, is now home to about 33 percent of the population, and the West is home to the rest.

In absolute terms, then, opportunities will remain best in the Northeast/Central region. Most people will be there, and if each person has equal needs for activity and leisure service, then the center of gravity of the industry will remain there. Even when migration over the remainder of the century is taken into account (see Figure 3.8 for the projections for 1990 and 2000), the majority of people will still live in the Northeast/Central regions.

However, when population *growth* is considered, the picture is dramatically different. Figure 3.9 shows the changes in the population by regions up

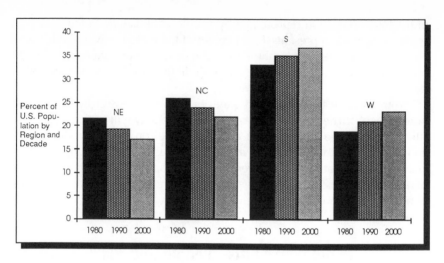

Figure 3.8 Population distribution by region (Wetrogran, 1983). Regions are identified in Figure 3.6a.

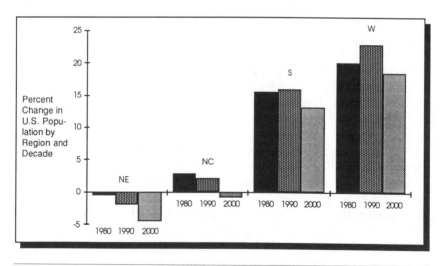

Figure 3.9 United States population growth by region (Wetrogran, 1983). Regions are identified in Figure 3.6a.

to the year 2000. This figure shows the startling effects of in-migration, that is, the movement of people within the nation. As a result of in-migration and immigration, the population of the South will continue to grow at about 15 percent per year, but the West will grow faster, at about 20 percent.

The growth of the South has resulted from a complex set of political, economic, and social factors. Of these, climate, the failure of the old labor unions to control workers and wages, space, and lifestyle are some of the most important factors. The result has been that it is cheaper to locate and relocate employment to the South and Southwest than to wrestle with the problems of the Northeast/Central regions that have been settled and industrialized for many decades. The decaying infrastructure of the "Rustbelt" (Wolf, 1974) and the evolution of the industrial base from extraction and manufacturing towards information- and service-based economies have hurt the North (Houston et al., 1984).

The growth of the West has been driven recently by the shift in the world trade market to the Pacific rim from the Atlantic rim. The rise of the Asian Pacific as a manufacturing and trading region has drawn trading activity to the West Coast. Trade has led to immigration and cultural exchange. Activities and employment associated with the import and export business and customarily associated with the Eastern seaboard are increasingly important activities for the Pacific Coast. Growth in employment and population will continue in the coastal states.

The major growth areas, according to Wetrogran (1983) will, however, be in the mountain and intermountain states of the West. Figures 3.10 and 3.11 show the picture of projected percentage growth of the states. The mountainous West, and the Northwest and Alaska (plus Texas via immigration and Florida via in-migration), will increase more than 20 percent through 1990 and then increase about 15 percent through 2000.

Self-Limiting Prognoses

The shift of population to the South and West is in full flood now. But such a trend is inherently self-limiting. Each in-migrant to those regions takes one job and consumes some of the resources of the area. In every way, in-migration eventually will be self-limiting.

Furthermore, the Northeast/Central region will intervene in the process. The leadership of the cities of the Northeast/Central region and the captains of industry that is placebound there will move to recapitalize and redevelop their infrastructure to increase the quality of life. When this is done, the advantages of old, established cultural elements in the environment of the North will become an attraction that the South cannot easily match. This process has already begun in earnest. The 1985 version of the national survey of the livability of the nation's cities revealed that the large cities of the North and East are already countering the earlier observation that the best cities in which to live are small and in any region but the Northeast/Central region (Boyer, 1985).

Another limitation stems from the fact that the people of the open lands in the West are increasingly resistant to the degradation of their environment. Forces for preventing unbridled growth, avoiding both human and chemical pollution, conserving the wilderness, and preserving the quality of the cities

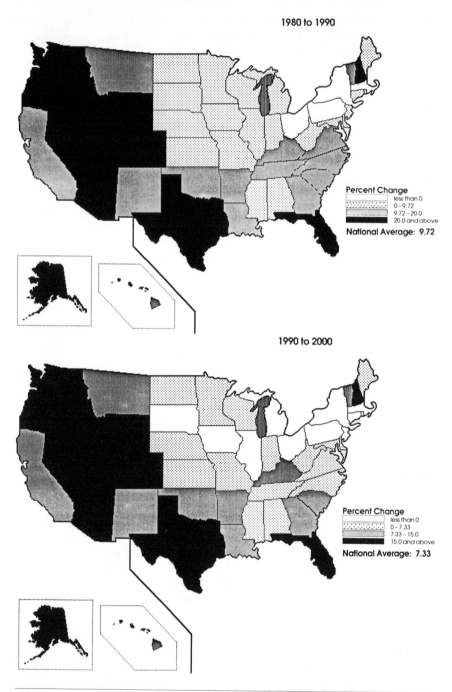

Figures 3.10 and 3.11 Projected population change in state populations for 1980 to 1990 and for 1990 to 2000 (Wetrogran, 1983).

are rising in power. They will continue to gain influence and will eventually be regarded as forces for economic development because new information and service industries will share the same ethos concerning the nature of people and their relation to the larger ecosystem. This tendency will lead to a control of the growth projected by the population statistics. In a sense these processes may be considered an "intervention" of the opposite kind to that expected in the Northeast/Central regions.

Thus it seems that the projections for growth generated from population statistics probably overestimate the likely effect of in-migration from the Northeast/Central regions. Although growth will occur, the naturally corrective tendencies to any population swing or trend will reduce the current attractiveness of the South and West. As a consequence, the loss of population from the Northeast/Central regions will not be as severe as population projections suggest.

The population statistics are based also on middle-range estimates of immigration. It is projected that immigration will level off at about a net addition of 450,000 immigrants per year. These Department of Commerce estimates include illegal immigrants, refugees, Cubans, Puerto Ricans, and returning civilian citizens. However, the figures seem low and predicting immigration by extrapolation is very difficult. Acts of government determine the rate of immigration in addition to the acts of immigrants. It is very clear that the open space and the opportunities in the U.S. will bring forth all the ingenuity of people who want better lives. People from Asia and Central America want to move to the West and South. There is no reason to believe that people from the rest of the world will exert less pressure to emigrate to the U.S. The future of the immigrant pool is uncertain, because while it is known that the pressure to immigrate exists, it is not clear what interventions will be initiated by the government to curb immigration.

Curbing immigration is difficult. The immigration legislation passed in 1986 attempts to curb immigration by controlling employment, although it is too early to determine the effectiveness of this legislation. However, it is clear that like in-migration, immigration has self-limiting features. When the impact of immigration exceeds the tolerance of U.S. residents, then government will be forced to intervene and to limit it. The prognosis is that the projections underestimate the effect of immigration to the Southwest and West. The growth of population in the Southwest and West will comprise a larger number of immigrants and fewer in-migrants than projected.

Changes Resulting From Population Shift

The overall changes to be expected are clear. The population will grow, and a substantial contribution to that growth will not come from new youth but from the longer lives of adults. The nation will become more heterogeneous with immigration and with the higher birthrates of black and Hispanic population segments. Opportunities for those wishing to serve youth will be enhanced, all else being equal, among blacks and Hispanics rather than among whites. For those planning to serve older adults, the future looks bright. The median age of the population as a whole is climbing fast and as the needs of adults and older adults are more widely recognized, they will become a major market for the activity and leisure industry. The increased age of the client population will, however, challenge the industry to reconstruct the activity content of the field and to find new ways to deliver it.

The geographic distribution of the population and the growth of the population send different messages. Although the majority of the people will continue to live in the North Central and Northeast regions, the major population growth will occur in the West and intermountain zones. To the extent that large numbers of people present opportunity, then opportunity will be found in the North Central and Northeastern regions. On the other hand, when population growth is important, the intermountain region is the zone of choice. This picture is complicated by the nature of the people in any region. This particular question is discussed in more detail in chapter 6, "The Changing Profession."

Discretionary Time and Income

People—distributed as they are across the nation in different cohorts and population segments—invest some of their discretionary time and income in self-enhancing activities. In fact, for many it is the discretionary activity that brings joy to their lives. The data presented in this section will show how much time and income are expended on the services of the activity and leisure industry.

The population is aging and the baby-boomers will soon be middle-aged and enjoying their midcareer incomes. To a great extent, the activity and leisure industry is unprepared for the windows of opportunity that will be created by the preferences of adult Americans. The windows of opportunity naturally will occur in the free market where potential clients spend their discretionary income. It is also true that these same potential clients are subject to a bombardment of rival claims for their dollar; competition is and will be intense. However, it is appropriate here to gain some view of the likely developments and size of two more basic phenomena driving the market: discretionary time and discretionary income.

Discretionary Time

Before discretionary time can be discussed, some definitions are needed. *Discretionary time* is presumed to be the amount of time left after working and traveling to and from work and unencumbered by obligations, chores, and sleep. It is the time at one's discretion. Work, a principal determinant of one's amount of discretionary time, is quite difficult to fix. The nominal work week is determined by custom, union agreement, and legislation. It is to the nominal work week that we refer when we discuss the forty-hour or thirty-five-hour week. The *nominal work week* is the normal duration of a regular week of work without any increases due to overtime, emergencies, and other exigencies and without any reductions due to sick leave, holidays and short-time, layoffs, and so forth.

Thus the nominal work week is not the same as the worked week. The *worked week* expresses the actual number of hours worked once overtime is added and vacation, compensatory time, or holidays are subtracted. Thus the worked week is usually substantially longer (but can be shorter) than the nominal work week according to the actual number of hours worked in that week.

A further complexity occurs when the total amount of work done in a year is averaged over the weeks in the year. Here the average work done per week, the *average work week*, is relatively small because holidays, vacations, and sick leave, are spread out as though they occurred proportionately in each week of the year. The data, of course, do not include salaried or self-employed people whose worked week and average work week exceeds the nominal work week rather substantially.

As you will see, there is confusion created by these definitions and the reader should be careful to know which definition is being used. In general, people in everyday conversation are referring to the nominal work week. The widespread belief is that the nominal work week is shrinking, thus giving the impression that discretionary time is increasing. Furthermore, there is also a belief that the amount of vacation time and the number of holidays are increasing, thus reducing the average work week. Here we look at the evidence, because changes in discretionary time are of importance to the activity and leisure industry.

In the last twenty years the nominal and the average work week in the U.S.A. have shrunk by about 10 percent. In 1964 the average work week was just under 39 hours per week. In 1982-83 it had shrunk to about 34.5 hours per week. Since then it has climbed back slightly to about 35.5 hours as we emerge from recession (see Figure 3.12). There are three possibilities for this trend: (a) a climb upwards toward the 40-hour average work week, (b) a return to the linear trend downwards towards a shorter average work week that was interrupted by the recession, or (c) some complex curve that results from something else.

The third choice is the most likely. The number of hours in the average work week will be influenced by several factors. Some factors influence the length of the worked week and others the amount of time spent on vacations and holidays. These two features of workers' time seem to be working in opposite directions.

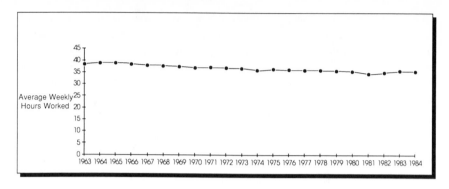

Figure 3.12 Average work week in the U.S. in hours (Valentine, 1984, p. L14).

One factor that will certainly tend to increase the length of the worked week will be the people's desire to work. People in general like to work; work has an important place in their lives. Improving working conditions so that the workplace and its activities have a more pleasant and leisurely character will increase this desire. Changes that will tend to reduce the worked week will be increases in productivity and changing social consensus that there is not enough work and that it should be shared. The amount of work done in a week will increase for some and decrease for others depending on individual circumstances. However, it is not at all clear that the trend towards the reduction of number of hours in a worked week will continue.

We can predict with confidence that the total amount of work done in a year will be reduced by a willingness to accept marginal unemployment such as unpaid vacations, leaves of absence, official holidays, and early retirement. Thus, across society at large it can be expected that the average work week for the entire population over the year will shrink.

Changes for the better in most people's work experience will make work more pleasant, and it will continue to occupy an important place in people's lives. For many people, work will not be an evil experience to be reduced to a minimum. It will be woven into a lifestyle in which the individual values the work experience yet seeks substantial blocks of time away from work in the pursuit of self-development.

The linear trend we see in Figure 3.12 would, if left undisturbed by new forces, reduce the average work week to thirty hours by 2004 to 2010. However, it is becoming clear that people like the process of working and will resist the trend. We will not move below a thirty-two-hour work week in the next twenty years. We will, however, see a greater variety of ways that the worked week is distributed—flextime, four-day work weeks, some work done at home, some at the office, plant, and so forth. Redistribution of the worked week and the overall reduction of the total period worked during the year will have complex effects on the amount and distribution of discretionary time.

It would be logical to assume that as the average work week (the total hours worked during the fifty-two weeks of the year) has been reduced, leisure has increased. However, this increase in leisure occurs during vacations and holidays, not during the worked week. The amount of leisure in a worked week has in fact declined. Valentine's official figures (1984), cited in Figure 3.12, are not in accord with a recent Philip Morris survey of the length of the worked week reported by workers. The Morris report is cited in a 1985 article in *Forbes Magazine*, "Upward with the Arts," and indicates that the worked week had increased from 40.6 hours in 1973, to 46.9 hours in 1980, to 47.3 hours in 1984. The survey went on to ask how much leisure time (that is, unobligated time other than working, traveling to and from work, chores, shopping, going to school, etc.) there was in the respondents' lives. Interestingly, the reported hours decreased from 24.3 in 1973, to 19.2 in 1980, and still further to 18.1 in 1984. Thus the survey found that the number of work hours in a worked week was increasing and that leisure time was decreasing. These observations were validated by a Harris poll that indicated that the worked week had increased from 40.5 to 47 hours, with leisure time shrinking from 26 to 18 hours in the period from 1973 to 1984 (data estimated by inspection from a figure reported by Solomon, 1986).

These data run counter to popular perceptions of the trends in hours worked. The notion of hours of work per week originated in the factories during the industrial revolution when there were few vacations and very little time off. Workers punched their cards and the customary duration of "at-work" time was codified as the nominal work week. It is to these agreements that people usually refer when they argue that the duration of the work week is shrinking. However, fewer and fewer people are working in punch-clock settings and the assumptions are changing for the majority of workers. There is an increasing expectation that workers will do what it takes to get the job done. White-collar workers and service workers have always worked longer hours than their colleagues in blue-collar occupations. There are increasing numbers of information workers, and the body of information to be processed is increasing dramatically. In addition, blue-collar workers are finding opportunities to work in small organizations or for themselves, and the work in these settings has intensified. Also, the competition for the opportunity to work from offshore has prompted massive "give-back" programs by workers that are unionized and in some cases workers have bought their own companies, thus becoming owners willing to work harder for themselves than for the stockholders.

When our concern is turned to the apparent reduction in discretionary or leisure time, we find a new factor that compounds the addition to the recent increase in the worked week. The number of women entering the work force has increased dramatically. This means that their former unpaid occupation, care of the home and the children, now has to be done after work. This work, whether shared equally with a partner or not, now reduces the total leisure time available in the households of the nation.

In summary, there is a perception in the activity and leisure industry that things are getting better—that the worked week is shrinking and leisure is increasing. This perception is not shared by workers. A Harris poll recently found that twice as many workers thought they had less leisure time now than workers who thought they had more (Solomon, 1986).

Although the agreed upon nominal work week is shrinking, as a nation we seem to be working longer and experiencing less leisure during each regular worked week. At the same time, the number of regular worked weeks has shrunk in a variety of creative ways. Thus, when working, Americans are working harder and longer in exchange for longer periods of vacation. In the end, the total amount of leisure available to the average American worker during the year has increased. This considerable redistribution of discretionary time during a working year has important implications for retailers whose markets are driven by the availability of discretionary time. However, hard-pressed workers are finding it more difficult to sustain earlier progress towards human development in the workplace—economic development is getting priority.

The Philip Morris survey also noted that, despite the fact that leisure time during a working week was shrinking, workers were budgeting their time more efficiently and were spending the available time so that their participation, at least in the arts, was rising. In 1984 it was reported that movie-going was up 9 percent, theater was up 7.4 percent, and attendance at popular concerts, ballet, and opera was up 18 percent, 46 percent, and 41 percent respectively. It is as if the work ethic has been applied to leisure, and that leisure is being used more efficiently. This tendency was noted very early by Linder (1970) in a book he called *The Harried Leisure Class*. He noted that people able to afford leisure lived harried lives, where leisure was managed with the same efficiency as their work. Linder noted the paradox that for the wealthy "leisure classes" there was actually little time available for leisure. On the other hand, people with time on their hands often did not have the wherewithal for meaningful leisure. Once again, the inequitable distribution of the benefits of our civilization is identified as a problem for physical education.

While the expectations for the reduced duration of a worked week will not be realized, other sources of discretionary time will expand. It is clear that people welcome extended periods of time to pursue some major life project. They want extended weekends and longer vacations, and if they cannot get them, they are often willing to value the time more highly than the earnings that the time would give them. Dropping out of the work force voluntarily will become increasingly common in a multitude of ways. The discretionary time this will create will also produce new opportunities for service. Supporting extended projects, travel, education, the donation of personal service, social interaction among like-minded people, joint ventures, and more will become new opportunities. To this source of discretionary time must be added retirement time. The number of retirees, their longevity, and the decreasing age at which people take retirement will dramatically increase this potential clientele.

Services building their success on short but regular attendance during the working weeks will have to recognize that unobligated time during the worked week is not growing. There are two choices open to those interested in creating programs that become part of the worked week life cycle that is experienced by most people for most of the year. One strategy will be to offer their services when the people are not working. Nine-to-five programs will not get the job done in this situation. Programs will have to be offered where and when the increasingly time-bound workers want them. Early morning, late night, lunchtime, and suppertime programs will have to become more common and the physical educators will not be able to count on office hours for their employment, at least in the adult sector.

The second strategy that will develop will be to take the programs themselves to the workers in their workplace. Here the increasing flexibility to control "time-on-task" within long hours at work will work to the advantage of the activity and health enhancement sectors of the industry.

While these developments take place, however, those services that require the dedication of blocks of time—weekends, vacations, whole days, and leaves—can expect that their clients will find it easier to find time. Thus time-extended workshops, trips, packages, touristic activities and adventures that involve active themes during long weekends and vacations will grow, offering physical educators increased employment and business opportunities.

Discretionary Income

Discretionary income when combined with discretionary time determines the absolute potential size of the market for activity and leisure services (see Figures 3.13 and 3.14). During each of the ten years from 1974 to 1984 leisure spending in the U.S. rose. It reached the sum of $191 billion per year in 1984, and this growth represented a compounded growth rate of 11.9 percent over

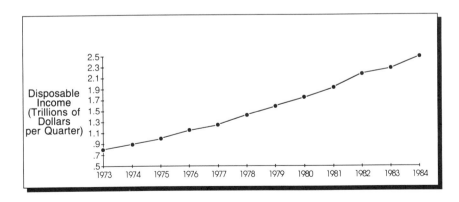

Figure 3.13   Estimated disposable income in trillions of dollars per quarter from 1973 to 1984 (Valentine, 1984).

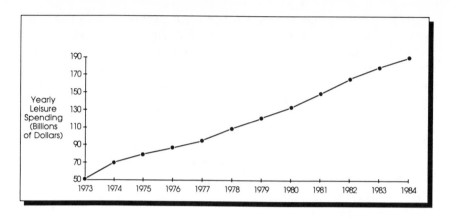

Figure 3.14 Estimated leisure spending in billions of dollars by year from 1973 to 1984 (Valentine, 1984).

that decade (Valentine, 1984). This growth in leisure spending mirrors the rise in real disposable personal income that rose similarly. By 1984 real disposable personal income rose to about $9.7 billion per year, and approximately 2 percent of it was spent in the leisure market. We can expect leisure spending to continue to follow real disposable income in the future. As a quick rule of thumb, we can project that the absolute size of the leisure market will be about 2 percent of real disposable income.

Other estimates of the market using data from different sources are consistent with the above data. Figure 3.15 shows that personal spending on rec-

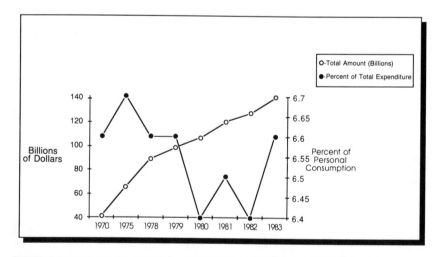

Figure 3.15 Estimated personal consumption expenditures for leisure from 1970 to 1983 (U.S. Department of Commerce, 1985, p. 377).

reation has risen consistently over the years. The pie chart, Figure 3.16, shows that recreation represents about 6.6 percent of all personal consumption expenditures. This figure has remained essentially constant since 1970, varying only from 6.4 to 6.7 percent per year since then. This suggests that the leisure market is inelastic. As income goes up, the proportion allocated to consumption increases and the share allocated to leisure remains the same.

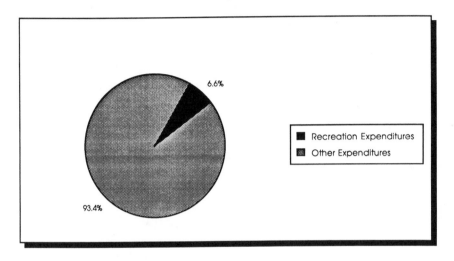

Figure 3.16 Leisure expenditures as a percent of total personal consumption expenditures from 1970 to 1983 (U.S. Department of Commerce, 1985, Figure 8:1).

Leisure expenditures are not all directed towards the activity and leisure industry. Figure 3.17 shows the major categories into which leisure spending falls. Professional physical educators may find access to the market sectors in a variety of ways suggested by the categories and their sizes. Retailing sport supplies and equipment, providing spectator amusement, writing the reading materials and contributing in the many ways identified in this book will fall into the large section labeled "other." Clearly these avenues are so new that the Bureau of the Census responsible for the original data has not yet categorized the activities.

The size of local markets can also be expected to follow real disposable personal income in a particular region. Knowing the size of the total U.S. market is of little real value to an entrepreneur in the activity and leisure industry, because there are limited opportunities to create services that are sensitive to market conditions of the entire country. Our services are fundamentally face-to-face. It is difficult to automate these exchanges and maintain the satisfaction of the client who has multiple personal and interpersonal motivations for purchasing the service. Thus opportunities lie with small business ventures seeking to create service on small scale in restricted locales.

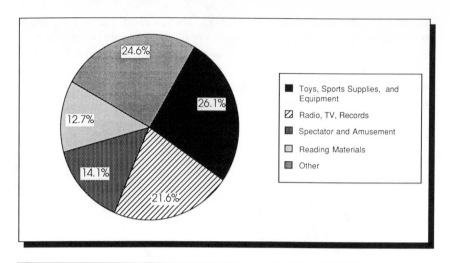

Figure 3.17   Distribution of leisure expenditures by category (U.S. Department of Commerce, 1985, Figure 8:1).

The secret will be to find small segments of the market and fill that need competitively, thus capturing some of the local leisure spending. Nevertheless, it is useful to view the large market picture to gain an insight into the overall patterns that are at work.

Manpower for the Leisure Industry

Manpower projections for nonschool-related employment in the activity and leisure industry are not easily obtainable. No agency or company is charged with making these projections routinely for the activity and leisure industry. Manpower needs are embedded in estimates for service occupations, manufacturing jobs, information tasks, and the like. No clear picture is possible and the last major leisure manpower study is now old and out-of-date (Hawkins & Verhoven, 1968). Recently, Kraus (1984) tried to estimate the size of the industry. He estimated that there were about 350,000 to 450,000 people employed by governmental, voluntary, and commercial organizations providing and operating park and recreation services, facilities, and programs. This number did not include clerical and maintenance personnel, and so it estimates only the number of people involved in professional and quasiprofessional roles. About half of the people were government employees.

Kraus also estimated that there were an additional 1 million people working in the allied entertainment industry. Other sources suggest that in 1983 there were a further 4.6 million people employed in the travel, tourism, and hospitality business (U.S. Travel Data Center, 1985). Travel, tourism, and hospitality form an industry that is second only to the health services as a private employer and is growing much faster than the economy as a whole. It has produced 2.6 million new jobs since 1973. Yet this industry employs disproportionate numbers of women (53 percent compared with 43 percent in all industries) and salaries are low. It is probably a principal cause of the obvious shift to a service-based economy here in the U.S.A.

When the activity and leisure industry is broadly defined to extend beyond municipal parks and recreation agency employment, to include private sector involvement and the closely related tourism and hospitality and entertainment, then the size of the employment pool is substantial. The people entering this pool come from a wide variety of specialties attracted by the opportunity to earn a living by dealing with people and their leisure activity. Sessoms (1986) points out that the occupations in the leisure side of the industry form a composite occupational category. Leisure service employees are not a unique occupational group. They come from prior training in such diverse and unrelated fields as landscape architecture, public administration, physical education, music, adult education, social work, and recreation and parks. Characterizing the employees and their occupations is not possible. The organizing principles that relate them to each other is the voluntary nature of the motivation for participation by the client. The size and diversity of the opportunity pool reflect the trend in the society at large to drift from manufacturing to service occupations.

The growth of the service sector is exemplified by the fact that 88 percent of the 9.1 million new jobs estimated to have been created in the economy since 1982 were generated by services. By 1995 it is expected that service jobs will outnumber manufacturing positions by 4.3:1 as opposed to 3.8:1 in 1985 (Russell, 1986). A major source of this growth in service occupations stems from the public and private sectors of the activity and leisure, health, travel, and hospitality industries.

Public Sector/Private Sector

For many activity and leisure professionals the decision to work in either the public or private sector is determined more by opportunity than by decisions based on careful planning. Since no agency or company regularly collects manpower projections for the activity and leisure industry, it is difficult to make direct projections as to whether future opportunities in the industry will predominate in the public or private sector. Some estimates can be made from the trends discussed above, which clearly favor the growth of the private over the public sector. However, the industry is not monolithic and in some parts of the nation the balance may be shifting the other way. Some estimate of how the public and private sector opportunities are distributed is desirable.

Clear manpower projections of the split between public and private sectors are not available; therefore, an indirect view of how the two sectors of the industry are balanced in the various regions of the country is necessary. The size and content of the public sector is, to a very large extent, determined by political decisions and the tax structure. The majority of these decisions are vested by the Constitution with the states. Thus it is the states and their intrastate local governments that control the large majority of the public sector's leisure supply. The exceptions occur when federal agencies like the Forest Service, Corps of Engineers, and the Bureau of Land Management are charged with creating multiple uses, including recreation, on their projects. Nevertheless public sector recreation can be considered to be a state and local government function.

The decisions made by state and local government to provide leisure services are in themselves limited by the total state and local revenue from all sources available to the politicians for expenditure. Furthermore, the number of people to be managed locally determines the degree to which local and state revenue is available for the advantage of individual citizens in the various political locales (see Figure 3.18a) of the nation. Thus the amount available to spend and the number of people to spend it on define the limits of the public sector leisure services in the local economy. These two data sets are combined in Figure 3.18b. The histogram shows the large variations in total state and local revenue available for disbursement per person compared to the average value for the whole U.S.A., which is $2,043 per person. The picture shows that revenues received by state and local governments per resident is greatest in the Rocky Mountain region.[2] The available revenue to be spent on each individual is greatest here. The revenue available per resident in the Rocky Mountain region is $2,533 per capita. The revenue available per person is smallest in the Southwest. Note that revenue per capita is higher than average in Hawaii, the Far West, and the Mideast. Other regions cluster closely to the national average. This picture would have been grossly distorted if Alaska and the District of Columbia had been included. Alaska was excluded because the tiny population there benefits from enormous oil industry extraction tax revenues (in 1984 the per capita revenue there was nearly six times the national average). The District of Columbia is also anomalous because of the considerable direct costs of operation of the federal government located within it (in 1984 the District of Columbia's total revenue per capita was more than twice the national average).

While it is obvious that each political entity within the regions varies in revenue, population, and tasks to be addressed, it is clear that the distribution of revenues per capita places different caps on the aspirations of people in the regions to acquire public sector leisure services. The wealthy and populous Mideast, and the relatively sparsely populated Rocky Mountains

---

[2]Census tract data are combined for specific regions that are identified on the map in Figure 3.18a.

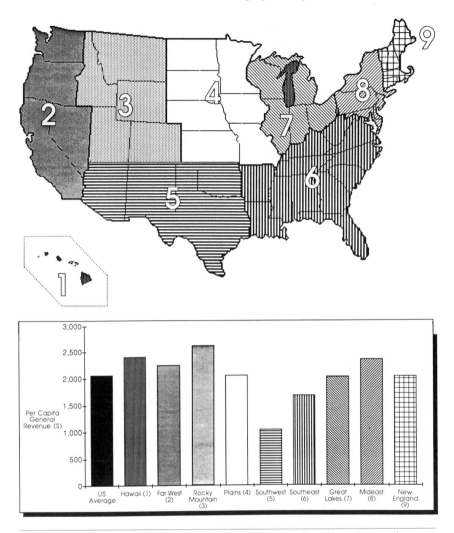

Figure 3.18a and 3.18b Map defining the regions used to determine total per capita state and local revenue received by region (data derived from Advisory Committee on Intergovernmental Relations, 1984, p. 53).

and the Far West, are best able to maintain high level expenditures on social services. Whether they actually do so requires more detailed study. However, the lesson is clear: If per capita revenue in state and local government is considered, then the populous Southwest will have most difficulty making public sector services of any kind available to its people.

It is possible to ask the question the other way around and address the capacity to support private sector leisure services. The question then becomes, In what regions do the citizens' personal incomes augment or offset the capacity of local and state government to deliver service? A way to answer that question is to chart by the same regions the per capita revenue received by state and local government as a percentage of personal income. If this is done, then it will express the relative weight of state and local revenue per person as a fraction of each person's personal income in the region. These data, obtained from the Advisory Committee on Intergovernmental Relations (1984), are charted in Figure 3.19. The state and local revenues in the Rocky Mountain region are very large relative to the rest of the regions in the U.S., and are also very large compared to the personal incomes of the residents of the region. Thus in the Rocky Mountain region the fiscal power of the state and local governments is considerable compared to the purchasing power and income of the residents of the region. The opposite situation holds true in the Southeast and the Great Lakes regions. Compared to the total income of the residents, the income for state and local governments is relatively small.

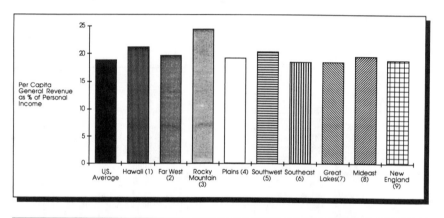

Figure 3.19 Total per capita state and local revenue expressed as a percentage of state personal income (data derived from Advisory Committee on Intergovernmental Relations, 1984, p. 53). Regions used are identified in Figure 3.18a.

These data can be summarized by thinking of Figure 3.18b as painting a picture of the regional differences in the absolute revenue available to the public sector for expenditure on private individuals. Figure 3.19 expresses the relative power of that income as a component in the total market of the region. Clearly, this information suggests that the public and the private sectors will fare differently in the different regions of the U.S.A. Such data should be analyzed carefully by those working in the activity and leisure industry because the shifts in balance between public and private expenditures will influence the nature of the delivery systems used by the industry to achieve its objectives.

Summary

The size of the activity and leisure market is determined by the number of people and their distribution, the time they have at their discretion and the way it is distributed throughout the year, and the money they have to spend. As a review, the principal changes and their implications for physical education are summarized.

The absolute size of the market will grow as the population increases. However, the composition of that population will change. People on average will be considerably older and the number of vigorous, older retirees will increase dramatically. Furthermore, the population will become markedly more heterogeneous with more black Americans and a substantial increase in the number of people of Hispanic origin. New content and practices for a physical education tuned to the needs of adults and the elderly will have to be added to content currently aimed towards youth. In the same way, it will not be possible to ignore the changing face of the nation as the black and Hispanic minorities become major population segments contributing to the heterogeneity of the populace.

The discretionary income spent by individuals on activity and leisure services is likely to hold essentially constant, so that the absolute amount spent on activity and leisure services will grow with population. However, that growth will occur among adults who will voluntarily determine their own expenditures on activity and leisure services. The proportion of the expenditures of interest to physical education will not be determined by legislation or political action, but by myriad purchasing decisions made by older adults. In other words, though the market is growing, it will not automatically be captured by funding formulae tied to population growth; rather, its growth will be tied to the physical educators' collective ability to persuade adults to purchase their services.

In addition to private discretionary income, there is also public sector income derived from taxation. A further feature of the market for physical education's services is that it is created by both private sector and public sector programming. The balance between the fraction of the total earnings captured into the tax base for public expenditure, and that portion left in the purse of individuals for their discretionary use, is not equally distributed across the states. This fact should be considered one of the features influencing the relative size of the markets created by the public and the private sectors.

The remaining determinant of the size of the activity and leisure market is the time available to engage in the programs offered by the industry. Discretionary time is also shifting. For those in the work force, the worked week is increasing as the U.S. economy is forced to become more productive. Workers' discretionary time during the worked week is decreasing and shifting into larger blocks of time that interrupt the flow of work during the year.

In addition, there will be more people outside of the work force who have substantial discretionary time and need for activity and leisure services. These people are the retired, the unemployed, and those who voluntarily leave the work force.

The notion that physical educators will work from nine to five, if it was ever really true, will be put to rest by shifts in discretionary time. Most physical educators will have to work where and when their adult clients are available in the future. The programs for working adults will have to fit conveniently around an expanding worked week or serve working adults freed temporarily for blocks of time during the year. Programs for those outside the work force will have to recognize that the discretionary income of these clients is often small, and public sector initiatives in these cases are clearly justified.

A final note: Each of these shifts will not take place independently of each other; they will interact. For example, as older people are shifting southwards, they will take with them their restricted taxable and discretionary income. As a result, the demand in the South for public sector services will not be matched by the public sector dollars. Each of the determinants of the size of the activity and leisure market identified in this chapter will interact with each other. The basic data are provided for those readers interested in specific population segments, geographic locations, and the public or private sectors, to help them create their own scenarios that combine the data in ways that are of interest to them. All of these scenarios may not come true; however, the virtue lies in the process of thinking about how we in physical education are to serve our changing nation in the future.

The Health
*Revolutions*_____

Health enhancement is a very important part of the mission of physical education. The factors affecting this mission are many and complex. This chapter deals with two major health care revolutions and their implications for physical education. Because this chapter is a long one, a "map" is needed to help guide you through its rather complex structure.

The chapter is divided into two major sections. The first deals with the way the health care industry is becoming a business; the second deals with two major governmental initiatives that seek to revolutionize the health status of Americans by promoting prevention rather than cure. These initiatives are the surgeon general's two comprehensive health enhancement initiatives. The first of these deals with Americans by age—a convenient framework for physical education—defining the specific health enhancement challenges that each age group presents. The second specifies the steps necessary to contain each of the major preventable disease complexes. Together, the two current health care revolutions—that is, the conversion to a business model and the conversion to preventive rather than curative medicine—have major implications for physical education.

Health Becomes an Industry

The health industry is undergoing rearrangement at a dramatic pace (Starr, 1982) as a result of three parallel forces all working to alter the face of medicine. These forces are (a) cost containment, (b) the shift to preventive medicine, and (c) the rising cost of malpractice insurance.

Health care has become enormously expensive and there are vigorous attempts by government and by businesses in general to contain the costs. The many efforts to prevent the continuing rise of health care costs are changing the face of medicine. Although eye-catching advances in curing disease continue to be made, it is clear to all now that it makes more sense economically and practically to prevent disease, and to promote the enhancement of wellness, rather than to cure disease once it has occurred. The pressures on the health care industry to become more like a business and to emphasize preventive health care are many and intense.

Containing Health Costs

Health care enterprises, particularly hospitals, have traditionally grown in size and cost at rates that far exceed growth in population, the number of elderly therein, or inflation. The health care industry has written its own ticket in the past and was largely run as a "costs-plus-profits" business. The total cost of health care as a percentage of the gross national product has grown from 5 percent in 1960 to 10.7 percent in 1984. It now costs the nation in excess of $350 billion. Health care costs and expenditures cannot be allowed to soar upwards indefinitely. Costs must be contained and the governments of the states and the nation, together with the third-party payers, are cooperating to restrict the process.

The drive to contain medical costs is altering the basic unit of the health industry. The basic unit used to be a tiny organization of one to a few physicians who did their best to serve a small group of clients over long periods of time. Now we see the emergence of a few health industry conglomerates establishing multifaceted, vertically integrated businesses that control massive systems from a distant head office. Increasingly, the physician is becoming just one of many types of employees organized by the standard business practices of a management that operates a large and complex business in order to make a profit.

Business Control of Health Care

The commercialization of the medical side of the health industry is proceeding apace. For example, the market share garnered by for-profit hospital companies, many belonging to multisite conglomerates, has already reached 55 percent in Puerto Rico, 43 percent in Florida, 39 percent in Nevada, 36 percent in Texas, and 33 percent in California. Although the market penetration of the profit-motivated health care complex is much less pronounced in the great plains (Kansas, Nebraska, the Dakotas, Iowa, Minnesota, and Montana average about 4 percent), it is clear that the tendency of big business to acquire control of hospital care is growing and spreading from the Southeast and Southwest into the heartlands (Cohn,1985).

Hospital care has become a major part of all health care delivered, and capturing a market share in the hospital care business can be very rewarding. Hospital and major clinic buildings and the associated staff exist as coordinated organizations in all major communities, and will be the bases from which the major expansions of the traditional health care industry occur. However, while the health care industry has grown substantially since Medicare and Medicaid were introduced, there are now very strong pressures to limit rising costs. Although profits are to be had from acquiring control of hospitals and attendant enterprises, those profits will have to be gained in the future from skillful management and cost control rather than simply from increasing prices. Because of these efforts at cost containment, the hospital profits are no longer rising as quickly as they have in the past. As a result, energy has been diverted to generating profit from the ancillary enterprises that surround health care. Thus real estate, manufacturing, and quasimedical services will increasingly become part of medical-industrial complexes (Starr, 1982). Physical education is a ripe target as an ancillary service for this kind of incorporation.

Prevention Rather Than Cure

A major cause of increasing health care costs has been the tendency to create more and more high technology medicine just because it is there, but there is no clear evidence that more and more sophisticated medicine necessarily produces better overall health. Hospitals have skimped on hiring people to improve the personal care of patients, yet have sometimes used their money to buy enormously expensive items—CAT scanners, for instance. It is clear that the future growth in profits must come from increased efficiency and from practicing preventive medicine.

Limiting Costs of Malpractice Insurance

Finally, the settlements in malpractice suits have grown so enormously that defensive medicine has become an accepted way of practicing. Physicians have had to order multiple and redundant tests to be on the safe side as a defense against potential malpractice suits. However, even this process is subject to cost analysis. The recent furor over the cost of insurance has led to efforts to reduce the costs of malpractice insurance passed along to the consumer by legislating limits on settlements.

Competition for Market Share

Competition is developing dramatically for a market share in the health care industry. The increasing surplus of physicians, for instance, is startling. In 1950 there were 79 medical schools preparing 25,000 students for careers as physicians. In 1984 there were 127 medical schools and more than 67,000 medical students. The number of doctors practicing medicine has also been augmented by the immigration of foreign-trained physicians. Starr (1982) reports that in 1975 there was one physician for every 545 people in the U.S.; it is projected that by 1990 that number will shrink to 404. There is now intense competition for the opportunity to practice medicine; and the opportunities for service, wealth, and influence are shrinking. More and more physicians are forced to contemplate new career patterns for themselves and to seek new avenues and settings among the ancillary services. In doing so, they threaten to enter the traditional health care domain of physical education.

A second form of competition for a market share in the health care industry arises from those in the allied health professions, who aggressively assert that they can contribute to the achievement of good health just as efficiently as physicians. Exercise physiologists, birthing specialists, psychologists, athletic trainers, physician's assistants, physical therapists, nutritionists, chiropractors, homeopaths, and osteopaths are all vying to contribute to health care and to share in the rewards. The activity and leisure industry has an important role to play in health enhancement and will participate increasingly in the health enhancement business. In fact, the recent report *Prospects for a Healthier America* argues that this process could be accelerated by the formation of dual-locus programs involving the primary providers (such as hospitals) and other community agencies (such as universities) to provide the desirable preventive and health enhancement programs (Farquhar & King, 1984).

Competition has resulted in a dramatically increased tendency for the health care industry to use conventional business practices to safeguard profits while containing costs. The struggle for efficiency and for customers has led to many new forms of health care designed to deliver the same service in different ways. Offering better locations, more convenient service, and lower prices, and dividing the market to skim off the most profitable segments of the business, have all entered the scene. Storefront health centers, home delivery, office surgery, mass-produced procedures, self-testing kits are all examples of competitive pressure forcing the industry to adapt to competition and become more efficient in order to survive.

Impact of Competition

Clearly, all of this competition will have a major impact on the way physicians view themselves and how they do business (Swanson, 1985). Although physicians may be recruited on the basis of their desire to do good, or to enjoy status and wealth, future trends will tend to frustrate both those ambitions. The forces for cost containment and demystification, and the increasing tendency toward self-help, will reduce the physician's profits. The glut of MDs and increasing market pressures will diffuse the responsibility for health care. Competition and eventually advertising, marketing, and even price wars will occur just as they have in other segments of the retail business. Physicians will be forced to branch out and create markets for their services, something heretofore neglected by a profession traditionally rooted in a relatively inelastic curative medical industry.

Activity and Leisure Industry Under Attack

As the activity and leisure industry enters competition with other segments of the health care industry, it will inevitably come under attack by physicians and hospitals forced to seek new markets. The less profitable fields, historically left to the activity and leisure industry, will become an arena for direct competition.

For many decades licensed physicians (together with some other health care professionals) have enjoyed a carefully regulated market for their services. Access to that market has been carefully restricted by the professional licensing boards and the vigorous policing of the boundaries of medicine by the county medical societies and other professional associations. Equally knowledgeable competing professionals have been prevented from providing health care, yet the boundaries preventing the extension of medical practice into new and adjacent fields, such as fitness, sport science, public health, health education, community development, and leisure counseling, have been less clearly defined.

When legal protections are added to the residual of the long-held mystical authority of the physician as practitioner, our field does indeed face a fierce challenge. Physicians will be forced by the glut, by the reduced rewards and opportunities of conventional practice, and by their newly adopted roles of employees within massive health conglomerates, to seek for clients wherever they can find them. They will find them increasingly in the schools, institutions, sport systems, gymnasiums, spas, and recreation centers. In short, they will find them where we find our clients today.

Physical Educators in Favorable Position

Although the historic authority of physicians will work to their advantage, the cost of delivered service will work to ours. The expense and duration of training and the expectations for earnings are all lower in the activity and leisure industry; but the expertise of activity and leisure professionals in their areas of specialty is often impressive. For example, exercise physiologists may be as well qualified as physicians to work in cardiac rehabilitation, although their personal investment in training is much less. The median debt of students leaving doctoral (PhD) study from public universities is $5,000, and from private universities, $7,975, while the median debt for those leaving both public and private medical schools is $21,000 and $25,000 respectively (Ehrlich, 1985). Furthermore, the PhD can be fully functional in three to four years beyond the bachelor's degree. It takes at least five to six years, and usually more, for a physician to do the same.

It will become clear, as market forces regulate the process, that medicine is not as attractive a means of entering the helping professions as it once was. As recruitment into medicine is negatively affected, recruitment into the activity and leisure industry will be positively affected. As a consequence, competition for entry into the helping professions via physical education, health education, and recreation will increase. The qualifications demanded for admission will also become more stringent. The result will be better qualified candidates entering the activity and leisure industry, an increasing capacity of the field to compete on an even footing with medicine, and a blurring of distinctions a generation from now. Individual physicians and high-level activity and leisure professionals will more frequently cooperate in their practices to improve the lives of their clients.

To summarize, as a result of the tendency for the health profession to run as a costs-plus-profits system, and as a result of the profession's practicing high tech curative and defensive medicine health care, health care costs have skyrocketed. These increases have been unbridled in the past because of the massive growth of third-party insurance payers. Because third parties have been paying for much of the care, there have been no immediate incentives to reduce costs. Now, however, government cost containment and efficient business practices restrain these processes. The health care complex has become an industry.

The Move Toward Healthy Lifestyle Management

A cheap and effective way to contain health costs is to involve citizens themselves in preventing costly disease. The federal government has recognized this and has focused the nation's attention on the role of the people in disease prevention. A major governmental goal is to encourage and reward good self-management of health nationwide.

Changing one's lifestyle and making sound decisions about diet, weight control, exercise, stress control, and early detection of disease have been shown to cost very little and yet produce great benefits (Richmond, 1979). The preventive health care approach is producing much greater gains in the nation's health than expenditures on exotic curative medicine, and with little expense. Thus physical educators have an important role to play in recruiting people to the processes of beneficial personal lifestyle management.

The preventive health care revolution began to flower in the 1950s. Epidemiological studies of cardiovascular disease gained attention when they showed that some occupations had lower heart disease rates than others. Alarming health status reports that showed that American children lagged far behind their European counterparts in physical fitness led to the formation of the President's Council on Physical Fitness. These reports began to sensitize Americans to their role in maintaining their personal health. Diet studies and studies on the role of obesity in mortality and morbidity followed; then came the alarm signals that smoking carried significant health risks. By the late sixties people had also been alerted to the problems of chemical contamination; we had seen our tiny earth from the moon.

By the 1970s personal health and community health had become concerns of many ordinary Americans. Since then the jogging phenomenon, the health food industry, seat belt laws, the environmental movement, and many other health-enhancing activities have become part of our lives. Consequently, substantial numbers of people now seek to manage their own lifestyles in a healthy way.

So powerful was this health consciousness revolution that by 1985 (according to a Media General/Associated Press survey) nearly six in ten Americans claimed they "exercise to keep fit" (Kilman, 1985). In the poll of 1,402 adults taken nationwide, 57 percent indicated that they exercised in addition to their normal activities. Walking was the most common form of exercise with about one-third claiming they walked to keep fit. About half the respondents claimed that they added exercise indoors to their daily activities, citing rope jumping, weight lifting, calisthenics, aerobics, and yoga as popular exercises. The important thing here is not whether these activities are necessarily capable of improving health, or even whether the frequencies of exercising are effective. Rather, the important message of the poll lies in the respondent's perceptions: Nearly 60 percent were persuaded by the prevailing data, or by the changing climate of support for exercise, to begin exercise programs for health reasons. Furthermore, three-fourths of the respondents who did not exercise claimed that they were prevented from doing so by time pressures. The notion that exercise is good for you has become so pervasive that only 10 percent of the sample admitted that they were too lazy to exercise, or did not like to exercise.

Even the advertising industry has accurately sensed the shift in people's interest and the new legitimacy of a personal concern for enhancing health. Themes related to health and fitness are frequently used to sell products. Images of beautiful, exuberantly healthy and active adults are commonplace in mass marketing schemes. The day-to-day bombardment of advertising with both the overt and covert message that good health must be achieved rather than just experienced has altered the consciousness of Americans. We have taken up healthy lifestyles in droves. It is now up to the activity and leisure industry to consolidate its role in health enhancement by actually delivering the promised products of a healthy lifestyle—reduced morbidity, enhanced status, better appearance, greater vigor, friends, and fun.

Health Enhancement at the Workplace

The people themselves are not alone in their new awareness of their own roles and responsibilities. Businesses have also recognized the need for a healthier work force and the role that health enhancement plays in their own profitability. When large numbers of workers choose to maintain healthy lifestyles, the company as well as the workers benefit (O'Donnel & Ainsworth, 1984). For example, only one year after health enhancement programs were introduced at 130 General Motors worksites, GM reported significant reductions in grievances, accidents, and lost time, and a massive reduction in sickness and accident payments. The company also estimated that it recovered three times its investments in health enhancement at these worksites (United Press International, 1984).

Other incentives for enhancing the health of employees are equally dramatic. Medical costs now exceed pension costs in most industries. O'Donnel and Ainsworth (1984) have indicated that a company saves $600 per year each time a worker quits smoking. Kennecott Copper experienced a 55 percent reduction in medical costs associated with those workers who participated in an exercise program. Evidence of direct financial benefits gained from enhancing employee health is accumulating rapidly.

Such benefits are so appealing to some employers that they are offering financial incentives, bonuses, and recreational programs for those who contribute to the financial health of the company by staying healthy themselves. These programs can be classified as Employee Assistance Programs (EAPs), which are any programs offered by the employer to "assist employees with personal problems (mental, legal, family, job-related, etc.) or illnesses (substance abuse, emotional illness) that can affect job performance" (Kiefhaber & Goldbeck, 1984, pp. 45-46). If eliminating illness is defined not only as attempting to eradicate existing disease, but also as preventing potential disease and achieving wellness, then this definition of EAPs can include all worksite health enhancement programs.

We can impute an employer's implementing an EAP to altruism, but there is also hard evidence that improving job performance reaps direct financial benefits for that employer in terms of immediate productivity, and indirect financial benefits in terms of reducing the costs of sickness. In addition, these programs have the effect of improving employee morale. The drive for increased profitability will inevitably result in many more companies and agencies creating EAPs for their employees (see Table 4.1).

The people needed to run these health enhancement programs at the worksite will come from a variety of helping professions, physical education among them. In a sense, a new industry will be created and will take its place among such revolutions of industry as mass production, time and motion study, and value engineering. But in this case the company's stock of human resources,

Table 4.1   Cost Savings Reported for Some Employee Assistance Programs (EAPs)

Company	Number of employees	Number using EAP	Annual cost savings (dollars)
University of Missouri	7,000	1,002	67,996[a]
Scovill Manufacturing	6,500	180	186,550
Illinois Bell Telephone (with families)	38,490	1,154	254,448[b]
U.S. Postal Service	83,000	?	2,221,362
Kennecott Copper (with dependents)	7,000	1,200/yr	448,400[c]
New York Transit	13,000	?	2,000,000
E.I. DuPont (with spouses)	16,000	176	419,200[d]
New York Telephone	800,000	300	1,565,000

Note. From "Worksite Wellness" by A.K. Kiefhaber and W.B. Goldbeck, 1984, in *Proceedings of Prospects for a Healthier America: Achieving the Nation's Health Promotion Objectives* (p. 54), Washington, DC: U.S. Department of Health and Human Services.

[a]Plus 40 percent decrease in use of health benefits.

[b]Plus 31,806 disability days saved; off-duty accidents decreased 42.2 percent; on-duty accidents decreased 61.4 percent; savings in reduced use of health insurance and job inefficiency.

[c]Total includes reduced absenteeism, sickness, accident disability, and health insurance use. A conservative calculation found a $5.78 return for each $1.00 invested.

[d]Alcohol program only.

rather than the efficient design and use of materials, will be the object of attention.

Federal Governmental Interests

As these health revolutions were taking place, the federal government entered the picture. It wanted to reduce the cost of medical care and improve the health of the nation simultaneously. Preventive health care became an issue. To emphasize new governmental policies, the surgeon general published a report, *Healthy People* (Richmond, 1979), that cogently defines health enhancement goals for the nation. In a companion report, *Promoting Health, Preventing Disease* (Richmond, 1980), the surgeon general proposed concrete objectives that will help us achieve our national health goals. The two reports establish a blueprint for preventive health care and health enhancement in our country between now and the end of the century.

The reports are organized differently from one another. The first report, *Healthy People*, identifies health problems of different age groups and offers solutions of a general nature. The second report, *Promoting Health, Preventing Disease*, is organized by disease complexes and defines specific goals for dealing with each. Both reports have much to say to professionals in the activity and leisure industry, the most important points of which are detailed in this chapter. The following section of this chapter includes those lessons to be learned from the first report, *Healthy People*. Then the discussion turns to the lessons we can learn from the second report, which considers the major disease complexes and specific objectives for the nation. This material speaks loudly to the activity and leisure industry as it accommodates to the changes taking place in the health care industry, which consumes about one-eighth of the total earnings of the nation.

Age Group Health Problems and Goals

During an individual's early years, the activity and leisure industry is presumed to play only an indirect or preparatory role in health enhancement. However, the surgeon general's goals for a healthy nation call on the activity and leisure industry to play a single and direct role in health enhancement during the adult years. A summary of the goals for different age groups follows, with a commentary on the role that the activity and leisure industry, and physical education in particular, will play in achieving them. (Indented text are summaries of the surgeon general's goals for each age group.)

Infants

Infancy begins at conception and ends at the age of one. The factors that influence infant health are determined by the health of the mother at conception and her capacity to support the developing child in the womb and during its first year of life. The health of infants does not depend substantially on the services of the activity and leisure industry. The major goal for infant health enhancement is simply to reduce the infant mortality rate by 1990 to that achieved by Sweden, the world leader. A major step toward achieving this goal will be the improvement of the intrauterine environment for the developing child, which will result in fewer underweight and unhealthy babies. Improved prenatal care and adequate nutrition for the pregnant mother will help to accomplish this goal. In addition, pregnant women must be educated to avoid smoking, alcohol, substance abuse, and exposure to harmful chemicals and pollutants in order to avoid chemically altering the fetal bloodstream. Accidents, inadequate birthing care, genetic counseling, and fewer pregnancies in younger and older women are also important considerations.

During the first year of life, adequate nutrition, preventive health care, and accident prevention become important. Educating the parents in how to offer their children play and affection is also vital. Finally, parents need to understand the importance not only of a warm and affectionate relationship with their baby, but of the baby's interaction with others. A significant failure to thrive can result from the social isolation of infants.

The activity and leisure industry is clearly involved in the health of the mother at the beginning of pregnancy. However, the industry's role in enhancing the health of young adults, including mothers-to-be, will be discussed later. The industry will find little opportunity to influence the developing child in the womb except with the cooperation of the pregnant mother in maintaining her own health. Once the babies are born, the activity and leisure industry may be able to find a role in enhancing the health of the new mother and creating opportunities for the new babies and their care givers to enjoy an improved quality of life together.

The challenge will be to create opportunities for pregnant women to remain in activity and leisure programs, and to welcome them back with their new babies after birth. Existing activity and leisure programs should be expanded to include mothers (and care givers) and their babies. Finding social and recreational activities for new babies and their mothers is a part of the industry's role of serving from womb to tomb. This market is already being tapped by private sector businesses that provide structured exercise and play programs and infant exercisers. These programs have names like "Gymboree," "Playorena," and "Babycise" to attract parents who want to provide nurturance and activity for their infants with the help of others (Kantrowitz & Joseph, 1986).

However, the size of the industry that provides activity and play for mothers and their new babies is likely to remain small, if only because of the brief duration of infancy. Furthermore, the population most needing such infant health enhancement activities is that part of the population least able to afford them. Because of the nature of our society's current evolution, the roles of public sector agencies are being minimized, and there will be little incentive for private providers to market services to the poor. Affluent people will make their presence felt by demanding opportunities to maintain good health during pregnancy and infancy. Unfortunately, this tendency will simply widen the gap between those infants born into impoverished situations and those born into affluent families. Because of this, the surgeon general's goals for infant health are not likely to be fully realized.

Children

Children are defined as those people between the ages of one and fourteen years. While the health of U.S. children is better than ever before, there are nations with healthier children. Our nation's goals are to reduce the deathrate and optimize the development of the next generation. In all the major categories of child death except cancer, nonwhite children have a higher deathrate than whites. The major preventable causes of death are accidents and homicides, and the causes over which we have less or no control are cancer, birth defects, and influenza and pneumonia. In any case, the morbidity and mortality patterns suggest that unequal distribution of benefits and health care is a substantial cause of the differences in deathrates between white children and nonwhite children.

The activity and leisure industry can assist in correcting the fundamental inequalities in the distribution of health care only by avoiding the dissemination of further inequality. Unfortunately, the funding of the activity and leisure industry tends toward a "user-pay" or "pay-for-play" basis, which will exacerbate the current biases in distribution. Because this issue of unequal distribution of health care is a general one affecting all people of all ages, its discussion is reserved for the end of this chapter.

Beyond a moral obligation to ameliorate this kind of maldistribution, the industry has a major, specific task. This task is to convince young children that activity is enjoyable. The industry must provide them with the basic skills and knowledge needed to use their bodies effectively at work and play later in their lives. With few exceptions, children spend much of their time in school. Because the role of physical education in the schools and the curriculum is a major topic in itself, extended comment will be saved for later.

Adolescents and Young Adults

Deathrates for adolescents and young adults aged fifteen to twenty-four years are higher in the U.S. than they are in Sweden, England, and Japan. These countries, with comparable affluence and stability, do far better than the U.S. in keeping members of this age group alive. The principal causes of death in this age group are accidents and homicides. Motor vehicle accidents kill 1½ times more whites than blacks. Homicide, on the other hand, results in about 6 times more black victims than white victims. Other types of accidents and suicide are the next two leading causes of death. Thus the most likely cause of death in this age group is violence in one form or another. This age group is the one traditionally served by the youth-oriented activity and leisure industry.

Reducing violent death cannot be a responsibility of the industry alone. However, the industry can contribute to accident prevention on one hand

and to improved mental health and healthy lifestyles on the other. The surgeon general suggests by implication that the industry might assist youth in making the transition from dependence to independence in a predominantly urban society. Direct action is needed in combating alcohol, smoking, and substance abuse. But the principal call is to contribute support and emotional stability, and to construct a network of agencies and programs to assist adolescents in becoming engaged with society in healthy ways. This cry for the active promotion of mental health among the young should be a major objective of the public sector agencies struggling to gain taxpayers' support. It is a cry reminiscent of the earlier cry for the playground movement and the public recreation movement. In those days the task was to prepare children of the new immigrants to meet the challenges of the industrialized New World. Now the cry is to prepare our youth for the newly emerging postindustrial society. It seems that the wheel has turned full circle.

With adolescents and young adults, physical education's role is clearly a preparatory one. This role is to lay the groundwork for health at later stages in the life cycle. Activity, at least as a preventive measure, is not going to produce much immediate effect during this relatively brief stage. The biological equipment is still relatively young and the symptoms of hypokinetic disease are usually latent. While the immediate motivations and interests of the young adult clients must not be ignored, there is a deeper agenda: to develop the attitudes, knowledge, skills, and biological capacities necessary for health in the later years.

Curricula for physical education during this stage must balance the immediate interests and needs of young adults with their future needs for managing their lifestyles effectively as middle-aged and older adults. Thus one side of the balance must be the knowledge and skills needed for cooperative, or non-zero-sum, activities conducted in socially rewarding settings and that call on the kinds of physical abilities expected during maturity. On the other side must be the knowledge and skills of the competitive sporting culture that serve so many youths and young adults. However, any program design that rests solely on the three traditional competitive team sports—baseball, basketball, and football—which usually can be sustained only through a person's early twenties, avoids a fundamental purpose of the field. Physical education that concentrates exclusively on competitive team sports does a disservice to its young adult clients. Youth and young adulthood is such a short fraction of the total life span that the physical education curriculum must create effects that reach far beyond the present.

A healthy lifestyle involves more than finding a meaningful source of activity during middle age and older. It involves attitudes and knowledge about nutrition, safety, smoking, alcohol and substance abuse, early warning symptoms, stress management, and communication skills in addition to exercise (Ellis, Edginton, & Howard, 1985). To prepare young adults for this lifelong effort to optimize health, the physical education curriculum needs to be reintegrated with health and leisure education during young adulthood. Only then will the new middle-aged and older generations be able to see the connections among all their lifestyle decisions and act accordingly.

A further goal must be to create good health-service consumers. The multitude of health-related services presents a bewildering array of choices when assistance is needed. The basic wisdom needed to avoid quackery and exploitation should be imparted early and through the curricula of the schools. Physical education and health education within the schools should be held accountable for this learning. In this regard physical education should most probably be considered part of the broader concerns of school and community health programs and curricula.

Adults

During adulthood, from twenty-five to sixty-four years of age, the protections of youth, the new equipment as it were, begin to fade. Earlier decisions on lifestyle management produce effects that accumulate during this, the longest stage of life. A person's actions throughout this period also have the potential to determine one's state of health. Earlier habits and practices carried into and maintained during this stage can have dramatic effects; it is during this time that people reap the benefits of earlier enlightened health and physical education.

The deathrates in the U.S. remain greater in this age bracket than in Sweden, England and Wales, and Japan. In every category the deathrates for blacks substantially exceed all other racial groups. Again, the surgeon general's goals are to decrease the nation's deathrates to those deathrates in the comparator countries.

The leading killer in this age group is heart disease, followed by cancer, stroke, cirrhosis of the liver, other accidents, and motor vehicle accidents. The rates diverge, after that point, with the homicide rate for blacks being startlingly larger than for all other races. Lifestyle decisions are implicated in all these categories. Although curative medicine may be extensively involved once an incident has occurred, often lifestyle decisions made prior to the incident produced effects that accumulated and contributed to the disease. Diet, exercise, alcohol and tobacco abuse, and unsafe behavior have contributed to one or more of these causes of death.

The sources of morbidity identified above are relatively well-known; however, a major new source of concern involves the mental health of adults. It is estimated that between 2 and 4 percent of Americans suffer severe depression or manic excitability at any one time. About 25 percent of the population are reportedly suffering mild to moderate depression, anxiety, or other mental disorders. It was estimated that in 1974 about

5 percent of all people had limited functioning due to mental health problems. Women had higher rates of manic-depressive states, while men had higher rates of personality disorders. Psychiatric disorders are highest among people with low incomes, little education, and menial occupations. City dwellers exhibit higher rates of all mental health problems, with the exception of manic-depression, which is higher in rural areas.

Modern urban life, replete with change, noise, bustle, and competition, has become an extremely stressful place to live. Stress has deleterious effects when it is chronic and there is no avenue to its relief or amelioration. Stress management skills have become an increasingly important part of each person's lifestyle management. The role of exercise as a way to purge stress has given a modern flavor to the meaning of the word catharsis—the word used by the Greeks to describe the process of purging disorganizing emotions. Today catharsis has come to mean the process of managing personal response to stressors in order to minimize their damaging effects. All professionals working in the industry will need to be familiar with stress management strategies and techniques of relaxation.

The precise words of the surgeon general's report summarize all these concerns:

Many adult health problems today—it bears reemphasizing—can frequently be controlled by the individual. And the measures required are often not particularly dramatic.

An individual's risk can be substantially reduced (or increased) by a few simple personal decisions with respect to smoking, alcohol use, diet, exercise, seat belt use, and periodic screening for major diseases such as high blood pressure and cancer.

The potential exists to promote substantial changes in the profile of disease and disability among American adults. . . . We can anticipate impressive gains in the health of adults. (Richmond, 1979, p. 69)

Adults will become convinced that simple lifestyle management practices are worthwhile for the long-term reduction of disease risk. As that population grows, the industry will find a huge adult market for its health enhancement services. Because competition for the adults' time is fierce, work and family responsibilities compete vigorously during the first half of this stage. But adults usually also have discretionary income with which to buy the services they desire. This is a fortunate alignment of forces. The shift in demand to adults, who have the best chance of supporting their own activity and leisure needs, coincides with the withdrawal of tax dollars from public sector agencies. In fact, there may well be a causal link as older adults use their political power to reallocate resources away from the young and the poor.

It is clearly a responsibility of the activity and leisure industry to realign its mission to include concern for the health enhancement goals of the nation's adults. Such a realignment will also be good business. Again, it is fortunate that the economic forces exerted by adults as a result of these new interests will be in line with, and will strongly augment, the underlying philanthropic intent of the field.

To achieve its goals, the activity and leisure industry will have to learn to cope with clients who have power. Their discretionary dollars can be spent anywhere, and the industry will have to learn how to attract and keep its clients in the face of competition. The services offered will have to be of a quality largely unnecessary with young and captive populations. Settings will also have to be of high quality, services excellent and reliable, and personnel personable and appealing to adults. Many lessons will have to be learned from the hospitality industry—the technologies of the theme park, tour, resort, and cruise operator will have to be transferred and mutated.

The principal lesson can be found in the concept of "time deepening" (Godbey, 1976), which shows that, to adults, time is a commodity that is best spent accomplishing multiple objectives simultaneously. For example, a prized experience for an adult might involve eating a needed meal with pleasant company in an intriguing setting with, perhaps, music, dancing, and alcoholic beverages. This principle is well understood in the hospitality business, although probably not by Godbey's name. It needs to be brought consciously to the fore in physical education's planning for attracting and keeping clients.

Time-deepened programs will set out to create programs that meet multiple motivations simultaneously for multiple adults. For example, a health enhancement business must go beyond providing the opportunity to work out. To this activity must be added another set of activities such as opportunities for the practice of personal hygiene, consultation with a lifestyle manager, some health checks, and personal record keeping and self-competition. To this should be added a variety of social opportunities that foster a sense of belonging. These could include lounges and meeting places, restaurants, and user group advisory boards that involve the clients themselves. If all these things can be brought together in a comfortable and high-quality setting, then an extremely potent motivational complex will have been created. To be attractive to adults, the services of the industry will often have to be combined with other services. Supermarkets of health enhancement activities for adults and their families will emerge in the private sector as a direct outcome of the competition for discretionary income. The burgeoning athletic clubs are good examples of the kind of high-quality health enhancement businesses that are a response to these tendencies.

The somewhat dowdy and staid YMCA movement has learned this lesson. Several of the larger YMCAs have decided that to survive, they must move to a new level of service and compete directly with the private sector. New, up-to-date, and glamorous facilities designed for immediate public appeal and the use of enjoyable, multifaceted health enhancement programs have been so successful that private sector providers of the same services have sued to remove the competitive advantage that tax exempt status brings to the YMCA movement (Toufexis, 1986).

This tendency towards the integration of activity, health enhancement, and leisure services in one locale and program will also call into question the wisdom of the separation of the professions into three major subgroups. Health educators, physical educators, and recreators will have to reintegrate their operations, professional preparation programs, and associations in order to be able to respond nimbly to the opportunities presented to them by the changing attitudes and wishes of the adult clients they serve.

Older Adults

The surgeon general's report categorizes older adults as those over sixty-five years of age. However, that age is selected more for social reasons than for biological reasons. By age sixty-five, health status is extremely varied. Some people are biologically robust and others are beginning to show the signs of chronic ill health that eventually leads to death. Nevertheless, Americans are living longer than ever. For example, the life expectancy for Americans born in 1983 was 78.3 years for females and 71 years for males, with the gap between men and women slowly beginning to close. The improvement has been created mainly by a 25 percent drop in the deathrate from heart disease and a 50 percent drop in the deathrate from stroke. Overall, the deathrate per 100,000 people has continued to decline steadily. It seems that Americans have been living more healthy lifestyles and that the effects are showing up in improved mortality and morbidity statistics among older adults.

Differences remain in longevity among the races with the whites living longer than blacks and other races by 5.6 years, although the gap here is also closing. Despite this optimistic picture, the deathrate for older adults is still not as low as that in the racially homogeneous nations of Japan and Iceland; however, it is still better than in Sweden, England, and Wales.

The major causes of death, in descending order, are heart disease, cancer, stroke, and "other causes." While these disease complexes remain important targets, the main goal for the nation, according to the surgeon general's report (Richmond, 1979), is to combat the chronic debilitating diseases that reduce people's independence and ability to function. Eighty percent of older adults have one or more chronic conditions on which they spend about 30 percent of the nation's health care dollars. The long-term goals are to create states of health and a service delivery system that maintains an independent existence of high quality for older adults.

Our common conception of the elderly is that they are infirm and are found primarily in institutions. The truth is that only 5 percent of older adults reside in institutions, and many of these individuals only temporarily. Accordingly, our industry's plans to improve the quality of older Americans' lives must be built around systems for reaching older adults who are relatively vigorous and who live in the community, mostly in their own homes, either with a spouse or alone.

The severe mental and physical decline associated with the stereotype of the senile older adult is not inevitable. Much of senile decline is caused by drug interactions, depression, metabolic disorders, chronic subdural hematomas, alcohol and chemical toxicities, lung disease, infections, and anemia. Many of these conditions can be cured by medical interventions. However, many other aspects of senile decline are behavioral in nature. Sensory deprivation and social isolation, withdrawal due to loss of sight or hearing—all lead to a kind of self-fulfilling hypokinesis, where failure to behave eventually creates adaptations that finally prevent activity.

The behavioral aspects of senility can be ameliorated by modifying the lifestyles of older adults. Education about proper nutrition and safety practices is important. Activities designed to exercise the body and maintain aerobic capacity, flexibility, strength, and agility are critical. The older adults have the same needs for social interaction as other people, and it is important to create networks of social interaction that sustain and reward participation in a life beyond the self. But most critical of all is the challenge to create programs that offer these activities in settings where older adults learn, grow, and contribute to the wider society. The critical aspect of maintaining function is to create in each individual a welcoming orientation to the future so that the functions being preserved are necessary for the life being planned.

The cohort of older adults is rapidly increasing in size. Creating healthy independence among them presents multiple opportunities for the activity and leisure industry. The professionals in the industry will become increasingly involved in habilitation and rehabilitation activities. Whenever these efforts are successful, the industry will then be called on to deliver experiences and programs that ensure high-quality lives for all older adults.

This challenge to the industry is similar to the challenge of another group of people who hitherto had not been included in the mainstream of everyday life: the handicapped and disabled people who have only recently been enfranchised. While it is clear that older adults, with the special needs, cannot be considered handicapped, it is also clear that the lessons we learned while trying to modify the activity and leisure industry to serve the handicapped and disabled people can serve us well. No one system of activity and leisure services can be applied to any group or cohort.

At one time handicapped and disabled people were largely excluded from society. A terrible isolation and self-fulfilling institutionalization resulted. These people adapted to their exclusion and could not easily be reintegrated. In reaction, the pendulum then swung the other way, and handicapped and disabled people were allowed to move into the mainstream. Soon, equally disturbing stories surfaced about woefully inadequate treatment and settings where the presence of the "mainstreamed" person hindered the development of others. Resentment on both sides, and sometimes worse, was occasionally the result. In fact, genuine concern has grown that a very large number of emotionally or mentally handicapped street people have been mainstreamed and are now living out their lives on "Main Street" with nowhere to go.

It would be a tragic error to assume that either separate but equal activity and leisure systems or completely mainstreamed programs for older adults are desirable. Both are necessary. The industry must prepare for growing numbers of older adults who wish to participate in mainstream activities and who also wish, on many occasions, to form affinity groups with other members of their cohort. The models used to determine how to serve older adults are the same as for all other cohorts. Private sector provisions will be driven by the market forces of the older adults' discretionary income. Public sector provisions will need to be especially sensitive to the needs of older people. If they are not, then they will be forced, by political "gray power" in the political forums of their communities, to respond.

The curricula of professional preparation programs and in-service programs for existing professionals will increasingly focus on the developmental problems and opportunities of older adults. All aspects of the content, methods, and technologies will be scrutinized to determine how best to serve the older adult. Existing programs will be modified and extended to include the older adult as the median age of the population continues to rise. New programs, many of them managed by older adults who are both professionals from the industry and laypeople, will develop. By the end of the century the activity and leisure industry will have achieved a new balance. In a few short decades the industry will have mutated from being youth- and competitive-sport-oriented programs into multifaceted services allocating resources equitably across all the nation's cohorts.

Health Objectives for the Nation

The surgeon general, in conjunction with others in the Department of Health and Human Services, has defined the major preventable health risks for the nation (Richmond, 1979). The surgeon general has also produced a series of national objectives designed to reduce those risks (Richmond, 1980). Many of these objectives involve educating people about health risk factors and persuading them to change their lifestyles; the objectives clearly overlap with the missions of the activity and leisure industry and highlight many responsibilities and opportunities.

The surgeon general's second report proposed a multifaceted program for addressing each of the nation's major health problems (Richmond, 1980). Each of these proposed programs can be classified under the same five general programmatic headings:

- Education and information
- Service
- Technology
- Legislation and regulation
- Economy

In the next section of this chapter, for each major national health problem, those elements that present a challenge to, or opportunity for, the activity and leisure industry are identified. Together, these elements present a manifesto for the industry's contribution to making Americans a healthier people.

Health Objective 1—Smoking Cessation

Cigarette smokers have a 70 percent greater rate of death from all causes, and smoking is associated with 320,000 premature deaths per year. Tobacco usage is involved in a complex way in causing cancers, heart disease, peripheral vascular disease, spontaneous abortion, retarded fetal growth, and slowed child development. Involuntary inhalation precipitates or exacerbates asthma and existing cardiovascular and respiratory disease, and causes many accidents and fires. Kiefhaber and Goldbeck (1984) report that a smoker costs an employer between $624 and $4,611 per year in lost production due to the effects of the habit at the worksite, absenteeism due to sickness, and health expenses. It is in the interests of all to prevent the onset of smoking and to help smokers to stop.

Smoking Cessation Programs.   Efforts to persuade people not to smoke are gaining ground. The number of people smoking has declined in response to education concerning its effects. The decline has recently accelerated and in 1978 only 33 percent of adults smoked regularly. In contrast, in 1985 Great Britain congratulated itself because for the first time in a good while there were slightly more nonsmokers than smokers. Perhaps because of the considerable concern in the U.S. about the costs of smoking the proportion of regular smokers in the population is smaller than in other countries, and the amount of tobacco consumed has declined 7 percent from its peak in 1981 (Rudolph, Leavitt, & McCarrol, 1985).

Smoking cessation programs have been least successful with women. Although the smoking rate for men decreased from 58 percent to 38 percent between 1955 and 1978, during the same period the percentage of women smoking for the first time increased from 25 to 33 percent before falling to 30 percent by 1978. However, among younger women the rate was on the rise, and in 1978 the proportion of smokers among women aged seventeen to twenty-four exceeded the rate for young men of the same age. This bodes ill for future smoking-related morbidity and mortality rates among women. They must be persuaded not to start smoking, or when they have started, to stop. Already lung cancer is rapidly approaching breast cancer as the leading cause of cancer deaths among women.

Strategies for Smoking Cessation.   Those in the activity and leisure industry must assertively identify with the surgeon general's goals for the nation in this respect. They must ally with others to support smoking cessation programs, wherever possible adding smoking cessation support programs to their ongoing programs. If this is not possible, they must at least become knowledgeable about local smoking cessation programs and act as referral agents.

The industry will soon come to recognize that it must manage its facilities and programs to support smoking cessation, to prevent initiation, and to minimize the health hazards of passive tobacco smoke inhalation. Health and market forces will support these actions, and it is now good management to control the settings in which the industry works in the interest, first, of the nonsmoking majority, and second, of the smokers themselves (U.S. Department of Health and Human Services, 1984).

Simple actions will contribute. Declaring public service facilities and all activity spaces and changing areas as nonsmoking or tobacco-free areas will protect the nonsmokers and provide incentive for smokers to delay or omit an opportunity to light up. In public areas reserved for eating and lounging, or for some other activity that is primarily social in character, smoking areas should be set aside in proportion to the number of smoking clients and staff. Tobacco vending machines should be removed from industry facilities, and concessions should be prevented from selling tobacco products. Information on the costs of smoking and referrals to smoking cessation programs should be posted.

The industry should take an active position with regard to its employees who smoke or chew tobacco products. Such employees set a bad example for clients on the one hand and are less valuable as employees on the other. Smokers have higher morbidity rates, offend other workers, and spend a significant portion of each day managing their smoking habit rather than working. It is worthwhile rewarding employees who already smoke for quitting, and refusing to hire smokers in the first place. For workers in the health enhancement side of the activity and leisure industry, absence of a tobacco habit is an occupationally relevant qualification.

Health Objective 2—Alcohol and Drug Control

Because alcohol consumption is legal it is possible to obtain data on its use. The same cannot be said for drug or controlled substance abuse. Users are naturally reluctant to reveal the nature of their drug usage. Both illegal drugs and prescription drugs are abused extensively and both create substantial health and economic costs. About 2.5 million Americans over the age of eighteen experience some form of drug problem, and the total cost to the nation is at least $10 billion per year. The statistics on alcohol abuse are reliable, but the statistics on drug abuse, when they exist, are best considered guesses.

Alcohol Abuse.   Alcohol kills directly by its effects on the body, and indirectly by its short-term impairment of functioning and the accidents that result. Alcohol abuse causes about 10 percent of all the deaths in the United States in any year (Richmond, 1979). It is implicated in deaths from cirrhosis, psychosis, and oral, esophageal, and liver cancer. It also induces about 1,700 birth defects a year. About 45 percent of all motor vehicle accidents involved a driver who had a blood alcohol level greater than .1 percent. Its consumption is vast—the equivalent of about 28 gallons of beer plus 2.5 gallons of spirits and 2.25 gallons of wine per person in 1979 (Richmond, 1979). Reducing alcohol consumption presents a difficult problem because alcohol is legal and forms a major part of the American social experience.

Strategies for Controlling Alcohol Use.   Alcohol consumption creates a challenge for those in the industry to operate all programs in such a way that alcohol consumption is controlled, that potentially impaired individuals are prevented from further consumption, and that actually impaired individuals are prevented from operating cars and equipment. The climate of opinion is changing to support these goals. However, real change will come only from the pressures of litigation. Litigation will present serious liability insurance problems as insurance premiums rise in response to settlements resulting from the failure of the industry's professionals to prudently monitor the effects of alcohol impairment. The activity and leisure industry must start behaving like the beverage and hospitality industry in dealing with this problem.

Reducing the cost of alcohol abuse is a high national priority. In 1975 the cost of all alcohol-related disease was nearly $43 billion (Richmond, 1979). About 10 percent of adults are considered problem drinkers and another 26 percent are identified as having potential drinking problems. These vast numbers will present the industry with a new market. Alcohol control and rehabilitation programs will need physical education, as well as recreation and health education programs, as part of their multifaceted attacks on the alcohol abuse problem.

A major problem facing the nation is to rehabilitate existing alcoholics. This presents an opportunity for the industry because the inclusion of physical education and recreation programs in alcohol rehabilitation programs can be justified in two ways. First, like anyone else, members of alcohol rehabilitation programs need to learn how to care for a biological system that has evolved to serve an active life. The fitness of these clients is especially fragile; they will need to have a reasonable level of health and fitness restored, and they will need to know how to maintain that level upon reentering their normal lives. Second, the clients will need to learn how to structure an enjoyable leisure life for themselves. To ignore the role that alcohol plays in the leisure supply and to fail to create a new leisure lifestyle for these clients is to send them back into the community without the skills necessary to control their alcohol usage.

The activity and leisure industry can make contributions to each of the surgeon general's general program themes, with the exception of the last, which envisions the use of tax incentives and disincentives. In the education and information programs the industry can help by understanding the problem and making information about problems, practices, and local rehabilitative programs available to its clients. In the service programs, the industry's professionals can be of assistance in rebuilding shattered lives and providing healthy alternatives to alcohol and substance abuse. In the technology programs, the industry should explore all ways to create new social technologies that are not so dependent on alcohol. Finally, by establishing informed policies and practices in activity and leisure programs, the industry can be part of the solution—not part of the problem.

Increasingly, alcohol and substance abuse will be treated as part of the adapted physical education and therapeutic recreation programs, and more of the industry's professionals will find employment in these programs. As a result, new activity and leisure technologies and content will be developed in response to the special needs of adults who are being treated for alcohol and substance abuse, and who are learning to maintain a new level of healthy functioning.

Health Objective 3—A Healthy Diet

The problem of dietary inadequacy has largely been conquered. Deficiency diseases like rickets are now rarely seen. The problem has become, instead, one of too much food and complex effects of changes in the diet that have occurred over the last few decades. There is now good evidence to indicate that certain foods are linked in complex ways to many health problems.

Good choices made by individuals about their diet not only contribute to enhanced development but also reduce the likelihood of some diseases, such as heart disease, tooth decay, obesity, and cancer, in which poor dietary regimens are implicated. It is in the nation's interest to educate people to make wise choices from among the bewildering array of foods, advertising claims, and misleading information.

The surgeon general's report on the national diet has targeted three main areas of concern: (a) obesity, (b) nutrition and cardiovascular disease, and (c) diet and cancer (Richmond, 1979).

Health Problems Involving Diet.   Obesity is associated with diabetes, gall bladder disease, and high blood pressure. It contributes to heart disease. It also impairs motor functioning and is associated with the psychological costs of living in a society that values slim, athletic builds. Obesity affects 35 percent of impoverished women between the ages of forty-five and sixty-four, and 29 percent of women the same age above the poverty line. For men in the same categories the figures are 5 percent and 13 percent. The problem stems in part from the abundance of food, from our tendency to weave eating itself into the nation's social fabric, and from our tendency to treat food as a reward.

Controlling overeating has proved to be very difficult, and the industry has contributed to the problem. Programs designed by the industry often include eating for life support and ceremonial eating as a way to enhance the quality of the experience or for convenience. Rarely are menus carefully considered to avoid exacerbating the problems of participants' diets. Too much unhealthy food is routinely incorporated into the industry's programs.

High animal-fat diets seem to be linked to high serum cholesterol levels, which in turn seem to be associated with atherosclerosis and cardiovascular disease. People living in countries with diets that are naturally low in saturated fats experience fewer heart attacks, and subgroups of Americans who have a diet low in fat, such as vegetarians, also have fewer heart attacks. The evidence now supports the notion that Americans should eat less fat, particularly animal fat. Evidence also indicates that the diet should be changed as early in life as possible, because our children are showing higher levels of serum cholesterol than children in many other countries. Similarly, overuse of salt should be avoided due to its association with elevated blood pressure. In addition, high-fat and low-fiber diets seem to be related to colon cancer and cancers of the prostate gland and ovaries.

Strategies for Improving Diet.   The activity and leisure industry has an important role to play in two of the surgeon general's five programs to ameliorate the diet problem. First, the industry's professionals can contribute to the education and information programs, and second, the professionals should provide good role models and be the source of accurate information about nutrition. They should publicize the latest information to their clients and should be ready and knowledgeable sources of referral to other agencies that provide assistance with weight control and good nutrition.

Providing Healthy Foods.   The industry can make its most important contribution by altering the eating habits associated with its programs. Eating is a substantial feature of the leisure industry. Many of the programs offered by the industry incorporate eating as a high point, ceremony, or reward. Whenever food is offered, the choices should be made consistently in favor of a healthy diet that features pleasing, low-fat, low-calorie, low-salt, and high-fiber menus. Vending machines that do not or cannot offer healthy foods should be removed. Social settings that cue unnecessary eating, or the eating of unhealthy foods like midmorning doughnuts and coffee, should be planned out of the agenda. Eating in the activity and leisure industry, like eating at home and in the food service industry, should be reformed.

Because the number of Americans with eating disorders is very high, designing and planning programs around such problems and providing social support groups for those wrestling with dietary change will be good marketing. These types of programs have been very successful in the private sector. However, they are profit oriented and often have narrow programs. Because activity level is a related concern for those whose calorie input exceeds their output, the industry is well placed to link these two elements in their programs and compete favorably for the opportunity to influence the lifestyles of those whose diets place them at risk.

Activity and leisure professionals will have to phase these reforms into their programs. At first they will have to offer leadership in developing the new national diet, but as the century runs on, the pressures for healthy alternatives will come from increasing numbers of clients who wish to eat nutritiously and safely. The industry's professionals should be taught the principles of good nutrition so that they may help their clients when practicing. Existing professionals will need in-service programs that will address these problems also. If proactive, the industry will start now rather than have to catch up with its clients later.

Professionals as Role Models.   The industry's professionals should themselves be good role models (Wilmore, 1982). The nature and quantity of food eaten by professionals should exemplify good health habits. Obesity, no matter what its cause, sends the wrong message to potential clients, and keeping one's weight in control must be considered an occupationally relevant criterion for success in the industry. Melville and Maddalozzo (1986) recently demonstrated convincingly that the appearance of obesity in physical educators seriously impaired their ability to communicate and to convince others that they were knowledgeable and likeable sources of expertise about exercise and health. For both thin and overweight observers alike, the physical educator was less effective when apparently obese. This finding supports the folk wisdom on this issue and begins the process of assembling evidence that workers in the industry are not effective if they are not good role models.

Obese employees involved in face-to-face client relations must also be successfully rehabilitated, using the procedures developed for clients, in order that they can be effective contributors to the mission of the field. Where there are choices among potential employees, those who have demonstrated abilities to manage their diets should be chosen over those who have not. These choices should stem simply from the obvious occupational relevance of being able to model appropriate health behaviors.

Health Objective 4—Physical Fitness and Exercise

In response to the increasing publicity over the concern for the sedentary lifestyles of most Americans, the number of people using exercise to prevent disease has increased. Exercise has many effects on people. According to Richmond (1979), people report that they feel better and have more energy when they exercise; some report that they need less sleep. They have less excess weight, are stronger, and are more flexible. There are also psychological benefits: Exercisers report greater self-esteem, self-reliance, decreased anxiety, and less depression.

Relationship of Exercise to Enhanced Health.   In addition to reports from exercisers themselves, research indicates that exercising is associated with lower risk of cardiovascular disease and sudden death resulting from it. The results of research on the effects of exercise are highly suggestive, though no firm causal connection has yet been determined. The situation is analogous to the time when the evidence connecting smoking and cancer was considered only suggestive. The evidence connecting exercise to enhanced health is still mounting. Before the end of the century, the body of evidence will surely indicate that a causal connection exists.

Regular exercise that involves the consumption of large amounts of oxygen—that is, aerobic exercise—requires the energy transport system (heart, lungs, blood vessels, and their attendant control mechanisms) to work at a high level. If the exercise is continued for at least fifteen to thirty minutes, at least three times per week, then not only does the oxygen-transporting capacity increase, but in some cases blood pressure, resting heart rate, and serum cholesterol are lowered. Regular exercise has also been claimed to be useful in ameliorating angina pectoris, recovering from heart attacks, and managing chronic obstructive lung disease and diabetes.

As the evidence mounts, it supports the decisions made by people to exercise. Even though there are clear, long-term health benefits, the immediate psychological benefits are most probably the incentive that prompts individuals to maintain exercise. The psychological payoffs from exercise are immediate and pleasant. Furthermore, the exerciser can also claim that there are long-term justifications with which to bolster resolve and to explain participation.

The surgeon general's report raises important questions for the industry when he points out that much of the staple content of physical education for the young involves competitive sport. The competitive team games popular in the U.S. can rarely be sustained into later life (Richmond, 1979, 1980). Furthermore, it was established that by the end of the seventies only about one-third of all children were estimated to participate in daily physical education. What is worse, under the threat of budget cuts and the reallocation of energy and resources to varsity athletics, physical education in the schools seems to be waning. If this is true, then the foundation for lifelong activity regimens for the nation is at risk.

Strategies for Increasing Exercise.   Despite the fact that physical education in schools seems to be losing ground, among the postschool population it seems to be gaining. Increasing numbers of people are exercising sensibly. *U.S. News and World Report* (Levine, Wells, & Kopf, 1986), citing data from American Sports Data, reported that 44 million Americans were exercising with aerobic equipment, 42 million were playing basketball, 40 million were walking for fitness, and so on in the tens of millions through swimming, exercising, weight training, jogging, and other activities. Increasing numbers of companies are offering health enhancement or employee assistance programs. To accelerate this progress, the surgeon general, using the five categories of promotion measures presented earlier, set goals for the nation. Many of the surgeon general's suggestions for the improvement of physical fitness and the use of exercise are pertinent to the activity and leisure industry. Because this area is of such central importance to the industry, a discussion of the proposed measures and their objectives is warranted.

Use of Electronic Media.   Educational measures point towards the use of the electronic mass media to carry the message. The field has begun to increase its public service messages and paid advertising concerning the importance of exercise in a personal health enhancement program. This advertising will continue, but its magnitude is swamped by the massive use of health and fitness related themes by other advertising campaigns. However, it can also be argued that this "indirect" advertising used to sell other products creates a climate of receptivity to the explicit messages from the industry. For the rest of the century this state of affairs is likely to continue and the "piggy-backing" of direct messages targeted to specific themes and client groups will be a fruitful source of influence.

Proactive Encouragement Through Health Care Delivery Systems.   The surgeon general's report suggests that all health care delivery systems use surveys of their clients' personal health enhancement activities when taking their health histories, and become routinely proactive in encouraging physical activity and weight loss programs, particularly among middle-aged and older adults. This will, of course, require referral to outlets for these services in the activity and leisure industry. It is also very likely to spawn attempts by the cash-starved health care industry to provide these services themselves. In the latter case, the cheapest way to do this will be to hire allied health professionals to deliver the service.

The infrastructure to support these activities already exists to a substantial extent in the public sector agencies. A common outcome of the increased attention to exercise and weight control by the health care industry will be the formation of joint-venture programming to promote the use of the existing facilities and the personnel of the industry. Such usage will benefit the private sector, which will be able to participate in the business without having to capitalize new facilities. It will also benefit the public sector, which is experiencing pressures to become more efficient and use less public money to reach its objectives.

Provision of Physical Activity Services. The surgeon general's objectives also recognize that in addition to educating the people of the nation, physical activity services must be provided. The first service measure mentioned is that physical education services must become a regular daily service to all school- and college-age people. The activities should be health related and directed to everyone, not just to the elite few. Next, the report argues for the practices and procedures of the activity industry to be extended into the workplace and into all health care provisions. Finally, if these are extended into the nonwork sectors of people's lives, then opportunities for daily aerobic activity graded to the needs of clients should also be moved into the leisure market.

Provision of Facilities to Promote Health. Technological measures identified by the surgeon general involve the dramatic increase in the provision of health-promoting facilities by private, corporate, and public sectors. Existing facilities should be upgraded, particularly in inner city neighborhoods. The facilities specifically identified are fitness trails, bike paths, parks, and swimming pools. These kinds of facilities can serve the entire population and should be developed before facilities for competitive sports, which serve a narrow and restricted population segment.

Legislative and Regulatory Recommendations. The surgeon general proposed that the federal government stimulate national, state, and local support for health enhancing programs via a series of legislative and regulatory recommendations. The major reform here would be to permit the expenditure of federal funds governed by federal regulations on fitness and health enhancement programs. Furthermore, it recommended that local governments encourage the use of bikes by building bike lanes and paths and redesigning existing parks for jogging and exercise. State governments are asked to mandate health-related physical education services in their schools and colleges.

The surgeon general's report also calls for the creation of tax incentives for the private sector to provide activity and health enhancement services for employees. These incentives would support the provision of services either at the workplace or elsewhere. In addition, the insurance industry should be encouraged by legislation to give reduced premiums to those who practice personal health enhancement.

In summary, both government and business are finding it worthwhile to stimulate personal health enhancement activities of the people they are responsible for. The federal government needs to reduce the share of the gross national product diverted to health care, and business needs to diminish the proportion of its costs diverted to health care that would otherwise be profit. These economic interests are in line with the realization of more and more people that they are personally responsible for their own health. These three forces are driving the preventive health care revolution. Fortunately, this revolution presents many opportunities for physical education.

Health Objective 5—Control of Stress and Violent Behavior

The stresses of modern life that threaten without requiring gross motor activity in response seem related to much disease. Human physiology is designed for action—for fight or flight. When inactivity follows stress, there is evidence that the reactions produce maladaptive symptoms such as headache, obesity (via compulsive eating), absenteeism (as a form of avoidance), illness, accident proneness, and violence.

Stress-Related Disease and Behavior. Stress-related disease is not well understood. Nevertheless, there are important indicators that suggest that management of the stressors of everyday life are important to the nation and will become more so as the century goes on. The surgeon general's report (Richmond, 1980) cites a survey in which 82 percent of the respondents reported that they needed "less stress in their lives" (p. 84). There are no good indicators of the general stress level. However, if violence is a result of stress, then the level is too high, because the surgeon general's statistics describing the level of violence are frightening.

- Suicide ranks ninth overall as a cause of death.
- There are somewhere between 200,000 to 4 million cases of child abuse per year.
- Minority groups' deathrates from violence exceed that for whites, and among minority youths are increasing.

As stress and stress-related disease and behavior have increased, the general knowledge of the population has not kept pace. The surgeon general's report concludes that one of the nation's objectives must be to develop and communicate three kinds of approaches to stress management.

The first stress management approach involves the development of individually focused efforts—that is, exercise, relaxation techniques, adequate sleep, and the development of self-control and coping techniques. The second approach involves the development of social groups—that is, networks of peers and friends who cushion stress and assist in meeting the challenges of everyday life. These two approaches attempt to solve the stress problem by altering the capacity of individuals to absorb or resist the effects of stressors in their lives.

The third approach to stress management recommended by the surgeon general's report is to attempt to ameliorate many of the social conditions that create stress. Here the task is much greater and will involve changing unsatisfactory environmental conditions. Improved housing to reduce overcrowding and the elimination of pollution and stressful working conditions will be necessary. Also, the social circumstances that exaggerate the incidence and severity of stress-related violence, alcohol and drug abuse, and the ready availability of firearms and weapons, should be addressed. However, the prognosis is poor. The nation has retreated from these kinds of interventions and it is most likely that little progress will result from efforts designed to reduce the fundamental problems.

Strategies for Reducing Stress and Violence. The surgeon general's report identifies five categories of measures that are recommended as a plan for dealing with the problem of stress and violent behavior. Of the many suggested measures, only those that potentially affect the activity and leisure industry are treated here. The first measure involving the industry is to join in a public awareness campaign to establish the links between stress and disease in the minds of the public and then extend the campaign to demonstrate the role of self-stress management in the control of disease. Activity and leisure are both involved in many ways in stress management, and all professionals in the industry need to be alerted to the connections and opportunities. Professional preparation programs and in-service training must alert professionals to the signs of stress and suicide, child abuse, and other potential violent behavior and the nature and availability of interventions available in the community. The surgeon general's report particularly asks that the topic of stress and its management be added to the curricula of all teachers.

Another recommendation calls for the reform of services along the lines identified for exercise and fitness—that is, the addition of stress management education and services at all levels in both the public and private sectors of the economy. A multiplicity of stress-reducing activity and leisure pursuits, counseling, the teaching of self-help skills, and the creation of social groups to offer support are identified in the report. In most cases, the activity and leisure professional is uniquely positioned to be of material assistance.

The surgeon general's report calls for employers, labor, and government to cooperate in reducing the basic level of stress in the workplace and in the environment. Finally, the report calls for increased legislative control of handguns and stiffer penalties for child abuse.

The Expanding Role
of Activity and Leisure Professionals

There is no question that the surgeon general's report tabulates a vast number of opportunities for the activity and leisure industry to contribute to the quality of life of Americans. As the nation evolves through the next decades the evolution will be towards a society in which there will be an expanded role for activity and leisure professionals.

The industry, like the other health care industries, sends mixed messages to its clients. Unhealthy settings, poorly chosen menus, encouragement of alcohol and tobacco use, wrong foods in vending machines, stressful management practices, overweight employees, and employees with conspicuous smoking habits all say, "Do as we *say*, not as we *do*." The activity and leisure industry's programs and the behavior of its employees and professionals must send a coherent message that health enhancement is largely under the control of sovereign individuals and that we practice health enhancement affirmatively ourselves. The programs themselves must be consistent with the health enhancement objectives just mentioned, as must be the behavior of the industry's employees.

Modeling correct lifestyle management for personal wellness has been identified in the report *Prospects for a Healthier America* as a major goal for all segments of the health enhancement industries (Farquhar & King, 1984). It is important for all to recognize that for employment in the activity and leisure industry, successfully living a healthy lifestyle is an occupationally relevant qualification. One of the criteria for the selection of new employees should be their demonstrated ability to model a personal lifestyle that leads to their own wellness. For existing employees, passive acceptance of poor health habits cannot be tolerated, and employee assistance programs for the industry's own employees should be started to correct the situation. In other words, "Health professional—heal thyself!"

Equalizing Accessibility to Better Health

Opportunities for health and welfare of the people of the U.S. are not equally distributed across the major ethnic divisions in the nation. Ethnic heterogeneity and a richly diverse gene pool are fundamental strengths of the American experiment. However, past discriminations associated with ethnicity still reverberate in our modern society. The resulting inequalities become threats to the good order of the nation and to all its residents to the extent that the differences are institutionalized. The major danger for the rest of the century is the move towards the creation of permanent underclasses in the social structure of the nation.

A permanent underclass locked out from health care, education, upward mobility, and a share in the American dream remains a major problem. This is recognized widely, yet the two strategies for dealing with the problem of unequal opportunity—the New Deal and the Great Society programs—have not worked well. Current "trickle-down" theories of the 1980s and the offering of increased incentives for success seem to be exacerbating the problems.

Major progress will not be made during the rest of the century in combating poverty and the inequalities that result from it. It is not possible to augment the incentives for success in a competitive capitalistic economy and at the same time remove all the effects of failure. What remains is a need to provide equal access for all to success and its rewards. Barring some people from access creates the loss of hope and the fomenting of discontent. Professionals in the activity and leisure industry must develop creative ways to provide improved access to their services despite the increasing tendency to require "pay for play."

The reason for improving access can be justified on the moral grounds of equal rights. If that is not convincing, then it can be justified on the pragmatic grounds that discontented and excluded people can destabilize society; the activity and leisure industry cannot thrive in unstable and uncertain conditions.

Hence, the activity and leisure industry will face the same problems that currently plague the health care industry in that some clients need the services and yet cannot pay for them. One of the results has been exclusion of some people from the health care system in ways that have resulted in the alarming racial and ethnic differences in morbidity and mortality. Another result has been the need for "cost-shifting" that accounts for some appreciable fraction of the rising costs of health care borne by those who can pay either directly or through increased cost of third-party payment schemes. The industry will increasingly have to address the moral and social problems of delivering services to those without the means to pay.

This problem will be exacerbated because many people see play and recreation as rewards for prior production. Access is earned and is not a right. Unemployment raises a particular problem. The unemployed have neither the means to purchase access to the system, nor, in some people's view, the moral right to gainful leisure. Yet these are the people with the greatest period of uncommitted time. They will be bored, and to the extent that they become angry, they will pose a threat to society. Because unemployment is unequally distributed, with the highest concentrations among the young urban poor, predominantly black, this problem clearly lies at the root of the many other problems that can be traced to poverty.

Although the problem of access to leisure is not as immediately threatening as some of the disease problems have been, it is potentially a most threatening situation. An inaccessible activity and leisure industry will be an important thread in the complex web that entraps the poor. The activity and leisure industry must remain an important part of the broader efforts to prevent the creation of a permanent underclass whose members have lost hope even for their children.

Schemes for equalizing access must be forcefully and creatively explored, developed, and implemented widely until they are no longer needed. Scholarships, vouchers, fees that are altered according to ability to pay, open access to all, and work-for-play schemes must all be explored. Such schemes must be creatively modified and extended until the activity and leisure industry uses a panoply of options to make activity and leisure as accessible as education. Accessibility will be the single most important moral and practical problem for the industry for the rest of this decade.

Summary

The health care industry is being taken over by business and is being forced to cut its costs. It has surplus capacity and is therefore eagerly diversifying into areas of health enhancement formerly left to others. Furthermore, the next major contribution to the nation's health will come from prevention rather than cure of disease. These pressures will bring the health care industry onto a collision course with the activity and leisure industry. Fortunately, the activity and leisure industry is well placed to compete and has many opportunities to create healthy lifestyles.

Creating healthy lifestyles involves modifying daily activities so that they contribute to health rather than to disease. The activity and leisure industry is positioned to manage, or at least make major contributions to, many of the programs identified by the surgeon general as required to reach the objectives necessary for a healthier America.

Twin challenges are presented by this revolution. The first will be to create physical education programs that prepare young people for the healthy management of their lifestyles when they become adults. The second complementary challenge will then be to serve the vast majority of the population between the ages of twenty-five and sixty-five. This group, not traditionally considered a market for physical education, represents the major opportunity of the next two decades.

Chapter 5

Content of the Industry

Clients of the activity and leisure industry, like all clients, are driven by a complex of motivations that change from moment to moment and over months and years. Their goals may be for immediate gratification and pleasure, or may well be long-term goals that require the mortgaging of the present against future benefits. The behavior of each client, then, is created by his or her own individual calculus for determining the costs and benefits of any activity and leisure choice. Choices are made to maximize the likelihood of a desirable outcome at the least cost in personal effort, money, and resources.

The activity and leisure industry meets the individual's needs by creating experiences that enable clients to reach their own goals. Although a member of the industry may, at a client's request, prescribe a goal or target, the client chooses whether or not to accept the advice. The notion of a paternalistic profession determining the direction of the industry and the individuals served by it should be laid to rest. We may have persuasive influence, and we may have decided on a particular direction on the basis of our special knowledge; but the final decision to accept or reject our professional recommendations rests with the client. We are placed in the position of persuading our clients that our advice is worth taking and then selling to them the products we have planned for them.

Market forces will change the content of the industry. This chapter is about these forces and this process of change. Demystification of the professionals in the industry and the consumer revolution will mean that although we are convinced that clients ought to do something, the clients will not if they are not convinced as well. Our beliefs, based on either data or philosophical analysis, will have to be sold. Thus any professional's day will increasingly involve the analysis of client wishes and needs. Professionals will have to construct strategies to convince clients that our desires for them are also theirs.

It is becoming increasingly clear that our clients' wishes are influencing the nature of the things we plan for them. As the number of people served by the industry grows outside of the conventional school-aged and youth sport culture, so the nature of the industry will change. Despite this, the industry will still serve the young in schools and youth sport programs, causing the field to become more heterogeneous. The first part of this chapter follows the clients through the chronology of their various interactions with the industry. It then turns to more general principles that underlie all the specific changes identified in the first part of the chapter, and to the effect that these general changes will have on physical education.

Physical Education for Preschoolers

Early childhood educators have recognized the role of play in the development of the very young child. Day-care centers pay more than lip service to the role of fine and gross motor activity as critical contributors to development. Despite this, at this point very few physical educators see a role for themselves as employees in day-care centers or child development centers for preschool-aged children. Furthermore, preparing for a career exclusively in early childhood physical education is still not possible. Yet the increasing pressures on both parents to work guarantees a high demand for early childhood developmental services.

Although early childhood educators are convinced of the importance of the roles of structured physical activity and the facilitation of play and dance in the life of the child, physical education has not generally regarded the young child as a client. To some extent that will change during the rest of the decade. A tendency will develop for early childhood physical educators to enter the vast early childhood services industry. Enlightened and successful centers will find ways to bring physical education's expertise to bear on their programs. Some physical educators will be involved in teaching early childhood workers. Others will be involved in delivering developmental services to the preschool child either as direct care workers or as consultants to owners and managers of preschool centers.

This tendency will be slight, however. Preschool centers are pinched between the high cost of delivering excellent care and the relative inability of those needing day-care and preschool services to pay. Young parents are usually new in their careers, and generally with low incomes. The cost of adding physical education services will be high, and only the very successful and large centers or chains will be able to support physical education specialists.

The most likely scenario will be the creation of a few programs in which some physical educators will also certify as early childhood educators. As employees, they will work with the general child population but also use their expertise and interest to create and manage enriched motor experiences for the children. This scenario will require the cooperation of the disciplines of physical education and early childhood education. Such cooperation between professional specialties has always proved difficult in the past, but in some cases the opportunities presented by the day-care and preschool market will engender cooperation on a limited scale.

Physical Education of the Young Child

Physical education in the elementary schools is in relatively good shape. While each elementary schoolchild does not have daily physical education taught by a specialist physical educator the gains made over the last few decades in this area are likely to be consolidated. Physical education at the elementary level is appreciated for its contributions to general development, and there is general consensus that prepubescent children should be protected from specialization and competition. Although sport skills are taught extensively at this level, other components are included. Broader goals for the social and affective development of the child are generally sought.

The protection of the system from the strong pressures of varsity sport has permitted such physical educators as there are in elementary schools to work unhampered by the athletic aspirations of school administrators and/or communities. Physical education is more educative at this level, and also less consumptive. Facilities are simpler and less costly. For these reasons, physical education in the elementary school is likely to continue to grow and develop as an integral part of the elementary school curriculum.

Threats From Athletics

One of the threats to this optimistic picture comes from the structure of the professional preparation programs in physical education. Until recently, physical educators bound for employment in the elementary schools have followed a separate curriculum, thus coming to be treated as specialists in the physical education of the young child. In past years, however, primarily for administrative and demographic reasons, the elementary subspecialty has been targeted for inclusion in a general certification for grades kindergarten through twelve. The distinction between those headed for elementary and those headed for secondary schools will no longer be drawn. The inherent attitudes and the goals of those preparing for the profession will no longer be reflected in the type of certification that they hold. The danger of this situation will come from elementary schools employing physical educators who harbor strong athletic/competitive aspirations. Under these circumstances, the K-12 general certification may well prove to be disadvantageous to the developing elementary school physical education system, because the system will lose one of its protections.

Another potential threat lies in the fact that elite athletes (and musicians, dancers, mathematicians, etc.) often start specializing at very young ages during the elementary school years. Gymnastics and swimming particularly, and other sports to a lesser extent, try to capture the interest and the effort of very young children and their parents in order to encourage the development of special skills that are prerequisites for elite performance. To date this effort has been limited because the schools have not permitted their tax monies to be used for the realization of such aspirations. Consequently, the private sector has provided the services necessary to achieve such aspirations; unsubsidized by tax monies, the real costs are substantial. Few can afford such aspirations.

Continued Growth Likely

Because the young child is so exuberantly energetic and enthusiastic it is appropriate that he or she experience vital physical activity. Because children are neither powerful nor threatening, permitting them to explore and create results in benefits with few costs. The curriculum within the school system can be expected to grow and develop slowly through the rest of the century. Content will continue to be child-centered, and the field will improve its ability to deal with individual children in classes or groups. The role of the physical educator as potentiator and enricher of young children's lives will become better understood among those in the profession and among those in society who pay for the profession's services.

Physical Education for the Older Child

The content of the physical education curriculum in the middle and senior schools is heavily biased toward competitive sport forms. In these schools the curriculum is predictably organized around the sports that are in season, and the children can frequently predict what their experiences will be in physical education classes. On the whole, the curriculum is redundant and unimaginative. Despite this, participation in sports is paradoxically booming among the young.

Physical Education and Sport

Participation in sports has doubled to more than 30 million children since 1975. Participation in youth sport programs is extensive, and increases through the ages of eleven, twelve, and thirteen. Thereafter the number of participants declines steadily with an attrition rate from 22 to 37 percent per year. Kids drop out of competitive sports like flies around the period of adolescence (Klint, 1985). By the early twenties those pursuing sport are few, and by the thirties almost nonexistent.

The organization of sport is in most cases pyramidal. Eventually the system recognizes one winner. This winner is then advanced to another level of competition, and again one winner is recognized. The eventual outcome is that most sport participants fail. New forms of organization designed to ensure that *all* are winners are desperately needed. Orlick and Botterill (1975) proposed reconstructing sporting forms so that they might be both competitive and process oriented rather than simply a procedure for discovering who was best (and by extension, who was not). Martens' (1975) notions of competition as essentially processes of competition-with-self have still not permeated the field.

Curriculum for Lifelong Participation a Failure

If lifetime participation in sport is a goal, then the current process fails miserably. Eventually, and sooner rather than later, most participants find they do not enjoy sport, and quit. Do they quit because the sports are poorly taught and poorly organized? Do they find other avenues to their goals? Are the costs to the purse and the psyche too great? Do they get injured? Is sport participation simply a phase of development soon outgrown? Is sport foisted on the young by adults as part of an acculturation process because sport exists as entertainment in which artificial drama can be created cheaply? The answers to these questions will determine the future role of sport in the activity and leisure industry. We do not know all the answers now, but we had better find out.

Competition in Youth Sport: A Rite of Passage?

Clearly people participate in sport for many reasons. Sport has its own contribution to make to the development of many people. While adolescents may participate in sport because it is available and there is time enough for it and society encourages it, older people who have more control over their activities seem to lose interest. Some of those who remain successful at sport reap its many benefits, at one level or another, as a means of self-expression. However, most people leave sport at a young age. The dropouts carry with them for life the benefits—and costs—of their early experiences, but reap no ongoing benefits. This problem has been expressly addressed by Farquhar and King in *Prospects for a Healthier America* (1984). They lament that "little attention has been paid to methods of achieving long-term adherence to both structured as well as less formal (i.e., routine) physical activity" (p. 34). They also argue that, "while some type of physical education program has traditionally been offered in schools, it often appears that these activities are competitive in nature rather than focused on teaching a lifelong pattern of pleasant aerobic exercise" (p. 34).

If sport participation for the vast majority is such an ephemeral activity then we must inevitably ask the question, Why is the school physical education curriculum so biased towards competitive sports? The answer is twofold: because sport participation can enhance biological, cognitive, and emotional development, and because competitive sport is entertainment.

The benefits of competitive sport for young people lie principally in the fact that it is, in essence, a rehearsal for life. It requires learning how to meet social contracts and obligations. It requires the mortgaging of present effort for future rewards. It permits some to enjoy a sense of instrumentality and even an occasional peak experience. It demonstrates biological adaptation and aids in the development of cognitive, social, and motor skills. It is a celebration of the capacity of a human to change at will. In a very real sense, it is the adult condition in microcosm, and is thus a highly potent tool for development. It is a part of education that deserves our best attention, yet we should expect it to be a passing phase. Withdrawal from competitive sport for many is simply a signal of success. We sample and learn and pass on to other opportunities in society. The declaration of withdrawal by a young participant is a declaration of independence, and it should be regarded not as failure but as a form of success.

Competitive Sport as a Common Experience

Sport is also an experience common to all in our culture. It is a topic, like the weather, that gives safe entry into conversation. It provides a kind of social concord, giving groups of people a sense of communality and shared joy and disappointment. These features are exaggerated by the media, which are interested in it simply as a recurring novelty well suited to their own marketing purposes. Indisputably, sport is enjoyed by most people as an activity tangential to their own real lives, as a temporary, entertaining escape. The sporting life is a reality in the culture of the Western world, and as such, children must be acculturated to it in the same way they are exposed to the written, visual, and performing arts. This is the second reason for spending time on competitive sport in the school curriculum.

If sport exists in the school to acculturate children, then it is clear that we cannot expect the outcome of sport education in the schools to be lifelong, active participation. As soon as the lessons of active participation are learned, they are applied to real life. The individual will have a store of experiences to draw upon, and can participate more comfortably in society because of the shared understanding of one of its major entertainment forms. However, it cannot reasonably be argued that sport participation is preparation for later sport participation; the numbers of people actually participating later is too small to support such a contention. The only reasonable conclusion to make is that, for youths, the basic role of sport participation in school and community is acculturation.

Acculturation as the Goal

Sport should, and will, be taught in the schools with acculturation in mind. Sport educators will cease to be driven by the need to teach a large number of sport skills quickly so that a few can be selected for special attention as members of varsity teams. Sport education, as the engine driving elite competition, will sputter and die. Why? One reason is that, in the future, physical educators will be coaches less often. They will find their own professional fulfillment in their contributions to the broadly defined physical education of their charges rather than in the success of their teams.

Parents Take Over Youth Sports

Another reason that competitive sport, as we have known it, is dying in the schools is that much of the sporting activity for young children is now purchased by parents from youth sport programs. Parents, by moving their children to youth sport programs in millions, have seized control of youth sport. An amalgam of part-timers and volunteers, often parents themselves as well as some physical educators, run youth sports as they want to. Some even claim as their goal the optimal development of their young children. Many want their children to learn about the magic of their minds and bodies and build a set of common experiences that will enable them to participate effectively in their culture. Others, of course, harbor aspirations of greatness and exert untoward pressures on all involved. Still others find these programs to be convenient and inexpensive baby-sitters.

Teaching for Understanding

Sport education will remain one of the many avenues open to physical educators in assisting the personal development of their young charges; nevertheless, the role of physical education in youth sport education must change. Physical educators must declare a new manifesto for their involvement in youth sport education. Their goal must be to "teach for understanding." Thorpe, Bunker, and Almond (1986) coined this term in England to describe an approach they used to teach games and sports that began with the structure of the sport, its rules, and its resulting strategies, and finally moved to the skills needed to participate. Thus the sport is developed from the top down. Their students appreciated the family resemblances among sports, the role of rules in sports, and the rationale for the necessary skills. They were engaged, from the beginning, in cognitive analysis of the sport and its task demands. They started with the "good part"—a basic understanding of the sport—and from there came to appreciate the need for practice, fitness, and strategy. Furthermore, when they found that they were not able to reach excellence in an objective way, they were later able to participate in a higher level of analysis as spectators. Teaching for understanding—for a genuine comprehension of underlying principles rather than a mindless acquisition of disconnected skills—will become an important feature of physical education.

Sport must be regarded as a developmental experience, a phase quickly over, and must be taught as such. Sport contains within itself the seeds of its own destruction. It is essentially a zero-sum activity and people are, in the final analysis, more interested in non-zero-sum activities. Non-zero-sum activities, like rat-ball, where the score is not kept, like conversations, hiking, group workouts, and square-dancing, can be sustained for longer because they produce an inclusive social climate more suited to a society that must cooperate on a grand scale to survive.

Lifelong Activity—Not Fitness—the Goal

Next, it must also be recognized that physical fitness itself is not the immediate goal of physical education lessons. In his 1985 *Alliance Scholar Address*, Wayne Van Huss argued convincingly that changes in physical fitness require far more time and effort than a thirty-minute activity period twice a week. The efforts needed to produce significant effects far exceed provisions currently made in schools. The profession should confess to itself and its clients that it cannot realize the fitness goals for the nation's children through school physical education.

Denying that the goal of school physical education is fitness directly contradicts the behavioral objectives for school health recommended in the report *Prospects for a Healthier America*. This report specifically recommended that the objectives for the nation be redefined with regard to school physical fitness and exercise. It also recommended that 70 percent of schoolchildren be systematically assessed for their physical fitness, and that 90 percent be "participating regularly in appropriate physical activities, particularly cardiorespiratory fitness programs that can be carried into adulthood" (Kolbe & Gilbert, 1984, p. 62). Furthermore, it specified that an objective for 70 percent of children should be "participating in daily school physical education programs" (p. 62). To achieve these fitness goals would require a massive increase in time and resources to offer physical education to all children everyday for at least forty-five minutes and preferably longer in well-equipped facilities.

An example of the kind of program that enhances children's fitness was recently instituted by Blue Cross and Blue Shield of Michigan, which became alarmed that signs of health risks were evident among children they insured. With Guy Reiff (1986) of the University of Michigan, they instituted a "Fitness for Youth" program to alert children to their health status and to recruit them into a lifestyle-management plan. In addition to emphasizing cardiovascular fitness (60 percent of the program), strength (15 percent), and flexibility (5 percent), the program involved the school lunch program, serum cholesterol screening, and counseling. The students in this imaginative and effective program, the result of a partnership between the public and private sectors, achieved major improvements in health status. But the program required the efforts of highly qualified and energetic people and a substantial grant from Blue Cross, the interested private-sector insurer. If this pilot project is effective in reducing long-term claims, other third-party payers may likewise contribute to the development of school health-enhancement programs throughout the nation.

It is not possible for the schools to reach these goals by 1990. Immediate fitness improvement cannot be the goal of the physical education lesson in school. Until the reforms necessary for the dedication of an hour per school day to physical education are in place, the immediate goal for the teacher must be to teach for understanding, enjoyment, and skills in a protected situation and in the company of others. The objective is *to potentiate activity outside the school* and throughout life. It is to teach the attitudes, knowledge, and behaviors that will potentiate the living of a healthy lifestyle through a dramatically extended life span. Kids should leave school physical education with the capacity to participate in the culture's activities comfortably and understand the principles of nutrition, training, and injury and stress management as well as the major sport entertainment forms. They should know how to set out to learn new skills and, as good consumers, how to discern the real from the fake in the burgeoning activity service industry vying for their earnings. They above all should have experienced success and had fun.

These goals are somewhat different from current practices. Many physical educators are caught up in the press for immediate accountability and performance. They demand that fitness norms be met immediately, even though their immediate achievement may sour the recipient's attitude toward a healthy lifestyle for life. The field will move gradually to an understanding that long-term goals take priority.

The idea that the goal of physical education is understanding the body and its functions, society's sports and games, and the informed management of lifestyle, is an idea that has come of age. However, failure to create these understandings carries with it a threat from Farquhar and King who argue, "It may be up to health professionals in other community settings to help foster such patterns in youngsters as well as other populations (e.g., inner city residents; adults over age 65)" (1984, p. 34).

Unwise Diversion of Resources to the Elite

Many physical educators in schools are required by principals, school boards, and a vociferous community to subvert the goals of school physical education to serve the highly visible elite sport system. Varsity athletics can produce benefits for all, providing a rallying point for the school and community. Elite sport can also demonstrate fleetingly that a school team is "better" than another in the sense that it can score more points than another team. Varsity athletics can permit others to bask in the reflected glory and can provide the media content to sell.

Unfortunately, this system is highly selective. Each selection of a recipient of the benefits of elite sport participation comes at the expense of the many who are rejected. Athletic performance is so seductively visible that the press for achievement may in fact convince the majority that competitive sport participation is not only unachievable, but not worth achieving. This state of affairs is tolerable if the rejected receive a rich and beneficial experience in physical education that prepares them for their lives. However, quite often varsity athletics consumes all the resources. There is little interest beyond the utilization of physical education as a platform for the mounting of highly competitive athletics for the few. This subversion of the goals and practices of school physical education will lead to a revolution in its content. Parents and taxpayers will revolt, and elite athletics will be divorced from school physical education as it has been divorced from physical education in the universities.

School physical education will then be able to acknowledge that seeking fitness and performance for the few is not a desirable goal. School physical educators will count themselves succcessful only when all children leave school with an informed appreciation concerning the role of activity in their lives and the means to create for themselves a lifelong rich and changing activity content. The changing pressures will permit progress towards these goals during the rest of the century.

Physical Education for Young Adults

The people who have just left school are struggling to establish themselves as young adults; this group is still in transition. They must leave the protected environment of school and launch out on their own. At this point, the cohort in the U.S. divides into two groups. In about equal numbers the young adults go on to college or into the world of work (or unemployment). These two groups have quite different experiences. The college-bound move back into a protective system where many enter professionally organized college physical education programs designed to entice them into enjoyable and healthful activity. The others are only rarely the beneficiaries of such concern. Getting a foothold in the world of work is the immediate challenge, not the development of the skills and knowledge needed for an enjoyable healthy lifestyle.

As emerging teenagers, both sets of young adults are struggling for a sense of identity and the confidence of knowing that they can do something well. Our sport-based programs have provided a potent avenue to that identity for many. To the extent that we serve well and contribute to the emergence of personality, this is a beneficial process. However, we oftentimes demonstrate publicly and incontrovertibly that an individual does not do something well. Our competitive sports often involve an objective and odious comparison that undermines a client's self-evaluation as a valuable and sovereign individual. As a result, these people drop out having served as the "cannon fodder" for others' achievements.

Young sport dropouts and those who never dropped in comprise the large majority of young adults. With increasing age and competing demands from their workplace or education, young adults, newly in control of their activity and leisure choices, tend to drift away from competitive sport. If their early experiences with sport-based programs were negative, their tendency to drift away is even more pronounced. For these early dropouts sport is not worth doing badly, and the current state of the art in sport is only too available to them in double-slow motion color television. Eventually only a small fraction of the population is maintained in sports activities, usually driven by the pursuit of excellence. Actual participation in the traditional American team sports does not attract many Americans for very long, simply because it does not serve to maintain their personal growth and their self-image.

Young Workers

Emerging adults in the work force can be reached only by mechanisms that deliver activity and leisure services to the worksite or through the leisure industry. No institutional mechanisms are currently in place to reach them, and none can be expected in the near future. Young working adults will be reached using the same mechanisms used to reach adults.

Students

For those in college or university enclaves, the story is different. Physical educators have one more chance to influence these young adults. The programs they design should give students the information, skills, and attitudes they need to design and implement their own lifestyle management systems. The programs should be optional so that university and college physical educators will be forced to persuade students to participate and learn, rather than legislate their participation. This feature of the programs is important because the students' participation will also be voluntary as soon as they graduate to the work force as adults. The creation of attractive, enjoyable programs designed to foster a sense of responsibility for one's own health must be the goal. The programs should simulate those in the adult world, preparing students for the time they must make their own decisions as adults.

Physical Education and the Adult

In a nutshell, older clients are less vigorous, less competitive, more knowledgeable (some would say opinionated) and assertive, and, of course, in control of their discretionary income.

As a result of the megatrends affecting our society, adult clients now seek activities that bolster their self-image as sovereign, growing individuals mastering challenges that they have selected. Increasingly, part of the self-image that is shared by individuals across North America is the notion that they are in some way responsible for themselves. Their health status and appearance, their longevity and vigor, their capacity to respond to and manage stressors are increasingly regarded as being, to a significant extent, under their control. The industry's clients are hungry for the opportunities to exercise that control. They wish to be healthier in mind, body, and spirit. They do not want rejection, odious comparison, and the discomfort of poor-quality surroundings. They have high aspirations, for themselves and their experiences, and they are free to choose.

Self-worth is the driving motive behind adult participation in the activities we have planned for them. To satisfy this motive, the chosen activity must have a reasonable chance of being beneficial to each client. A few clients cannot be sacrificed for the benefit of others; they will not tolerate such a situation for long. The notion of voluntary and informed participation will dramatically redesign the content of the activity and leisure industry.

By the time people have reached adulthood, there has been a dramatic reduction in interest in competitive sport and an equally dramatic rise in interest in non-zero-sum activities that foster cognitive growth and encounters with the physical environment. For example, in the United Kingdom, the two fastest growing leisure activities are coarse fishing and lawn-bowls (J. Jeffery, Loughborough University, personal communication, 1984). In a longitudinal survey of changing patterns in the U.K., Veal (1982) concluded that cycling, jogging, "keep-fit" (an English generic term that is best translated as "aerobics") and home activities were climbing fast. The losing activities were spectator and team sports. Thus in the U.K. the activities that were growing were those for which one could create a personal agenda and that could be followed by individuals or by very small face-to-face groups.

The same tendency can be seen in North America. Competitive activities with clear winners and losers will not be capable of capturing the adult portion of the market. Activities that will sustain the participation of adults permit evaluation with reference to themselves rather than with reference to the performance of others. Adults already know who they are. There is much less need for trials and for the establishment of rigid hierarchies. In fact, the establishment of rigid hierarchies in the adult world is regarded as bad manners because it tends to resolve the issues and break up cooperating social groups.

Thus the content of adult physical education will first have to satisfy the needs of individuals for personal growth. It will have to honor their standards for personal comfort. It will also have to honor their needs for ongoing social interaction and enjoyment. The activities themselves will have to permit the development and maintenance of related social groupings.

Adult Participation Rates

The interest of adults in self-development has taken many by surprise. An enormous number of people seem to have changed their lifestyles and adopted some form of exercise, improved their diet, given up smoking, or decreased their consumption of alcohol. However, the actual number of people exercising is much smaller than it appears. A Media General (Kilman, 1985) survey reported that 60 percent of people exercised for health reasons and another 30 percent were prevented from exercising for one reason or another. Only 10 percent courageously reported they did not want to exercise. Thus this survey demonstrated that nearly everyone believed exercise was socially acceptable and reported that they, too, understood and were part of the health revolution.

The reports that show a majority of people participating in exercise grossly overestimate the rate and intensity of their participation. A recent paper by Brooks (1985) addressed just this issue. Brooks reported that one of the surgeon general's 1980 objectives for the nation was to have 60 percent of American adults by 1990 meet the standards for regular active participation in beneficial physical activity. Regular active participation was defined as engaging in physical activity involving "large muscle groups in dynamic movements for periods of 20 minutes or more for three or more days per week, and which is performed at an intensity requiring 60% or greater of an individual's cardio-respiratory capacity" (Richmond, 1980). To assess progress towards that goal, and to assess whether the goal is realistic, good baseline data were needed for 1980. Brooks set out to provide that data.

Brooks found two studies that had asked subjects to keep time-expenditure diaries in the years 1975-76 and 1981. These time diaries were kept in each season of the year and included data on participation in physical activity. It was this data that Brooks mined to generate the baseline data on activity participation. The samples were comparable in age, followed the same procedures, and reported participation in seven physical activities selected for their potential cardiovascular benefits if undertaken frequently (walking, team sports, racket sports, swimming, exercising/yoga, bicycling, and jogging). The decisions used to categorize participation were probably biased in favor of inclusion and thus likely to overestimate the participation rates. Table 5.1 summarizes the findings.

The Media General report and an article in *U.S. News and World Report* (Levine, Wells, & Kopf, 1986) suggest that we have already achieved the national target for 1990. However, it should be noted that the percentage identified as "active" by Brooks fell far short of this target percentage. The percentage was only about 7 percent in 1975. Although it increased by 42 percent to 9 percent in the five to six years between studies, it is still far short of the target even if liberal rating standards are used (i.e., the simple reporting in the time diary of activities with potential cardiovascular effects). Even if participation continues to climb at that rate, it will still be less than 20 percent by 1990.

Table 5.1   Summary of Baseline Participation Rates of Adult Americans in Regular Physical Activity (Brooks, 1985).

Study Year	M & SD Age (years)	M % Active	M & SD of Activity Duration (minutes)
1975 to 1976	46 ± 17	6.7	56 ± 49
1981	47 ± 16	9.5	51 ± 40

Brooks also used data from a major survey determining the frequency of participations. This survey accumulated statistics on activity dosage rather than merely counting those who participated. Again, if all the activities presumed to have cardiovascular effects are considered, the percentage of people who participated at least once during 1982 was 82 percent. However, the percentage fell rapidly to only 11 percent for sixty participations during the year (i.e., approximately once a week).

Brooks also cautioned that respondents quite often reported other activity concurrent with their participation. In other words, sometimes participants also listened to the radio, had conversations, and so forth. It was clear that the activity reported was labeled, for example, "racketball," but included all the peripheral activity of the setting, such as changing clothes and socializing. Consequently, durations reported were overestimates of the actual time spent performing the activity itself.

Finally, Brooks tried to estimate the percentage that met the standard set by the surgeon general for regularity and duration. She combined the data for about five hundred respondents with complete reports over the four seasons to try to calculate the numbers of people who were participating three or more times a week for the required duration. She concluded that in 1980 only 8.7 percent of this subset of highly reliable and consistent respondents met this criteria (a percentage closely approximating the 9.5 percent regular participation rate reported in her earlier study).

Surgeon General's Goals—Impossible.   The data just discussed demonstrate how few people have met the standards set as an objective for the nation. There is a very large disparity between the time diary data and the telephone survey conducted by Media General. The difference is almost an order of magnitude and the conclusion is simple and compelling: While we have created an awareness of the role of exercise in health enhancement, we have been markedly less successful in persuading people actually to exercise. It is clearly impossible to reach the surgeon general's 1990 objective for adult participation in regular physical activity.

There are two ways to look at this conclusion. On the pessimistic side is the very small proportion of people who are sufficiently active to reap the benefits of exercise. On the other hand, the industry has thrived in the last few years and it has done so as a result of a very limited market penetration. There is immense scope for future improvement.

Less Intensity and More Consistency.   The major improvement will come not from emphasizing high-intensity programs and "hyping" competition but from reaching the masses in the population who know exercise is good, believe they are involved in health-giving programs, but who are actually deluding themselves and the pollsters. The goal for physical education is to persuade the majority of people to do something beyond the infrequent walk or workout on the basement rowing machine. Regular, gentle participation of the masses will produce more impact on the health of the nation than intense participation of the few. The central question for researchers in physical education is to discover how little exercise is enough, and for program designers the question remains how to entice millions more people to enter and remain in personal health enhancement programs.

The professional task for physical education will be to find pleasing and gentle, low-impact and sustainable, enjoyable and sociable activities that can be built into the lifestyles of adult Americans. The normative, self-critical, intense activities that emphasize how much can be achieved will have limited impact in achieving the national goals for physical activity.

Estimates of the Popularity of Activities

As mentioned earlier, the content of adult participation has changed by moving away from zero-sum competitive team sports. We will survey some evidence for this shift; however, most physical educators will already have their own examples.

Brooks (1985) used the adult data reported by the Simmons Market Research Bureau to establish the way men and women were changing their participation in physical activities, which, if undertaken regularly, were likely to influence health. The simple graphs in Figures 5.1 through 5.6 indicate that patterns of participation were changing in the period 1975 through 1981. The most obvious change is reflected in Figure 5.1 where it is clear that women were an increasing proportion of the exercisers; this trend will undoubtedly

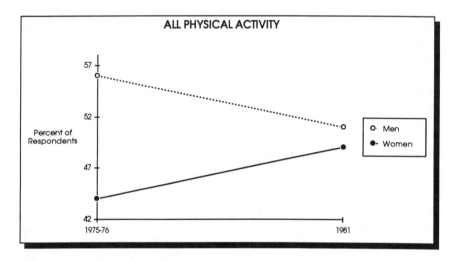

Figure 5.1 Change in the percentages of men and women exercisers in all activities from 1975 to 1981 (Brooks, 1985).

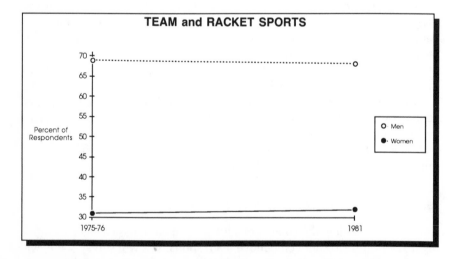

Figure 5.2 Change in the percentages of men and women reporting team and racket sports as exercise from 1975 to 1981 (Brooks, 1985).

continue. Note that the mean age for these respondents was from forty-five to forty-nine years depending on category, so these data refer to middle-aged and older adults.

Brooks analyzed the adult data available to calculate which activities were responsible for this shift. Again, an examination of the graphs in Figures 5.2 through 5.6 reveals no shifts in the breakdown by sex in team and racket sports and little change in the breakdown of joggers. However, from 1975 through

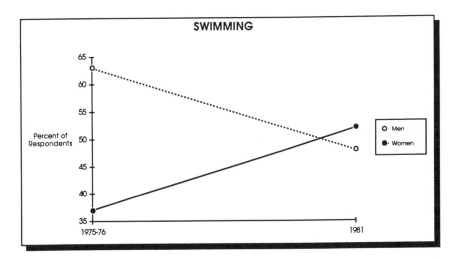

Figure 5.3 Change in the percentages of men and women reporting swimming as exercise from 1975 to 1981 (Brooks, 1985).

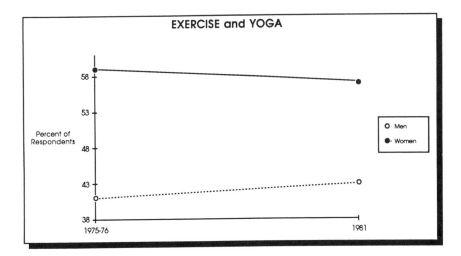

Figure 5.4 Change in the percentages of men and women reporting exercise/ yoga as exercise from 1975 to 1981 (Brooks, 1985).

1981 the differences in the participation rates of men and women decreased somewhat in exercise and yoga and decreased startlingly in walking. In swimming, women became the majority participators by 1981.

Much time has passed from 1981 and new trends continue to develop. Not only are more people participating, but the number of women participants is gaining. In fact, the exercise-for-health phenomenon can no longer be considered an activity biased towards male participation. This will require a

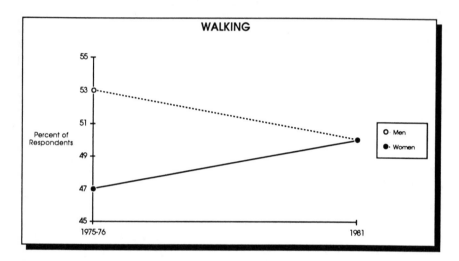

Figure 5.5 Change in the percentages of men and women reporting walking as exercise from 1975 to 1981 (Brooks, 1985).

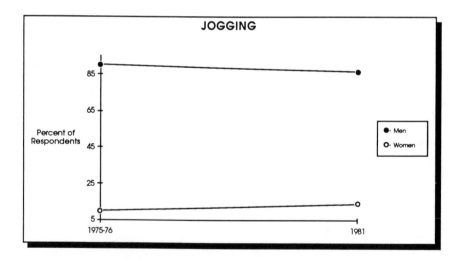

Figure 5.6 Change in the percentages of men and women reporting jogging as exercise from 1975 to 1981 (Brooks, 1985).

massive redesign of facilities to accommodate an equal number of men and women. It will also require preparation of equal numbers of men and women leaders for the popular health-inducing activities.

These graphs refer to middle-aged and older adults, but similar questions can be asked of a younger age group. In answer to such questions, readily available data describing the participation rates in instructional programs at the University of Oregon were split into categories of activity to reveal long-term trends.

Figures 5.7a and 5.7b show the percentage of the total enrollment in eight categories of classes in the years 1980-85. It is easy to see which types of

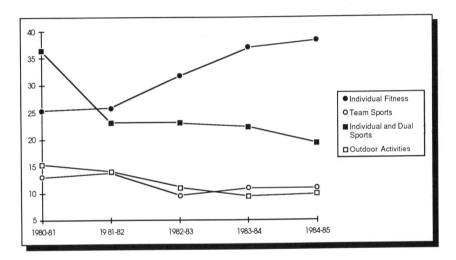

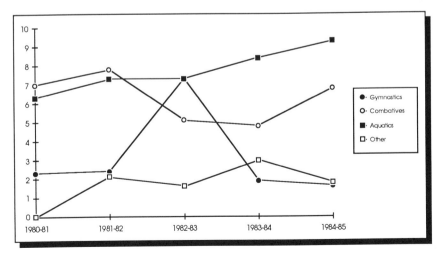

Figures 5.7a and 5.7b   Changes in the percentage of young adults enrolling in eight different activity categories at the University of Oregon since 1980.

activities have been gaining in popularity, and which losing, at the University of Oregon. Individual fitness and aquatics have steadily improved their share of the total participation. This gain has come at the cost of team, individual, and dual sports and outdoor activities. Other categories exhibit variation but no apparent consistent trend.

No records indicating gender participation are available because affirmative action requires that all classes be open equally to men and women. The participants in the Oregon sample are considered representative of the university student body where the mean age is about twenty-five years. The data from the University of Oregon are not strictly comparable with that presented by Brooks. However, they are consistent with each other and there are lessons to be learned from both data sets. The first is that middle-aged women have increased their participation startlingly since the midseventies. By 1980 they were more or less equally represented with middle-aged men in noncompetitive activities, such as swimming and walking, and were increasing their participation in other activities. Team and racket sports and jogging seemed to be still predominantly male activities in the Midwest where Brooks found her data.

The second lesson from the University of Oregon data is consistent with the Brooks data. When given the option to register and pay an extra fee for the privilege of participating in activity classes, younger adults were moving away from competitive sport activities and moving toward individual and self-developmental activities such as fitness and aquatics (Ellis & Ulrich, 1983).

It may be that the industry's clients are smarter than the industry. The clients seem to be selecting exactly the activities they should for optimal impact on their health. The rapid gain in activities like aerobics, individual fitness, walking, and swimming coincide closely with Kuntzleman's (1978) ratings of the activities for health impact. Kuntzleman rated activities for their presumed impact on endurance, strength, flexibility, balance, and coordination/agility. When all five effects are included (and when activities that may produce dangerous increases in blood pressure, i.e., football, baseball, basketball, and soccer, are excluded) swimming, ballet, and cycling are rated highest. Following closely are rhythmic dancing, tennis, bowling, golf, walking, and jogging. These activities are all "soft" in that sudden, violent responses are not called for. Also, they can be maintained throughout life and can include social elements to make them more enjoyable. Ironically, very few professionals will identify these activities as the principal components of physical education.

A revolution is in process in the content of the field. The activities themselves will no longer be so important. They will become the medium through which a variety of motives are satisfied in addition to mastery. The activities will become embedded in a context of support services within which participation is initiated and maintained. It will not be enough to be just a skilled performer or just a good teacher or coach. Being a good listener, counselor, and friend will be as important.

Reflections in the Retail Market

A recent article by Dunnett (1984) indicated that the popularity of swimming and pool-related activities among clients of sport and health clubs was so great, that all other things being equal, people are twice as likely to join a club with a pool than without one. Dunnett also reports that swimming is the most popular sport-like activity in the U.S.A. (105 million participants compared to 20 million tennis players) and that usage per square foot will be higher in a swimming pool complex than in any other area of a club. He explains that it is a family activity in which everyone, infants to seniors, can participate together at his or her own level with benefit. He argues that the creation of a swimming pool complex is the single most important marketing/sales tool for sport and health clubs because of client wishes and cost per square foot per participation.

A recent informal survey of private sector providers conducted as part of a special feature section of the *Seattle Post-Intelligencer* (Carter, 1985) revealed clear changes in the market for activity services and supplies. Buying patterns reveal changing tastes consonant with the aging population. Activities preferred are slower, softer, involve less risk at all times, and take less time. For example, Recreational Equipment, Inc. (REI), long synonymous with adventure activities and the mythic confrontational wilderness lifestyle of the Pacific Northwest, reports substantial changes in its market. Although it has maintained its lines of crampons, hiking boots, and ice axes, its real profits come from goods like family tents, sleeping pads for station wagons, footwear for the supermarket, clothing, bedding, and gifts. Many other "hard" item retailers have left the business. Adults have things other than confrontation on their minds when they think of activity and leisure. Substitute activities seem to be cooperative and experiential in nature. Even J.C. Penney has adapted to the changes. Marketing for this retailer has built its product lines on the idea that instant gratification is an important factor in adults' choices. Adults do not want to spend time acquiring difficult skills; they want to be proficient the first time they do something. Complex, skillful activities seem to be losing their popularity with the now mature baby-boomers who dominate the market. J.C. Penney has also found that adults like to buy high tech goods that relate to their health and fitness. They buy sophisticated exercise machines and fashion apparel to go with them. The consumption-oriented purchasing patterns associated with affluent middle America have finally come to the health enhancement market.

These tendencies have been demonstrated in the programs offered by the Seattle Parks Department, for example. Increasing numbers of adults and seniors seek activities that lead to personal wellness and fitness. Activities that are kind to aging joints and that permit all to win are gaining in popularity. The popularity of swimming for health among the adults in the population has led to increasing competition for scarce pool resources and to political fights whenever lap swim times are preempted for high school swim meets.

There has been a surge in interest in biking and dancing, and the bowling leagues have returned in numbers comparable to the peak enrollments of the early seventies.

The baby-boomers have not only matured, they have joined the affluent middle class. This fact is producing another effect evident in the changing tastes of America's middle class. An example can be found in the promotions created by the Bonaventure Hotel and Spa Resort in Fort Lauderdale, Florida. In addition to seeking the customary hospitality, lodging, and convention business, this hotel features the fact that it is a residential health club. It has its own quarterly newsletter, *Body Talk*, and has created packages of up to a week's stay at the hotel to participate in an adult residential fitness plan. While this may be dismissed as merely promotional hype, the plan includes a wide variety of activities that usually occur only in health care facilities and fitness laboratories. The stays typically include medical screening, body composition analysis, fitness evaluation, nutrition counseling and planned menus, fitness classes, tennis, racketball, squash, golf, use of the pool complex (swimming, steam baths, jacuzzis, whirlpools), massages, and a supervised children's activity program. It would be easy to dismiss all this simply as marketing fluff. However, if the Bonaventure is successful, its effort is likely to be emulated throughout the Radisson Hotel chain of which it is a part, thus creating opportunities for professional work for many activity and leisure professionals who have not previously thought of the hospitality industry as a base of operation.

The hospitality/travel industry is a vast industry, which has begun to recognize that health, fitness, and appearance enhancement are powerful motivations for most Americans. It has made use of these motivations together with motivations for fun, luxury, and novel settings, to create fitness sessions in which adults and children can move enjoyably from one positive experience to another in an environment that permits both business and pleasure. The fact that the hospitality business is planning and conducting these activities does not mean that the content is unprofessional. It is as easy for a hospitality business as for any activity and leisure agency to employ physicians, exercise technologists, activity leaders, and nutrition counselors—and produce good results. In fact, market forces will work directly, forcibly, and rapidly to ensure that the services provided are appreciated by the clients.

The hospitality industry and the health care industry have added the content of the activity and leisure industry to their portfolio of services. We in the activity and leisure industry have not been so quick to see the opportunities. We have not responded to the major opportunity presented by those clients who are already served by a complex of industries dealing with business and tourist travel, vacations, resorts, cruises, dude ranches, conventions, sales and management promotions, and the like.

To summarize, the content of the field attractive to adults is different from that which we have designed for youth. The activities are softer and less competitive. They permit individual participation, albeit in a social matrix; that is, other people present are part of the social experience but not necessary to the outcome. The activities are process- rather than outcome-oriented and are less likely to involve skill acquisition for the purposes of competition. They should take place in surroundings that are much higher in quality than those the clients can provide for themselves in the more mundane settings of home or work.

Enjoyment, Understanding, Then Skill

The changes in the adult market will manifest themselves in the purchasing decisions of adults. The market forces created by these purchasing decisions will be inexorable. The roles for physical educators in such markets will be quite different from what they have been. For example, the classic prescriptive role of the physical educator leading a class of beginners in a normative mode will be relatively rare. Adults will demand to be treated as individuals and will resist demeaning comparison with others. Teaching will have to be individualized and result from the desire for self-improvement generated by participation. Thus early enjoyment, if not success, will be absolutely necessary. Adults who are licensed to leave, and even to stop payment on their checks, will no longer settle for the mere possibility of success after a long period of preparation and skill acquisition. Ironically, this tendency towards enjoyment calls for an exact inversion of our current practice of teaching skills first in the hopes of later understanding and enjoyment. The new strategy is the strategy called "teaching for understanding" that Thorpe, Bunker, and Almond (1986) advocated for school physical education. Adults will struggle for skill acquisition only after they are personally committed to the activity. Enjoyment of the process itself, and the quality of the attendant social experience, will have to precede the realization that later effort is worthwhile. In short, physical education leadership will have to reverse the traditional assumption that the first stage of participation in any activity is the acquisition of skill followed by understanding and finally enjoyment. With adults, enjoyment will have to precede understanding, and understanding will have to precede efforts to acquire skill.

The characteristics of the adult clients will involve physical educators in new client relationships that were not well developed when the field was almost exclusively oriented to youthful clients. Counseling and referral, recruiting and connecting, the offering of indirect advice will all become more important. While these may not be enough to sustain full-time positions, they will become a part of most physical educators' jobs.

Older clients are less robust and will require more sophisticated handling to adapt activities to meet their individual capacities. Adapted activities and the knowledge needed to create and dispense them will also be more important. In addition, athletic training or sports medicine will rise in importance as the median age of the active client climbs. The technologies developed for special populations, both advantaged and disadvantaged, will increasingly become part of the day-to-day practice of those dealing with adults.

Finally, the normative assessment scales built over the years for classifying captive clients in schools and the military will label too many clients below average. This aversive practice will rapidly be replaced with systems for tracking individuals' performance changes against their own goals. The classic system of test and measurements will be replaced with two new technologies: marketing and individual assessment.

Motives for Participation

Not much effort has been expended by professionals in the field to determine the reasons for participation. The notion of marketing, as opposed to sales, has not been part of the thinking of physical educators. Marketing involves discovering the products and services desired by future clients. Selling involves persuading clients to buy products that already exist. In physical education the services offered—the products—are usually presumed to exist already. Our programs have always been taught essentially in the same way. The captive nature of child clients permitted the field to prescribe the activity content. Sophisticated marketing was unnecessary and even selling was not critically important. Now that a larger portion of the market for activity and leisure services consists of adults who must be persuaded to participate in our programs, marketing has become an increasingly important activity.

Marketing involves divining the motives for participation so that desired services can be designed. Our understanding of motives for participation has now become critical; more and more effort will be spent conducting studies of such motivation. We are also beginning to understand that the motives for participation differ markedly with increasing age. These motives proceed along a continuum from external to internal locus of control. In other words, the young child can be convinced to participate wholeheartedly to satisfy a parent, a teacher, or other authority. But as children pass through school, they eventually reach adolescence and begin to place the self into context, often in sport. Finally, as adults, motives become internal. Adults seek personal goals of health and vigor, improved appearance, and pleasant company. An understanding of these simple but fundamental differences should drive the provisions we make for our clients from womb to tomb.

Summary

The shifting motives for participation require an understanding of the roles that activity plays during the different stages of life. In fact, there are many physical educations, and we must prepare for them all.

The preschool child needs activity to facilitate physical development and to explore and learn about the physical and social world. We think of the field's content as play at this stage, but physical educators need to learn how to enhance this play. By the time the child is in school, the physical educator should be concerned about developing skills and capacities in the human form, and showing how these can be changed over time. Furthermore, the school curriculum must not only acculturate the child, but also prepare the child to take an active part in designing his or her own lifestyle for health and enjoyment in later life.

Adults have become a new market for physical education. They are clients who are in charge of their own decisions and the content of the field must be designed to attract and maintain their interest. Furthermore, the increasing age of the people in the society will require physical education to design activities that serve a matrix of needs and goals simultaneously. Competitive sport is unsuitable for the vast majority of adults and non-zero-sum activities will predominate. For old adults, the maintenance of existing capabilities rather than the development of new ones will take precedence. Throughout the adult market, prescription will be out and persuasion will be in.

Simply put, much of the content of physical education will no longer be determined by the physical educators, but shaped by the power of the adult market.

■■■ **Chapter 6** ■■■■■■■■■■■■■■■■■■■■■■■■■

*The Changing Profession*_____

The health enhancement industry is peopled largely by professionals from three main sources, that is, from the three university-level curricula that prepare neophyte (a) physical educators, (b) health educators, and (c) recreators. These three fields have become increasingly differentiated and separate from one another academically. In essence, they have matured into separate academic fiefdoms. It was not always so. As the industry was developing, these specialties were considered merely facets of the same enterprise. Many of the long-term career professionals in the upper levels of the three professional groups were prepared in curricula that had not yet been differentiated into health education, physical education, and recreation. However, members of the old guard are becoming fewer and farther between because the fields gradually split into separate curricula and departments during the two decades after World War II. These pioneers are towards the end of their careers; the old breed of generalists has become rare. Paradoxically, these generalists are becoming increasingly valuable as the industry responds to new circumstances.

The old forces that forced the split between physical education on the one hand and health education and recreation on the other have reversed their directions. Real pressures now exist to create young professionals who can work flexibly in the areas of the industry where the fields overlap. This chapter identifies the areas of overlap between the fields and the major pressures for change in physical education that result. The first theme to be discussed involves the changing profession in the schools. There will be approximately 20 million children in schools from now to the end of this century. Despite the dramatic developments occurring elsewhere in the field, schools will remain an important area of concern. The second theme involves the pressures for change in the professional areas serving adults.

Physical Education and Health Education in the Schools

Chapter 1 provided a thumbnail sketch of the recent history of the profession. It pointed out how physical education had been separated from health education and recreation, and that for much of its history it had concentrated legitimately on teacher education. It showed that the most recent developments—back to basics, the tax revolt, and the reduced number of children in the schools—have administered sharp shocks to the profession as teaching became less attractive and harder to enter. The sharp shocks induced change at a fortunate juncture. They occurred just as adults were developing their interest in health enhancement, and just as alternative careers developed for physical educators in the private and adult sectors of the market. Nevertheless, during the last decade or so, the teaching situation has been somewhat gloomy for school physical education as the center of gravity of the field shifted towards serving adults rather than children.

Despite the above tale of woe, the absolute number of teaching jobs in primary and secondary schools has been increasing throughout the last fifteen years. In the decade between 1970 and 1980 the total number of teaching positions increased by 151,000 to a total of 2,439,000, despite falling student enrollment. This gain was created by reducing the teacher-pupil ratio at a rate far higher than the reduction of the number of teachers due to dropping enrollment. For example, in public schools the number of teaching jobs created due to the reduction in teacher-pupil ratio increased by 15.9 percent while the rate at which the number of teachers was being reduced as a result of falling enrollment was −10.6 percent. In private schools the figures were an even more startling contrast: +22.8 percent to −4.3 percent respectively (Frankel & Gerald, 1982. p 72).

Surplus Teachers

The problem for the profession was not that the teacher corps had failed to grow, but that the numbers of new teachers far exceeded the demand. Figure 6.1 displays this relationship. While the demand for new teachers fell slowly, the number of new teachers available exceeded demand by about 600,000 in 1975. Although the number of new graduates fell precipitously during the next five years, the backlog of would-be teachers, returning teachers, and new teachers flooded the market. Those health and physical educators among them had to do something to earn a living, and the curricula creating new health and physical educators had to respond to falling interest in preparing for a teaching career. These two closely related forces accentuated the pressure to create alternative avenues to service and resulted in a revolution. Physical education went into business, and health education moved into the community. There are interesting parallels between the current turmoil in the teach-

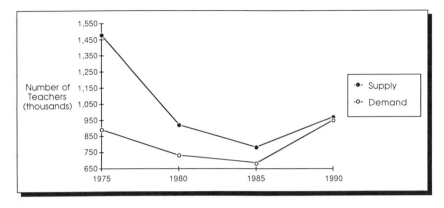

Figure 6.1 Estimated demand for new additional teachers in elementary and secondary schools and estimated supply of new teacher graduates. Totals for five-year intervals (Frankel & Gerald, 1982, p. 71).

ing profession that occurred with a surplus of teachers, and the turmoil among physicians in the health care industry as the surplus of MDs was created.

The picture above deals with the general teacher corps of the nation. It is possible to break these statistics down to consider the relationship between supply and demand by region and by specialty. When this is done, the news is not encouraging for teachers of health education and physical education. The data presented in Figures 6.2 and 6.3b (pp. 134 and 136) are indices of the perceived demand for teachers relative to the supply reported by teacher placement officers across the nation. The higher the number from 1 through 5, the higher the demand relative to the supply. Thus the indices can be considered to be ratings of teaching employment opportunity.

Opportunity changes from time to time according to economic and demographic circumstances. Figure 6.2 shows how employment opportunity has changed during the last decade for both health education and physical education relative to the numerical sciences. It is clear that opportunities are not as good in physical and health education as in the numerical sciences, a well-known fact that is of little comfort to those in the industry wishing to enter the teaching profession. Both teaching specialties reached their nadir in 1983. Since then opportunities have improved, and will most probably continue to improve as the overall picture indicates that demand and supply in the teaching profession in general will come into balance sometime between 1990 and 1995 (see Figure 6.1).

Multiple Majors

If the Association for School, College, and University Staffing report on teacher supply and demand (Akin, 1985) is studied carefully, one may conclude that

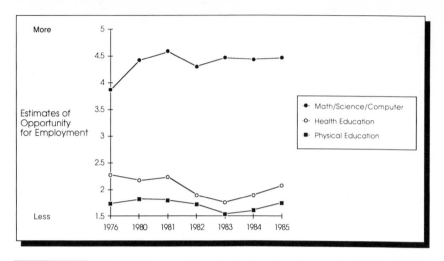

Figure 6.2   Trends in the employment opportunities for teachers in the numerical sciences, physical education, and health education during 1976 to 1985 (Akin, 1985). Units of measurementa are subjective estimates of opportunity for employment provided by educational personnel officers.

for those determined to teach health education and/or physical education, the best strategy is to combine an interest in a discipline that has a low demand with an interest in a discipline that has a high demand. Thus earning a double major seems a sensible strategy. The disciplines that are in greatest demand, in descending order, are: mathematics, physics, chemistry, computing, bilingual education, special education in its various forms, industrial arts, general science, biology, and librarianship.

Furthermore, although the health education and physical education professions and the curricula leading to them have completely separated themselves from one another, these subjects are still regarded as closely related for scheduling purposes at the level of individual school operations, and are often treated as inseparable by the legislation enabling the curriculum. Indeed, the separation of certifications and curricular content into specializations involving different people has been a nuisance to the school systems. The fundamental relationship between the concepts of a healthy lifestyle in both health education and physical education remain fixed in the minds of the employers. They would to this day prefer the flexibilities inherent in hiring the old generalist who is equally at home with the teaching of both health and physical education.

In a down market the wise beginning teacher should prepare to face the demand for occupational flexibility. A combined preparation in health and physical education, the traditional preparation essentially eliminated during the last decade or so, now seems eminently attractive.

Isolation of Health and Physical Education

While new physical and health educators can be exhorted to go the extra mile at their expense to personally reintegrate the fields of health and physical education, such action does not in itself remedy the isolation of the fields from each other in the curriculum and in the informal life of the school. All involved with the two fields must address both the problems that derive from their mutual isolation and the initiatives occurring in the rest of society. The recommendations of the recent national conference, Prospects for a Healthier America, convened by the Department of Health and Human Services, called for coordination and collaboration to produce effects in the schools similar to those being produced in the workplace. A major planning conference for the two professions was called so that

> school health educators and school physical educators might collaborate to ensure that school health and physical education programs synergistically facilitate the development of health related fitness and life-long enjoyment of exercise. (U.S. Department of Health and Human Services, 1984, p. 19)

The simplest way to achieve that goal will be to have the synergies occur inside the thinking and the practice of one individual responsible for both.

Now to return to the employability of teachers in the industry. Given the increasing emphasis on the harder sciences in the curricula for physical education and health education, the overlap between general science, chemistry, and biology make these natural targets for double majors and certifications. A prognosis is simple here. Increasingly, employed physical educators and health educators will have the capacity to teach other subjects that are in great demand. Furthermore, the health and physical education curricula in the universities will be reformed to permit students to combine health and physical education with a major in the sciences supporting them. Eventually, these more versatile degree programs will take five years to complete. Their increased cost will be offset by the increased chance of employment for their graduates.

Location of Teaching Opportunities

In addition to differences in opportunities at different times, there are differences by region across the nation. Figures 6.3a and 6.3b indicate the dramatic differences in the balance between supply and demand in the eleven regions used in the 1985 Association for School, College, and University Staffing (ASCUS) survey (Akin, 1985). In 1985, the best opportunities for physical educators existed in the Middle Atlantic region. Intermediate opportunities existed in Alaska, Hawaii, the Southeast, and the Great Lakes regions. For health

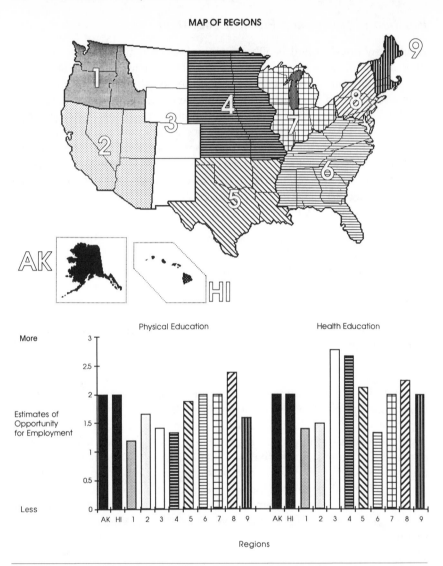

Figure 6.3a and 6.3b Regional differences in employment opportunity for physical educators and health educators (Akin, 1985). Units of measurement are subjective estimates of opportunity for employment provided by educational personnel officers.

educators things were best in the Great Plains/Midwest and Rocky Mountain regions, with intermediate opportunities in the Middle Atlantic and South Central regions, Alaska, Hawaii, and Great Lakes and Northeast regions.

As startling as these differences are, they are still minimal compared to the differences between fields. The message, however, remains clear. Unless would-be teachers live in areas of great opportunity, it is highly likely that they are going to have to move. The Northwest, with its self-proclaimed active lifestyle, is paradoxically caught in a trap. It produces and attracts far more physical and health educators than it can employ, and consequently, employment opportunities there in both disciplines are among the lowest in the nation.

For physical educators with a second major in mathematics, the best opportunities are in the Great Lakes and Middle Atlantic regions. For double majors in health education and mathematics the greatest opportunities exist in the South Central and Middle Atlantic regions. While these data will rapidly become dated, academics and neophyte physical educators and health educators can similarly project the opportunities for future teaching employment by using the annual ASCUS survey.

Flexibility Desirable

The changing demography of the schools that will experience the boom in babies from the baby-boomers during the next two decades will also require flexibility on the part of teachers. Large numbers of students will pass through the schools during the professional lifetimes of those entering the profession in the middle to late 1980s. Opportunities will pass through the age/grade structure of the schools like a wave. The more flexible teachers who can move from elementary level teaching through junior high/middle schools and eventually teach in senior high schools will have more opportunities.

These projections lead to one unmistakable conclusion: Specialization in a narrow band of content and the acquisition of a very limited certification to teach will become a barrier. Teachers with mastery of a broad range of skills will be more valuable. A teacher who can teach physical education and health education, some general science, mathematics, physics, chemistry, special education, or a foreign language will become a prized and highly paid employee. Our curricula must reflect that fact and recruitment into teaching within the industry must emphasize higher mathematical and language skills. Furthermore, we must explore the reorganization of our curricula to eliminate the subspecialties of school physical education and school health education. The two subspecialties will not be able to stand alone comfortably in the schools.

Need for Accountability and Health Enhancement

However, there are two more powerful forces developing that will accelerate the trends identified earlier. The first is the response to the multiple task forces on achieving excellence in education. The widespread dissatisfaction with the performance of children in our schools has caused much finger pointing. As a result, numerous multifaceted attempts to improve matters have sprung up all over the nation. Some of these efforts involve state task forces attempting to interpret the problems for their states and to correct matters locally. Others have been efforts mounted by task forces of the national organizations of superintendents and principals. These national organizations have responded to the calls for reform and improvement of the nation's schools. They have made recommendations for all subjects including health education and physical education.

The second force, related to our concern about achieving excellence in education, is the need for the enhancement of the health of our schoolchildren. School health promotion and enhancement has become a major concern. The separation of health education, safety education, home economics and nutrition, and physical education in the schools is producing splintered and disorganized curricula; it is failing to beneficially influence the wellness of children and to prepare them to become proactive in their search for wellness in later life. People are demanding curricula directed at health promotion and enhancement. For example, the National Professional School Health Education Organization believes that the curriculum should "motivate health maintenance and promote wellness and not merely prevent disability" (1984, p. 4). A cognitive component is also being added and the curriculum should "develop decision-making competencies related to health and human behavior" (p. 4). The call is for the curriculum to be reintegrated and modernized to include attention to the following areas:

- Community health
- Consumer health
- Environmental health
- Family health
- Growth and development
- Nutritional health
- Personal health
- Prevention and control of diseases
- Safety and accident prevention
- Substance use and abuse

From the physical educator's point of view, the absence in this list of concern for sport, exercise, dance, and play as elements of our culture, and for the role of exercise in a healthy lifestyle, is startling. To be charitable, one may assume that concerns for movement and its educational and health effects are naturally included under each of these headings. Furthermore, persons concerned with the role of human sexuality will also have an interest in many of these headings. If the list, or the curriculum that it spawns, is expanded to include these missing topics, then the list of concerns will truly be an enlightened one. But if it is left as is, then it is just a further example of the failure by the authors to truly consider integration and modernization by including all elements that contribute to health and learning in schoolchildren.

Oregon's Proposed Curriculum—An Example

In Oregon, the call for curricular reintegration and modernization is interpreted by a proposed amendment of the administrative rules that govern the curricula of the schools statewide. The curricula offered by health educators, home economists, and physical educators need to be integrated to ensure that students practice appropriate and positive health behaviors to enhance the learning process. The rules recognize that good health enhancement practices are desirable not only to carry over into later life, but also to produce immediate beneficial effects on current learning performance. It is as if the health enhancement curriculum is now perceived as occupationally relevant to the task at hand for the child. The argument is that health enhancement is necessary for the school to accomplish its educational mission effectively.

If physical educators, health educators, and home economists do not enhance the health behaviors of children, they will fail to enhance the effectiveness of all other efforts made in the school. In other words, the teachers in the fields that influence the students' health are going to be held accountable because the effects they are capable of creating are too important for the enterprise as a whole to allow for failure. The Oregon curriculum is going to demand that an integrated curriculum address four areas of learning: (a) nutrition, (b) substance abuse, (c) stress management, and (d) physical activity to promote fitness for learning. These areas are expressed in outcome goals and the students will be expected at Grades 3, 5, 8, and 11 to demonstrate that they have acquired them. The standards permit individualized treatment so that students are optimally stimulated to reach high standards. Table 6.1, from *Essential Learning Skills* published by the Oregon Department of Education (Duncan, 1985), contains those skills that will have to be cooperatively achieved in Oregon schools by mandate.

These mandated performance standards are designed to empower the professions in the face of attempts to divert resources to other functions, like athletics, and to require that everyone concerned integrate their curricula to produce demonstrable learning by the children that will have beneficial effects on their total school performance. Health educators, physical educators, and home economists will need to create a health enhancement curriculum in cooperation with one another. As a result, eventually there will be strong pressures to create a single curriculum for school health enhancement specialists that will cross those lines so carefully drawn by the societies and by academe over the years. Similar strands for learning have been identified for the other areas of learning in the schools, and other teachers will similarly be expected to produce the effects desired by the taxpayers of Oregon.

The forewarning has already produced dramatic reform of the curriculum in physical education in one school: Sam Barlow High School in Gresham, Oregon has eliminated all sports skill instruction from its physical education curriculum. The time available for physical education is given over to the

Table 6.1 Appropriate and Positive Health Behaviors to Enhance Learning

Grade 3
- Identify foods that enhance learning.
- Identify common substances that can affect mental and physical performance.
- Identify common stressful situations.
- Identify physical activities that promote physical fitness.

Grade 5
- Explain how a balanced diet based on dietary goals for the nation relates to physical and mental performance.
- Explain how substance use can produce healthful or harmful effects on mental and physical performance.
- Explain how stressful situations can affect physical and mental performance.
- Explain how physical fitness contributes to optimum student performance.

Grade 8
- Evaluate components in personal diet that affect physical and mental performance.
- Evaluate the effects of substance use on physical and mental performance.
- Evaluate the impact of stress or stressful situations on individual lifestyles.
- Evaluate personal fitness habits that affect physical and mental performance.

Grade 11
- Implement a personal dietary plan that will enhance individual physical and mental performance.
- Apply information concerning substance use that will enhance physical and mental performance.
- Implement a personal plan to minimize the negative effects of stress that will enhance physical and mental performance.
- Implement a personal fitness program designed to enhance individual physical and mental performance.

Note. From Duncan (1985).

understanding of the role of physical activity in enhancing health and self-esteem. In addition, a large variety of activities and learning experiences have been added to the core curriculum. Attendance is booming and the argument is that the students at Sam Barlow are now good consumers who understand the role of activity in their lives and act accordingly.

Physical Education for Credit

In a parallel development, some school systems in Canada and Australia have installed physical education as an examinable and accredited requirement for university admission. This indicates that the understanding of the role of movement in human life is ranked alongside the effects of exercise and the acquisition of skill as viable goals for physical education in those schools. These efforts are altering the status of physical education in the school and in the curriculum of universities already admitting students relatively sophisticated in the "academic" content of the field. It is clear that physical education in the schools is on the brink of interesting and challenging reform.

Physical Education and Recreation in the Schools

The preceding section demonstrated how the interests of physical education and health education in the schools can overlap. In this section the interests of school physical education are shown also to overlap with those of recreation.

Increasing Use of the Outdoors

The tendencies towards self-expressive and cooperative activities can be expected to influence the school curriculum in physical education. The search for new activity content that avoids zero-sum outcomes will lead naturally to the use of the outdoors as a source of adventure. The outdoors, and in some parts of the U.S. the wilderness, will come to be seen as an increasingly attractive locus for the development of curricular content. Although costs of transportation and equipment do exist, capital and operating costs are small, and during the school year there is usually surplus capacity in the outdoors: The challenges are real, there is great potential for linking to other subject areas, outdoor activity produces few injuries, and most importantly, does not have a zero-sum outcome. All students on a trip can confront the challenge and win while simultaneously learning about themselves, their companions, and their environment. The fact that interest in outdoor and wilderness activities can be maintained over a lifetime will further enhance the importance of such activities. During the remainder of this century, outdoor leadership—an area of traditional concern for recreators since World War II—will become an increasingly important part of the physical education curriculum.

Social and Cultural Goals

The organization of recreational, social, and cultural activities, including intramural sports, is necessary if schools are to make a contribution to the acculturation of the nation's children. The kind of managerial expertise needed to make such activities an enriching and supportive part of school life is required as much of those in recreation as of those in physical education. If the national trend towards attention to lifelong participation as part of a healthy lifestyle continues, then increasing overlap of the two areas will occur. The social and experiential elements that are central concerns of those in recreation will have to be grafted onto the physical educator in the future. Together, recreation and physical education will be seen increasingly as essential elements of the morale of staff and student alike.

Finally, the community education movement will continue to make the case that schools are not just for children, but are a prize resource for the community that built them. The use of school programs in community development requires expertise in both the life and content of the school as well as of the community. Community recreators or community physical educators working with one foot in the school and one in the community will remain important. Acquiring the necessary skills to work in both settings will require a preparatory curriculum that includes significant elements from both physical education and recreation. The content of community physical education and recreation programs, of course, will have to be sensitive to the needs of both children and adults, which obviously overlap. The structural distance maintained between the specialties of physical education and recreation will increasingly become an impediment to the development of high-quality services for children and adults.

Let us return to the Sam Barlow High School. The health enhancement curriculum there places understanding of the role of physical activity in lifestyle management at the core of a cooperative curriculum. The school then provides a means to achieve the goals for health enhancement in a variety of beneficial, educational, and enjoyable activities. Voluntary participation in these activities mimics the circumstances that will occur immediately after leaving school. Not all students participate in a voluntary system, but the number is growing rapidly. To create a serviceable number of voluntary activities the physical educator needs to cooperate with others in the school and behave as a community recreation specialist would. Physical education and recreation will thus eventually be brought back together again under the externally applied pressure for improved health enhancement services to school-age people. A model that accomplishes this will be proposed in chapter 8, "Physical Education in School, Community, and University."

Sport Education and Coaching

A further trend involves an area customarily thought of as the preserve of physical education—coaching—passing into the hands of others. Until quite recently, coaching a sport—or two or three—was considered to be part of the job of the physical educator, at least by principals and by society at large. As teachers' unions have gained the power to bargain and enforce agreements concerning working conditions, this situation has changed. Teachers grew tired of the delegation of school-related duties and activities, without their input and as a matter of course. Teachers' unions, in their negotiated agreements with school districts, have whittled away at these extra responsibilities as they sought better working conditions. Physical educators were often successful in convincing their employers that coaching was not necessarily part of their job. Such developments were regarded as gains by physical educators; whether they were remains to be seen.

Physical educators were pleased to add their coaching duties to the roster of additional rather than integral job-related duties for two reasons: first, because the job market had tightened up and upward mobility was restricted. The old, accepted pattern for the young physical educator entering the profession was broken. Traditionally, new physical educators entered the profession with full teaching loads, coaching three sports in season, homeroom duties, and duties associated with intramurals. They could carry this load for a short while before burning out; then they moved upward or sideways in the organization. During the last decade there have been fewer teachers moving upward and sideways because organizations have ceased expanding. Fewer new teachers have been entering at the bottom and existing physical educators have been stuck with the duties they started with. The second reason that physical educators have been pleased to relinquish coaching duties is that they have been growing older during this time of occupational stasis. What at one time would have been an arousing and joyful force became a stressor as they had to balance teaching and coaching with other needs and interests that accumulate with time.

Physical educators worked consistently to reduce the pressures of their jobs. Without consensus or plan, as individuals and as members of local union chapters, they resolved the conflict in their lives in three ways. First, they worked to have the load of extra coaching responsibilities removed via their bargained agreements. Such massive time commitments were precluded in one way or another by the language of the agreements. Second, and alternatively, they pushed for extra payments for coaching duties newly defined as additional responsibilities. The third way is the one with which we are most familiar: The physical education curriculum itself was redefined as the extra duty. Coaches then gave pride of place to athletics, neglecting physical education. Some, to our professional chagrin, have managed to combine these solutions.

The modifications to the working conditions of physical education teachers plus the increase in the average seniority of physical educators due to occupational stasis has increased salary costs. Furthermore, to make matters worse, there are now often additional payments tied to coaching duties. These changes were taking place at the same time that Title IX had raised the consciousness of the nation and young women were being granted access to athletics in addition to young men. Costs rose dramatically and with that ascent came a dramatic increase in pressure for cost containment. It was clearly less costly to avoid hiring expensive physical educators to coach, and thus it became practical to hire part-time coaches, recruit volunteers, and use university students and past varsity athletes to coach.

A recent study conducted by Sisley and Capel (1985) confirmed these observations. This study, which examined those paid for coaching sports in Oregon schools, demonstrated that coaches with a background education in physical education were in a minority. The study surveyed the duties and backgrounds of 4,238 paid coaches associated with varsity sport programs in Oregon's high schools. Only 34.5 percent of them had degrees in physical education. Interestingly, 31.3 percent reported that they minored in coaching. If the notion of "minor" is interpreted to mean that they had taken an organized and recognized set of courses targeted toward the improvement of coaching, this raises interesting questions because official minors in coaching are rare. Varsity athlete status was claimed by 54.6 percent of the coaches.

While only 34.5 percent of the coaches reported degrees in physical education, 85.6 percent reported that they were certified to teach. The remainder were not certified. The conclusion of the survey was obvious: Laypeople and teachers of other specialties, who were varsity athletes earlier in their lives, were doing most of the coaching.

There are two concerns here that have import for our future. Coaching in the schools has become a subspecialty that is not reserved for those in physical education. Also, if competitive elite sport is moving out from under the purview of physical education in the schools, what role does the education of children in competitive sport play in physical education in the school curriculum?

Coaching Education and Physical Education

Given that the Sisley and Capel (1985) study of Oregon can be generalized to the nation, we are left with the fact that coaching in schools is in transition. It is moving rapidly in the direction of being handled by people other than physical educators. If others are going to be doing the coaching it is incumbent on those with the knowledge base about sports and coaching to create systems to transmit that information to would-be coaches outside of the traditional physical education system. The need is great to educate the lay coach both in the school system and in the community at large.

Many of these coaches will be teachers with specialties in other fields who will be doing the coaching either as an avocation, to supplement their income, or to enhance the prospect of gaining employment. Coaching preparation programs in universities will have to be organized to prepare other teachers to coach; coaching minors and specializations on a large scale will also be needed.

Many coaches will be uncertified laypeople with an interest in coaching who are recruited from the surrounding community by the administration. These coaches will be recruited from existing sport programs and will also need coaching education. Finally, in-service programs will have to be created for those already coaching without the benefit of degrees in physical education.

Needs for Coaching Development Programs

These three needs have not been properly addressed yet. Coaching education is being planned, but not on the scale that is needed. If the Oregon study is applied to the nation in general, it would indicate that there are about one-half million paid coaches working in the schools of the nation. The majority of coaches should receive some coaching preparation prior to entry, and once they are in place, they should receive some kind of in-service education on how to realize the benefits of athletic participation.

It has been estimated that some 33 million children are participating in youth sport programs of one kind or another in the U.S. and Canada. The bulk of this participation occurs outside the schools. The youth sport participation of six- to sixteen-year-olds has doubled since 1975 (Klint, 1985). Youth sport has grown so large and affects so many children that it has supplanted sport education in a major way in the schools. The unmet demand for meaningful and developmental sport education experiences for youngsters is so great that a paraeducational sports system has been developed in youth sport programs.

Some may see this as a sign of failure of physical education in the schools. However, to meet the demand for sporting experiences for the vast numbers of children who need them at a price the taxpayer can afford would have been impossible without massive volunteer effort. This is not to say that physical educators did all that they could. Many physical educators were subverted by the demands of athletics for the few. However, while physical educators were distracted by these demands for elite sport for the few, the demand for sporting experiences had not waned but appeared elsewhere under the control of parents and volunteers.

The Volunteer Coach

Most of the adult personnel in youth sport programs are not professional physical educators or coaches. They are parents and volunteers interested in youth sport for a variety of motives. They donate their time and have considerable impact on the participants themselves. This impact, and its potential for lasting effects, has created widespread concern about the quality of the leadership offered to young participants.

In Canada the federal government has taken an active role in the process of assisting parents and volunteers to coach in ways that develop rather than destroy young people. The Canadian Coaching Development Scheme has been in operation for more than a decade and has assisted thousands of Canadians to understand the processes of coaching and to help rather than hinder the development of the young athlete. This special instruction is divided into two parts. The first deals with the generic knowledge and skills necessary for all kinds of coaching. It deals with child development, elementary physiology, motor learning, teaching processes, organizing practices, and goal setting. It also attempts to sell a developmental philosophy and scheme of behavior. The second part deals with the content unique to the sport: skills, strategies, tactics, biomechanics, and developmental activities.

The Canadian scheme also grades the content so that there are ascending levels of coaching expertise to which a coach can aspire. The purpose of the scheme is to improve the likelihood that a young athlete will be coached by a person who has some knowledge of the process. In a sense, the scheme was designed to form a cadre of well-prepared paraprofessional coaches. It has within it the potential for certification and thus the potential to deny adults who are deemed undesirable access to young people. It addresses the fact straightforwardly that most sporting education is taught outside the schools by volunteers and parents and that it is in the nation's interest to make that experience a worthy one by preparing coaches well.

In the U.S. there is equal need for the management of youth sport programs in the interests of the children who participate. However, there is no central government arm responsible for sport. The United States sports scene is organized by private sector committees, congresses, federations, and councils. Some are dominated by professionals and some are lay organizations. There are only a few major recognized organizations that are charged with handling more than one sport. The three most important are the U.S. Olympic Committee, the National Collegiate Athletic Association, and the Amateur Athletic Union. Each of these organizations, however, deals primarily with elite sport competition, and none have taken coaching development at the grass roots seriously.

Against this background there is little wonder that no nationwide program of coaching development for young players, sponsored either by the government or by the major coordinating organizations, has emerged. In a manner characteristically American, the problem has been left to the private initiative of the citizenry to solve. In response to the need for a coaching development scheme Rainer Martens, while at the University of Illinois, initiated the American Coaching Effectiveness Program (ACEP) via his publishing house, Human Kinetics Publishers.

ACEP has features like those of the Canadian scheme. It uses graded series of materials about coaching in general in addition to materials about coaching specific sports. However, it is funded by receipts and not by government funds. The program is organized like a business with a coaching development director in each state, and is in a sense a franchised organization. ACEP is a well-designed program in its early stages of development. The need for such a program is pressing, but it remains to be seen whether it grows into a national scheme or whether it spawns imitators that contribute further to the fragmentation of U.S. sport. If it is successful, it will inevitably grow to great size and present many physical educators with professional opportunities.

Prognoses for Coaching

Paraprofessional coaches are already the norm in both school- and community-based youth sport programs. Coaching effectiveness programs will inevitably grow as those involved take an interest in doing a better job, thereby providing some additional professional opportunities as the community systems for delivering youth sport programs stabilize. In time, youth sport organizations will become multilayered in organization. The programs will be managed by professionals under the supervision of committees of parents and interested lay citizens. The actual coaching of the myriad teams will be done by lay volunteers.

The large-scale migration of competitive sport to the community will create new occupational opportunities. Organizing youth sport programs and recruiting and training volunteer coaching and officiating cadres will become a new industry. These opportunities will occur both in the public and the private sectors, and professionals well qualified to teach adults how to serve young athletes will be in demand.

Eventually coaching development schemes will become thoroughly incorporated into the system, thereby dignifying the role of the lay volunteer coach/trainer with sound and professional preparation. When coaching preparation systems are readily available, adequate preparation for coaching will come to be expected. Prudent boards and professional managers, prodded by legal precedents, will begin to demand certification of their coaches as a means of both safeguarding young athletes and demonstrating their concern for that safety.

To summarize, if coaching is no longer a substantial part of a physical education teacher's duties, important questions arise about the role of competitive sports in the curriculum. Physical educators will have to decide which of three missions their curriculum is serving: They may operate a curriculum of sports education designed to serve as training and screening for varsity sport; they may design a curriculum that uses sport as a means of enhancing a healthy lifestyle; or they may teach sport as an entertainment form and a process of acculturation, rather like the teaching of music and music appreciation.

Prognoses for Teaching Physical Education in the Schools

As the responsibilities of coaching the elite pass into new hands, and as extra-curricular youth sport programs are established in the communities, both the tasks of the physical educators and their numbers will diminish. Those physical education programs that are a front for varsity sport programs in junior and senior high schools will perish. Communities not committed to physical education will be able to deliver athletics more cheaply by hiring others to do the job.

Although the immediate effects of this reduction in personnel will be negative, in the long run both the children and the profession will benefit. Physical education will once again become an educational and developmental curriculum where all children can be served equally. The old tasks of imparting knowledge and skills in the cognitive, affective, and motor domains will return to center stage.

Generally speaking, and for a while, there will be less physical education. The struggle will be to demonstrate that children *can* be physically educated, and that will take time. However, the physical educators challenged with that task will not be distracted by the problems of winning on Friday night. Meanwhile, the reduction in the scope of physical education in the schools will result in health education and physical education reuniting. These circumstances will also happily require physical and health educators to teach other subjects that are in high demand.

Finally the rapidly changing demography of the schools in the next twenty years will place a premium on the teacher who can teach successfully at any level. Increasingly, physical eduators will be asked to obtain teaching certification for all grades, kindergarten through twelve. This prognosis—that coaching elite sport teams will cease to be a central role for physical educators—is based upon the simultaneous development of the extraschool sport systems, the changing demography of the schools, the aging of the profession, the pressures to reunite health and physical education, and the tendency for physical educators to teach other subjects. The movement towards both K-12 and double certification will accelerate because of the freedom that results for school managers and the occupational mobility that results for physical education teachers.

Merging Curricula for the Adult Market

The interests of physical education, health education, and recreation are merging in the adult market as well. As we may easily conclude from the previous discussions in this book, adults have multiple interests in the benefits to be derived from all specialties. Health enhancement in the workplace, and in activity undertaken in discretionary time, will involve a complex of knowledge and managerial expertise that currently reside in all three specialties (and in others).

Whereas the certification of physical education and health education teachers has restricted entry into schoolteaching to those with specialized undergraduate and graduate degrees, the same cannot be said for those attempting to practice in the adult area. Although there are some narrow specialties that require certification, general entry into the area of adult physical activity and leisure services is not restricted. New practitioners usually enter with degrees, often from physical education or recreation, but sometimes with degrees in other disciplines. In some face-to-face situations and entry level positions, and particularly in the private sector, people may enter with no degree at all. Thus there is no stranglehold on the means of entry into the adult segment of the industry as there is into teaching. Adults are presumed to be able to protect themselves in the marketplace.

The open entry into the adult market means that competition will come from all sides. In fact, physical educators will be competing with recreators for the same opportunities in many cases. Both specialties produce the "people skills" useful in entry level positions and necessary for the multitudinous face-to-face meetings with clients that comprise the stuff of the service industries in general. As physical educators seek to practice in the community, they will attempt to learn the content of the recreation profession. Physical educators will increasingly learn about public health, community development, business practice, marketing, and budgeting in order to take their wares confidently into the workplace and the community. On the other hand, recreators, perceiving the utility of participating in the health enhancement boom, will increasingly seek to develop the skills needed to manage fitness activities. Physical educators and recreators are both likely to be involved with sports and facility management, club operation, community center programming, outdoor education/wilderness trip leadership, community schools, military and prison programming, resort and tourism activities, summer camping, and specialist camping. In fact, the overlap is so substantial that it raises the question whether the two curricula leading to these careers can be kept separate for much longer.

Unregulated Access to Adults

There are a few areas of specialization that require certification for work with adults and that tend to favor one curriculum over the other. These specialties include certification by the American College of Sports Medicine and by the

National Athletic Trainers Association that normally follows after an undergraduate degree in physical education and sometimes in health education. Examples of certification that may not require a degree and that are granted on the basis of passing short courses and maintaining currency are the certifications of the American Red Cross, the National Outdoor Leadership School, and the Professional Association of Diving Instructors. A keen interest in the activity, a short course or courses, and some experience are the principal requirements for entry. The organizations controlling these requirements are as likely to control selection for employment as a degree.

Movement to the Outdoors

If today's tight budgets and the shift to a preference for group-oriented, non-zero-sum activities influences one's selection of activities, then the use of natural settings in the outdoors or wilderness becomes an important alternative. While the immediate direct operating costs of outdoor/wilderness activities are higher, the capital costs are lower relative to more conventional activities. Thus in sum the costs are lower. To elaborate, outdoor/wilderness pursuits are labor-intensive and often require transportation. Small groups under close supervision of trip leaders and instructors are necessary to control the risks inherent to the activity. The participants need to be transported from the city or town (or if they live in rural settings must be assembled for the activity) to the outdoors site. The high leader/participant ratio and transportation costs increase the direct operating costs over traditional, gymnasium-based activities. However, the total cost of the traditional activities must include the capital cost of the facilities and their maintenance and security. Other segments of society bear these costs as an indirect subsidy. When these costs are added to the cost of the traditional activities, a different picture emerges favoring movement to the outdoors.

Cost Effectiveness in Use of Outdoors

Physical education is a very expensive field when the total costs of servicing the construction and maintenance of the facilities are considered. For example, in 1975 I was required to compute the cost of operation (excluding debt servicing for construction) of a simple university gymnasium and an ice rink. This was a difficult task, because there were no mechanisms for accurately dividing the costs. Simply by guessing, I concluded that operating the facilities would cost fifty and sixty dollars per hour, respectively. We decided to charge fifteen dollars per hour to community groups to use them. Obviously, the activities conducted in the gymnasium and rink were subsidized on the basis of political judgments regarding the worth of the activities themselves and the goodwill they produced. Correcting these estimates to produce the hourly cost of operating a gymnasium or rink today is also difficult. While fuel costs are lower than 1975, inflation and increases in labor costs have occurred. Furthermore, we have all sought efficiencies in operation since the 1973 oil embargo in order to drive down costs. Unless there is data to suggest otherwise, a reasonable and conservative rule of thumb is to assume comparable figures for facility operation today. The operation of the activity and leisure industry's physical plant is very expensive.

Adding direct operating costs and the original costs of construction (and perhaps the ongoing debt service on construction loans) to the cost of traditional gymnasium activities makes the comparable total costs of outdoor pursuits, even though they have additional leader and transportation costs, very attractive. For outdoor activities, the subsidy flows the other way: There are no capital costs to the activity and leisure industry: Access roads to the outdoor activities, lodges, and a safety net system are frequently already in place, often built originally for another purpose, such as extraction of timber or minerals. The encouragement of their use for adventure and for outdoor education and pursuits is part of a goodwill campaign designed to generate controlled multiple usage of the outdoors. Under these circumstances the subsidy flows from the extractive industries or the federal government through the Corps of Engineers, the Bureau of Land Management, the United States Forest Service, and other related agencies, into the activity and leisure industry. Consequently, the activity and leisure industry can be expected to expand in this area.

Everyone's a Winner

The nature of the outdoor activity itself is in line with the changing needs for adults to experience cooperative success. This tendency and the belief that *all* can "stand on the peak," lend themselves to a rejection by many of activities that clearly reinforce hierarchies, and in which all but one eventually become the "losers." Adults, and increasingly children, want to be winners, at least in a subjective sense. It is easy to be so in the outdoors. Furthermore, social interactions there are important and close. There is meaning in the enterprise, at least for the moment, and it is very different from normal life. The outdoors should be promoted as an area of activity for the field. It will become a more important area for school programming, and will continue to provide many people with useful and enjoyable employment as adult adventures in the outdoors are packaged and sold.

Summary

We are living the story of this chapter as the profession is changing around us. A dramatic shift in emphasis from the child to the adult, from the school to the private sector, and from competitive activities to activities that do not involve self-criticism is apparent. Physical education has made great strides and is poised on the threshold of an expansion into the private sector and adult markets. This situation will create strains in program content, professional preparation programs, and the organization of the field as the field struggles to respond. However, the response of the field to early warnings has been quick and encouraging. The outcome will be more integration as the disciplines of physical education, health education, and recreation learn to respond to the fundamentally integrated nature of the activity and leisure industry.

Some of the information in this chapter appeared in preliminary form in "The Business of Physical Education" by M.J. Ellis (1987), in J. Massengale (Ed.), *Trends and Futures in Physical Education* (pp. 69-85), Champaign, IL: Human Kinetics.

The Role of Sport in Physical Education___

Competitive sport, particularly team sport, has been the centerpiece of physical education for many decades. Yet it will present major problems as the field reconfigures for the future. This chapter reviews the role sport has played in physical education until now. It then turns to the problems inherent to sport as it shows signs of becoming simply a short, youthful episode before being converted into entertainment and constructed news.

Elite sport currently tends to recruit progressively younger initiates in its search for perfection. Longer preparation, however, is needed to match ever-increasing standards. To achieve this before the vigor of youth subsides requires the would-be athletes to start training ever earlier. This trend is occurring at just the same time that the median age of the population is climbing and the activity and leisure industry is being called upon to serve adults.

The problem is that these two counteracting trends are pulling the content of physical education in opposite directions so that the field must attempt to serve two diverging markets. More young people are participating in youth sports than ever before, but they participate for a short time only. Most drop out early and do not actively participate again. Working adults participate in sport vicariously, if at all, through television or through the sports pages of the print media. The early loss of participants and the tendency to use spectator sport only for entertainment or for marketing purposes presents a dilemma for the activity and leisure industry. Why has the dropout rate increased so alarmingly? Is the teaching of sport meant to encourage lifetime participation or simply to acculturate? This chapter analyzes these questions and tries to derive implications for the future of physical education.

Sport as the Centerpiece of Physical Education

The prevailing mythology in physical education is that sport is the centerpiece of the industry. Much of the industry's content is designed with the major team sports and their seasons in mind. This is justified on the grounds that the industry prepares individuals for long-term participation. Furthermore, it is argued that participation in the major sports has developmental benefits and will contribute to health and enjoyment of life.

These expectations, however, are not realized. While sport participation in youth sport programs is booming among pubescents, the participation thereafter drops precipitously. There is substantial evidence to indicate that participation in youth sport programs is short-lived—fewer than four years on average. Participation in competitive and organized sport is a developmental phase in which young people engage for a short while before moving on to other things.

This variance between the mythology and the reality needs to be explored. Despite the efforts of the American Alliance for Health, Physical Education, Recreation and Dance to popularize "lifetime sports" over the last two decades, many physical educators are still driven by the notion that people naturally relish competitive struggle and that it is inherently beneficial and worthwhile. Yet many adult clients leading active lifestyles disagree. The demands of team sports for vigor, organization, and sacrifice do not correspond to the motives of adults. As a result, team sports are largely irrelevant as a means of achieving the goals of physical education with postpubescents. The danger is that we will not recognize this fact and will fail to act accordingly.

Benefits and Costs of Sport Participation

Each participant in sport carries on an inner debate about the costs and benefits of continued participation. The aggregation of these decisions determines the number of sport participants and hence the market for sporting activities. A review of the factors that these individuals consider in reaching their decisions is necessary for a reasoned view of the role of sport in the activity and leisure industry.

Benefits

The benefits of sport participation are many. Sport presents each participant with an opportunity to confront an irrevocable reality. The challenges in our world cannot be fudged. Meeting those challenges brings not only satisfaction, it affirms the potency of being human. In a small way the sport experience is a microcosm of the challenges that all humans have been forced to meet throughout the evolution of our species. Challenges met and conquered are a celebration of capacity. In sport, people set out to do something, and when they do it, they are fortified by the experience.

Sport participation, especially team sport, requires the participants to establish and abide by social contracts and to cooperate in order to sustain the game. Each game presents an intriguing set of questions. The foremost, of course, is, Who wins? But within the game the ebb and flow of strategies, tactics, and skills also pose questions. Each game contains much information, most of which derives from the acts of the other humans. Hence the participants learn about human nature from the process. These experiences are inherently beneficial.

Sports and games are usually vigorous, and participation requires a great deal of adapting. There are three major kinds of adaptation involved in sport. First, the participant may adapt to biological stressors, thus acquiring increased capacity to respond: Some combination of greater endurance, flexibility, and strength will result. Second, the participant may acquire the skills necessary to meet the behavioral challenges of the sport. Finally, the participant may learn the cognitive skills necessary to organize and meet the logistic, social, and strategic necessities of participation.

Each one of these extensions of the participant's human capacity is inherently worthwhile. However, there is a further advantage to be obtained from these kinds of adaptation. Participants learn, from watching themselves adapt, that they are plastic. Knowing that one has the capacity to control the nature of one's capacities, at least to an extent, is an important lesson. The knowledge that one is not immutable is perhaps one of the major lessons to be learned from sport. Sport provides an arena in which the adaptability of humankind is demonstrated to each participant.

Subjective Competition

Sport competition—in fact any competition—can be defined both objectively and subjectively (Martens, 1975). The zero-sum results of a competition, the score or the time, the finishing position, the record, the league standings that result are all signs of objective competition. The outcomes are reported and are clearly in the public domain. On the other hand, individual athletes will have set up for themselves personal, internal goals. They have hopes to beat their best time or just to finish, or to have a better scoring percentage in the second half than the first. Thus even in the face of objective failure an individual can feel, subjectively, successful; and it is this process that sustains participation in the face of objective failure. Athletes identify with, and attend to, elements that mean "success" to them.

Sport success defined subjectively (in the sense that an individual sets up realistic personal goals) requires planning, discipline to implement the plan, confrontation with failure, revision of the plan, and continued attempts in the search for a personal success. When this process works, the memories of it suggest that new challenges can also be met satisfactorily, and so individuals gain a general confidence in their abilities.

These benefits are justification enough for physical education, as Seidentop argued long ago in "Physical Education as Play Education" (Seidentop, 1972). There is no doubt that a successful sport experience produces potent and lasting beneficial effects for participants.

Costs

Subjective failure, of course, produces the opposite effect. Each of the potential benefits has standing behind it a potential damaging feature that also can last a lifetime. While it is possible to establish personal, subjective goals for competition, to a large extent the outside world is concerned only with the objective reality. Failure is objectively as likely as success because of the zero-sum nature of competition. In fact, given the pyramidal structure of sports in which winners advance to higher levels of competition until there is an absolute winner, the likelihood for objective failure is overwhelming. Confronting this fact is at best unpleasant, and at worst genuinely damaging.

Meeting and cooperating to honor contracts that sustain the game or sport can lead to the understanding that antisocial practices, offenses against the spirit of the rules if not the letter, and immorality often lead to advantages only in the short run. A win-at-all-costs atmosphere, however, can lead to harmful attitudes that are not conducive to beneficial participation in a cooperatively based society.

The challenges to adapt may also suggest that the adaptability of the individual is decidedly inferior to that of others and contribute to a loss of confidence in one's plasticity. At the metalearning level, sport participation can demonstrate the inability of the individual to rise to the challenges found within sports and thus lead to loss of confidence.

Finally, sport can induce chronic and acute disease. Rarely does the athlete contemplate the long-term effects of participation on health. Athletes are usually conscious of the immediate costs of injuries in pain and in the effort involved in recovery, but not of the long-term, chronic effects. Sport is responsible for a lot of disease. For example, for college football players there is a 93 percent chance of a time-lost injury each season they play (Christie, 1979). This is an astounding statistic, and one that should raise serious questions about the role of this sport in our field. Only with boxing has there been any real attempt to raise the issue of the deleterious effect of the sport on the health of the participants. As a result, boxing has been essentially dropped from the content of the field. In the case of other sports, it is as if there is a conspiracy of silence among physical educators who rarely identify disease as one of the costs of participation.

Sport, like anything else, can produce good or ill effects. However, there is a general unwillingness within the profession to face the deleterious possibilities created by sport participation. We base our practices and content on the blind assumption that by actively promoting sport participation, we are doing good. Yet the clients soon realize that the costs and benefits of sport participation are precariously balanced. When they reach the realization that the costs exceed the benefits, they drop out. These costs may be those just identified, or simply the opportunity costs of the time spent participating, which then, of course, become unavailable for other discretionary activities.

Dropping Out of Sport

Dropping out of sport participation may be either a positive or a negative thing. It is positive when the athletes have achieved their subjective goals, feeling both satisfied and enriched. They will then carry the positive fallout from their participation to other activities. The struggle will have been worth the rewards.

The experience will be negative, however, when the athletes are unsatisfied and have failed to reach their personal goals. In many cases, they will have accepted the bitter truth that, despite their following all the rules, they were just not able to meet their own ideas of success. The motivational aphorism that any goal can be reached with enough effort and determination is revealed simply as hortatory rhetoric. Such notions rest on the assumption that the athlete is responsible for his or her own failure, when the fault in fact lies in the genes or in the situation.

Subjective Failure

Athletes may also fail subjectively when they or others set unreasonable and unattainable goals. The failure here lies in the possibility that even though the athlete performed to capacity and ought to be proud of that performance, comparison with personal goals reveals failure and not success. The problem is the creation of unreasonable expectations. Television and even the print media contribute to this problem by supporting a climate of expectation that is often unrealistic. It is not possible to set subjective goals these days without being aware of where those goals stand objectively. There is a tendency to aim for targets so high that failure is most likely.

Objective Success Unlikely

There is no question that the athlete who has failed objectively can still have had fun and have learned much during sport participation. Eventually, however, the increasingly demanding and selective pressures diminish considerably the number of athletes who can be objectively successful. If the athlete's subjective goals are less demanding than the objective goals, then participation can be sustained. The goal may be simply to improve, to maintain, or to have a pleasant trip to a competition; but the external pressures often do not permit such subjective goals to coexist comfortably with objective ones. A dangerous situation arises when an athlete meets subjective goals and yet, because of objective goals, is not supported by others.

For the vast majority, the system is inevitably limiting. Eventually athletes climb up the ladder of achievement to a point where they fail both objectively *and* subjectively. At some point the costs of continued failure outweigh the benefits, and athletes drop out. Rarely can athletes compare their subjective goals to objective realities and remain comfortable in the sport. Even in master's level competition many rekindle their hopes for eventual success and look forward to crossing into the next age category where they can then compete successfully again for a short time due to an advantage in age.

Except for a very few, serious competitive sport participation is a process fraught with danger. Eventual failure is guaranteed. Most participants know this, draw their sights sensibly on intermediate and subjective goals, and drop out with the balance sheet showing a net benefit. Some, it is hoped only a few, are hurt by the hype, the unrealistic expectations, and the eventual disaster.

Fortunately for the industry, most adults who remain in the sport setting have redefined the competitive sport situation with the result that the competitive elements and forms are largely informal and the attention paid to objective outcomes is minimal. Unlike children who are struggling to find an identity, many adults simply use competitive sport forms as a social matrix. They acknowledge that objective failure does not contain implications about success and failure in other areas of their lives.

Continued Participation in Sport

A competitive, selective, zero-sum base of operations is inherently limiting. Such a base of operations has been acceptable for physical education in the past because we have been charged with the delivery of services to children and youth. With a growing population, a youth-oriented society, and a platform for service in the schools and universities, such a competitive, sport-oriented base did no harm to the profession. As people dropped out, other people entered. Such a system, however, will not be available in the future. Population gains will be modest and physical education in the schools is now either static or in decline. The new markets for physical education lie with those who have already dropped out from competitive sport—the adults. The marketing challenge for physical education lies in creating systems that are not inherently limiting. The goal must be to create continuing participation throughout the life cycle, not just an intense and brief three- to four-year involvement during adolescence. Without the creation of new markets for the industry's services among adults and older adults, the field will not thrive.

If It's Worth Doing, It's Worth Doing Badly

Continued participation will require the development of many kinds of sport experience. Some may be competitive, but many will have to be personalized and individualized. Grand zero-sum pyramids of competition will not achieve the profession's purposes. We are going to have to create systems where there is consensus among professionals and clients that if it is worth doing, it is worth doing badly. Only then will it be possible to avoid the limiting nature of the objective search for excellence. There is little doubt that the field will respond to this new challenge. The market will demand it, and the rigors of making a living in such a setting will dramatically change the nature of the field and the attitudes of those who work within it.

Continued participation among the general population requires that sport maintain the possibility of subjective goals and a variety of benefits that balance the costs. Some sports have been able to do this well. They permit identification with low or intermediate goals and are usually conducive to enjoyable, process-oriented social and learning activities. People do not want to be "athletes," but instead want to enjoy the game at their own level of skill over a long period of time. Golf, tennis, and sailing are good examples; it is possible to play badly at the objective level, but still attain subjective goals and enjoy social and other benefits in the process.

Adult Social/Sport Clubs.   Such sports are usually conducted in adult social clubs that emphasize one sport exclusively. The club is heavily dependent for its existence on continuous membership. Failure to treat the poor players as prized members leads to both loss of membership and economic disaster. Consequently, the club will develop a variety of strategies to permit a great range of possible goals and styles of competition while simultaneously providing a network of other enjoyable activities. The principal goal of all this is to minimize or postpone for most members the ultimate zero-sum outcome— that is, the establishment of one winner and many losers—because that tends to increase the dropout rate.

Unfortunately, most sports have not yet been developed to the point where they can be sustained in the leisured environment of adult social/sporting clubs, and so there are fewer incentives for continued participation by those at the lower levels of expertise or throughout one's lifetime. For the majority of sports, participation is intense and short-lived and the sport is not an avenue to leisured participation or extended maintenance of a healthy lifestyle.

The Fun Run.   Another example of a system that promotes and maintains the performance of the average and below-average performer is the so-called fun run. These affairs have successfully created a medium to mix the very able runners with the less able, while maintaining the interest of all. The term "fun run" reveals that subjective goals are taken seriously. Times for every runner, jogger, or walker are carefully recorded to assist and encourage subjective competition. Participation itself is often dignified by giving everyone T-shirts. Other incentives just to finish, such as drawings for a car or a ten-speed bike, emphasize that struggling with one's own goals in the company of many others is worthwhile. When to such goals is added the opportunity to socialize, to anticipate, to prepare, and to share with others who are similarly motivated, a meaningful sporting experience for many people is the result. The fun run has been a successful innovation that has captured the attention and allegiance of multitudes of people, of all ages and abilities. Without question, more such innovations will result as the field strives to find ways of including large numbers of people who, in the objective sense, perform badly.

New Games.   The New Games Foundation has recognized the inherent limitations in the structure of formal competitive sport and has set out to construct activities that do not have zero-sum outcomes. A host of such activities has been developed. Unfortunately, however, these games are usually not complex enough on a cognitive level to permit long-term evolution and are thus also incapable of sustaining long-term participation. Another initiative in this area comes from Orlick and Botterill in Canada whose major contribution is captured in the title of their book, *Every Child Can Win* (1975). They present, and argue the case for, a series of strategies for modifying the structures of games and sports that de-emphasize the objective winner and deflect attention instead to the process of participating. Orlick and Botterill advocate the creation of self-sustaining games and sports that do not lead directly to an incontrovertible outcome, but are ongoing processes that permit the realization of many possible subjective goals. In short, they advocate the principles of rat-ball—the informal, pick-up, no-final-score, single-hoop style of basketball that has operated continuously in thousands of gymnasiums throughout North America for years.

Lessons of Rat-Ball

Rat-ball conveys many of the lessons that physical education needs to learn if it is to be successful. Rat-ball is social, process-oriented, plastic in that it can respond to a great variety of skill levels, cheap, good exercise, unspoiled by absenteeism, and anyone can play. Ironically, rat-ball is often organized independently of physical educators. It is managed by the players themselves and in the spaces left unoccupied with formally scheduled programs. Physical education is increasingly dependent on fomenting lifetime, long-term participation. Understanding the motivation for ongoing participation in activity by adults is the most pressing question facing the field; a careful study of rat-ball would be a good place to start.

The Role of the Media

Lifetime participation must be a goal for physical education. Short-lived, intense involvement may be a potent source of developmental experiences with certain life-long benefits, but social and health benefits do not come from memories. Every effort should be made to encourage continued participation in activities that have social, cognitive, and physical rewards. Directing athletes exclusively towards sports in which there is intense, but necessarily short, involvement is not desired practice. Offering a broad exposure to lifetime sports is. Why, then, is the physical education curriculum dominated by sports in which there are no possibilities for leisurely participation throughout the life span? The answer lies within the communications media and chauvinism.

Stephenson, in his book *The Play Theory of Mass Communication* (1967), identified the important role played by the media in a democracy; that is, the media share the information necessary to allow the people to take an informed interest in the affairs of the nation. However, that function does not pay the bills. Consequently, the media have added entertainment to the process to ensure that they make a profit through advertising and the sale of a sufficient number of products. Accordingly, the media reached far beyond the presentation of news and information necessary for the democracy to work, and grew instead into a massive communications and entertainment industry.

TV, radio, newspapers, and magazines—the various forms of the communications media—have a vested interest in a ready and cheap supply of entertaining information. Hence the features columns, comics, and especially the heavy allowance of time and space for sports information. These things are not necessary for democracy to work, but they are enjoyed by readers and watchers simply *because* they are not critical, or important, or threatening. In fact, these elements are a kind of pabulum of constructed "news" with the sole purpose of entertainment.

Sport news and sport reporting is a very potent source of constructed news. Sport has its own drama created by the zero-sum feature of its competition. Against the broad canvas of critical world events, political upheaval, and wars created by the competition between political systems and nations, the artificial sport wars permit a needed and welcome escape. Sport provides competition and drama that are noncritical, contrived, and therefore somewhat playful.

The significance of this "constructed reality" of major league and local league sport is reflected in the amount of time and space that is dedicated to sport news reporting. Sport is clearly of interest to a vast number of people; it sells. A ready supply of daily sports news and stories is needed. The media have a vested interest in the continued functioning of competitive sports at all levels because the action on the sporting scene provides them with much of the copy they need to sell their newspapers and magazines, and their radio and TV programs.

To guarantee the ready supply of sport competition, the TV industry has begun to manipulate the competitive sports scene. It contributes money to the maintenance of the system and asks for favors in return. Sports events are now often scheduled during times of the media's choosing, and not necessarily during times that are best for the athletes or for local fans. Game rules have been adjusted to suit the medium of television. Rather than the media adapting to the system's needs, the system has adapted to the media's, including their special needs for scheduling, information, and advertising whenever and however they determine.

Sport as an Entertainment Product

It is true that the media simply exaggerate what is already the wish of the people. They are only partly to blame for this subversion of sport. The need for the daily fix of sports information as an escape from the trials and tribulations of the "real" news is probably healthy. The needs of the athletes, however, have been subordinated to the needs of the media trying to sell their products. The result has been the creation of the athlete as celebrity and an unrealistic set of expectations for the average person participating in sport. This set of circumstances has both professionalized sport and made it an entertainment product.

Unrealistic Aspirations

The unrealistic expectations of many sport participants have been induced by the media. For example, an unrealistic proportion of young athletes want to become professional athletes. Far, far more than can actually earn a living from professional sport aspire towards a life in the professional sport leagues. This kind of goal can damage an athlete by hindering reasonable preparation for life, even after a high-level, professionalized, but very brief sport career. These high costs of professionalizing sport have received much attention, and I will not pursue them further here.

What needs to be pursued is the effects of the media attention on the would-be participant. The media, via their glorification of sport, have done much to eliminate athletes from participation and to convert them into consumers of other's participation. In order to present sport attractively to the spectator as entertainment, the media have to attend to the unusual, the outlandish, and the startling. They have to use ever more sophisticated means of telling the story and recruit the latest video technology whenever possible. As a result, the spectator can become thoroughly familiar with the performances of a few superstar athletes. We are regaled with stories of their sacrifice, the fruits of success, the luck they had to experience to be where they are. The would-be participants are also very familiar with outstanding performances via double-slow motion color reruns. A would-be athlete knows exactly what is required for success in a sport.

A healthy, realistic athlete knows that it will not be possible to be successful like the superstar. Unless athletes can create satisfying, subjective goals based on local standards for their own participation they will not be able to enjoy the challenge of performing badly.

The Media and "Odious Comparisons"

Before the media took such a great interest in sport as entertainment, the competition itself resolved the issues as to standards of performance. Standards for sporting achievement were those as seen in competitions in which the athletes participated. The system of escalating competition presented the participating athlete with an escalating set of demands and possibilities. It was rare to the see the truly outstanding, and goals could be set in terms of local or regional significance. Nowadays, every athlete can assess his or her standing relative to the ultimate objective possibility. Day in and day out sparkling pictures of the world's best-ever performances and records are as close as the TV set in the family room. Each athlete these days cannot set his or her sights on the performance levels of the school, the county, or the state without also having available immediate access to the standards of the world.

One of the reasons for the incredible dropout rate from sport programs around the age of adolescence can be explained by the theory of the "odious comparison." After some years in the sport, an adolescent has developed a very clear picture of what it will take to be objectively successful, and the likelihood of actually being rewarded with success. While those close to the athlete can reward subjective success, the media cannot. When the costs are weighed against the likelihood of objective rewards, the majority of athletes conclude that the game is not worth it and drop out.

Those that drop out after a few years remain interested in the sport itself and become informed consumers of the sports information provided by the media. So the odious comparison accelerates the reduction of the pool of participants to a much smaller pool of objectively capable athletes without harming the capacity of the media to sell sport.

The objectification of sport with data, replays, exaggerations, and emphasis on the startling, contains within it the means for destroying sport, at least as a lifelong pastime. Why bother to do something badly? Why bother to sacrifice in order to perform well below the average in a society where such performance is not understood or respected? It is no wonder that young athletes drop out; they already have the answer to their questing aspiration. It is no wonder that adults are turning to activities that cannot be so objectified. They seek to maintain or develop themselves as unique social beings and will have nothing to do with activities so minutely dissected and so objectified that their levels of performance can only be odiously compared with those of the successful.

Chauvinism and Sport

Another reason that elite sport is maintained involves national, regional, and local aspirations. The reflected glory of a successful team is welcomed by the citizens as an affirmation of the success of their nation, region, or town. As such, it is politically expedient at all levels to be supporting elite sport as an indicator of the region's potency. At the national level, it is clear that the world's politicians welcome the fact when their athletes reflect well on the nation. Some governments actively promote the likelihood of winning for the ideological advantages that may be gained. Others do not, yet all want their nation to receive the advantages of being winners. This tendency repeats itself in smaller ways all the way down to the local level, because athletic victories are "good politics" and good for business.

The lionization of athletes and the use of sport for chauvinistic, political, or business reasons are now being called into question. The universities are beginning to resist the manipulation of their programs; school athletic associations are beginning to insist that the sporting tail not wag the educational dog. There are signs that more people are waking up to the fact that the participants, while young and vigorous, are being exploited for the community's own goals. Pressure from these people will build, but the vested interests of business and chauvinism are powerful. Professionalization of sport will continue, but most probably with stronger checks on the system and fewer young people eager to participate, as the real costs and benefits—the real likelihoods—become general knowledge.

Sport and Government

In the U.S., involvement with sport has historically not been a governmental function. Its promotion and organization has been left by default to the private citizen. As long as that system produced winners on the international scene, the system was left undisturbed. However, it is now manifestly clear that benign neglect will not permit the nation to compete well against other nations. The political aspirations for sport will not permit it to remain beyond the reach of national policies. The U.S. Olympic Committee was politicized in 1980 over the Afghanistan issue and it will be forced to fight for control over the daily affairs of sport in the U.S. The situation will remain in flux until a satisfactory system for coordinating the elite sport system is created. While the Los Angeles Games were a scintillating example of private initiative, there are not enough Ueberroths to organize the daily affairs of the myriad sports and clubs in a way that can compete with nations using government power to organize sport.

In Canada the federal government has declared an interest in sport by creating a ministry and a cabinet-level post responsible for sport. Such "top-down" interest has maintained Canada as a powerhouse in sport far beyond the expectations of its population size. Sporting superiority is a source of great pride for Canadians, the majority of whom are happy with the large expenditures of tax money and lottery receipts to maintain the process.

The U.S. will move in a direction similar to Canada's through the rest of the decade, but it is unlikely that a Department of Sport will be established. Two features of the current system will be maintained or augmented to create a successful elite sport system from a uniquely capitalistic system of incentives: First, business will continue to donate money to sport in return for publicity; second, there will be increasing professionalization of sport. Rewards via celebrity status and product advertising at all levels capture the attention of likely candidates for success. Previously, a potentially successful athlete had always to choose between sport and an occupation. That is no longer true for many gifted athletes; thus they can remain in the sport for a longer period of time.

The professionalization of sport that has served the U.S. well in the last decade or so will become more pronounced over the rest of the decade. Local clubs, coaches, and athletes will experience decreasing control over sport systems and their governance. Instead, control will pass to bigger systems to enable the coordination necessary to maintain a competitive position in the world of sport.

Summary

Although sport will continue to exist in all its current forms, it is not a growth area for physical education. Youth sport participation involves millions, but for a short time only. The real market will become adult participation, and the motivations of the majority of adults are at variance with that demanded by current competitive sports. Adults will not be seeking identity and affirmation, but enjoyable, developmental, and healthful activity in the company of others. Competitive sport will be dislodged from its place as the centerpiece of physical education.

As sport is professionalized and as it develops, it will provide an arena for personal growth and development to fewer people. Involvement with sport may be intense, but it is self-limiting. Objective failure is assured for the majority, and sport will come to be seen as a rite of passage for young people as they are socialized into one of the entertainment forms of the nation. It will not be seen as the precursor to lifelong active involvement by the majority.

The major challenge for physical education will be to harness the motivations for participation and activity that exist outside formal competitive sport structures. We can catch glimpses of the needed activity forms in fun runs, New Games, and rat-ball. There is a great need for activity and sport forms that can be sustained beyond adolescence and that act as matrices for adult social interaction.

Sport for fewer and abler athletes will be maintained by two influences. The communications and entertainment industry—the media—will use it as entertainment and constructed news to sell advertising time and space. Furthermore, many adult citizens, politicians, and business people will continue to support sport for the younger participant as a way to bask in reflected glory. The profession will be unable to resist these influences. Sport will continue much as it is now, but it will become a less important feature of the field's content because so relatively few people will be actively involved.

Chapter 8

*Physical Education in School, Community, and University*_____

As the turmoil of change all around us was surveyed in previous chapters, many different topics were introduced. It is clear that a new map of the field is necessary to guide our future. This chapter attempts to weave together into two models some of the informational threads from these previous discussions, one model for physical education in the school and the other for physical education in the community. These models should guide our efforts to play a strong role in the schools and communities of the future.

School stimulates the transition from the young and dependent child to the fully independent citizen. The fact that this transition takes many years and is becoming increasingly complex and demanding does not change the situation. However, school represents two radical life changes with a long learning phase in between. The first change occurs when a child enters kindergarten, and for the first time must essentially stand alone.

Mother, father, or caregiver are no longer there to shield and to solve the problems of existence. This transition from home to school life, however, is dealt with somewhat sympathetically; children are integrated gradually and on a part-time basis (regrettably this is often not so with day-care). Going to kindergarten is a temporary foray into what is usually a new and exciting world and soon the child is back home. The first transition is gradual, giving the child the opportunity to adjust.

More than a decade later, at the other end of the school period, the young adults graduate. One day they are big fish in a small and protected pond, and the next day they face adulthood. Competition for earnings and for their own place in the sun is fierce. No real attempt is made to make their transition into the community gradual. The second transition is not as well-managed as the first; if it were, the high school would gradually fade from the lives of older students as they enter progressively the world of adults. Unfortunately, graduation represents instead an abrupt, almost rude expulsion from the lifestyle of the school into another.

Discontinuities Between School and Community

The discontinuity between the high school lifestyle and the adult community lifestyle is considerable. Such discontinuities affect all disciplines, but we are concerned here with physical education where the discontinuity results in a failure to implement an active and healthy lifestyle after graduation.

Physical education's primary goal must be to instill in the individual a lifelong interest in a wise and healthy lifestyle. Opportunities for such a lifestyle can be created for the student in school far more easily than they can in the community. But simply creating such opportunities is not enough. Students must want to carry over the habits of a healthy lifestyle into their adult lives. They must be taught how to use those opportunities in the world outside their schools. Taking advantage of the habits of a healthy lifestyle outside of school demands different social and organizational skills from those skills required in school. For example, entry to a health club or a sport team requires an overt act of the kind that most students are not accustomed to making. Furthermore, managing a healthy lifestyle requires considerable self-discipline because participation is voluntary. Many high school graduates can function exceedingly well in the carefully structured and protected environment of the school; however, the break to adult society often finds the graduate unprepared for the organization and self-discipline necessary to maintain a healthy lifestyle in the working world or in college.

There seem to be two main solutions to the problem: (a) diversifying the curriculum and (b) encouraging community development of healthy lifestyle opportunities. The curriculum must be diversified so that it is representative of the myriad activity and leisure choices available in society at large. Unfortunately, it is impractical to expect any single physical educator to arrange an introduction to the wide variety of activities that exist in the community. One solution might be the host of affinity groups, clubs, and providers in the private and public sectors. All of these organizations practice their arts at high levels of expertise either for profit or simply for the sake of the art itself. Each maintains itself by developmental programs designed to recruit and introduce people to their particular activity. The developmental programs offered by the fly-fishing club, the ski patrol, the badminton club, the health club, and so on, must be incorporated into the enriched high school curriculum.

Physical educators must also cooperate with those in recreation, and others, to ensure that there is a rich supply of opportunities for graduates in their community. Physical education must also address the question of community development; it is not sufficient simply to address individual development. The goal must be a community enriched by the existence of many clubs, affinity groups, and other providers that create leisure and health opportunities. Paradoxically, despite being enriched by the presence of these organizations, the community often does little to assist them. Many clubs and affinity groups could put to good use the facilities controlled by physical educators that exist in abundance in the school systems of the nation. These costly facilities, however, are for the most part shut down in the later afternoon and withdrawn from the community's facility supply. A solution that would create both curriculum diversification and community development would be to bring into the school the clubs, organizations, and affinity groups that generate many of the leisure and activity services in the community. We need a mechanism to permit the community's clubs to share school facilities, and enrich the curriculum in the process.

Linking School Curriculum to Community

An organizational model depicting the optimal relationship between school and community appears in Figure 8.1. The model refers to the school as both a worksite and a leisure resource. It is a worksite in the sense that it is held accountable for a curriculum. The students have a clearly defined job to do and will be held accountable for achieving the goals that the community has for them. Faculty and staff of all kinds also work in the school; thus for them, too, the school is a worksite. Thinking of the school as a worksite has dramatic repercussions for physical educators. A worksite must be conceptualized in terms of the efficiency of its functioning. Both students and faculty and staff should be regarded as potential client/workers and therefore subject to efforts to help them achieve wellness and efficient learning and functioning. The school is also defined as a leisure resource by this model. The school is preparing young citizens for their lives in the community, and the school has facilities and resources that contribute to the leisure supply in the community, if properly used.

The school has two overlapping curricular functions, each open to the community. At the top of the figure is the formal curriculum dictated by the community's mandates. The system is open at this point to receive new people, resources in the form of taxes, volunteers, and directions. At this point mandates are debated and formed, a political process determined by the constitution and the law. School boards must take into account laws, administrative directives, taxes and the income they generate, the influence of PTAs, the

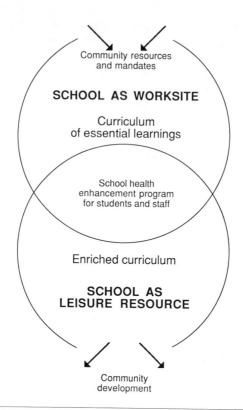

Figure 8.1 Link between schools as worksites and schools as leisure resources in a community.

demands of community pride and chauvinism, and last but not least, the media. School boards, after weighing all these things, issue policies and procedures designed to tailor the schools and their curricula to local needs and demands.

The faculty and staff, based on their own perceptions of the school's role and community input (as relayed to them by the school board), create a core curriculum. For physical education the essentials of this curriculum should involve the knowledge and skills needed for lifelong management of healthy lifestyles—that is, the matter analyzed earlier in chapters 5 and 6.

The second function of a school is its enriched curriculum, an expansion or extension of the curriculum in both formal and informal ways. These school activities and instructional extensions are made possible first by the efficient management of the required core curriculum, and then by the creation of new avenues for pursuing those lessons learned in the core curriculum. The enriched curriculum is linked to the community resources, signifying that this is the place to smooth the transitions to the occupations, activities, and leisure of the community. The enriched curriculum should be constructed to facilitate the transition of students on the brink of being edged from their secure nest into the turbulence of the adult society in which they must live.

By the time students leave school, they should have established their links to the activity and leisure patterns in their communities. They should know about and have become members of community groups and organizations in which they can maintain participation. The challenge is to have structured the curriculum to facilitate this transition.

High School Curricula

The two-function school curriculum depicted in Figure 8.1 is applied to high schools in Figure 8.2. This figure goes one step further and identifies the content of the core curriculum and enriched curriculum. Physical educators, health educators, and home economists will be required to cooperate if this model

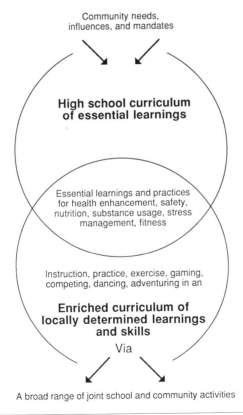

Figure 8.2 Relations between the high school and its curriculum and the community.

is applied. In effect, the core curriculum is the academic content needed to understand and implement personal health enhancement programs. According to this model, all students will be required to attend to the design and implementation of a personal health enhancement program that addresses many different problems such as smoking, nutrition, fitness, and so on. The identification of a core curriculum involving physical education will prevent health enhancement from being preempted by elite sports. Furthermore, when a health enhancement program for faculty and staff is requested by employees or approved by school boards, then a new market—the health enhancement of colleagues—will open up for school physical educators and health educators.

The lower circle in the model illustrated in Figure 8.2 indicates that the enriched curriculum is the school's activity and leisure supply that acts as the link to the community. The enrichment programs of the high school should be meshed with similar programs in the community at large. The students, faculty and staff, and the community will benefit from such a situation. Simply put, the community/school recreation program should be formally incorporated into the structure of the school in such a way that it enriches both school and community. We will return to this point again.

Elementary and Middle School Curricula

Figure 8.3 represents a model for the elementary and middle schools. Students at these levels are not yet on the brink of confrontation with the adult world; consequently, the enriched curriculum is not directly associated with the community leisure supply. The more conventional curricular models where the children inhabit a closed and protected environment still applies. The core curriculum has the same goals for the health enhancement of students and faculty and staff, and the enriched curriculum will still concern itself with teaching what is necessary to help the students develop healthy lifestyles. The model, however, indicates the essential closure of the enriched curriculum from the community at large, leaving the school a small community in itself. While some crossing into community activities may occur, this is not as much a goal in the elementary and middle schools as it is in the senior high schools.

The elementary and middle school model is at variance with reality in one respect. As the demand occurs for ever-younger athletes in gymnastics and swimming, aggressive recruiting of elementary-school-age children into youth sport programs is beginning to occur. However, these programs are usually single-sport programs. Even though they enhance the experience of the participants, the vast majority of the engagements do not last long because they are competitively oriented. The school itself must resist this early specialization and build a foundation for the long-term development of the child.

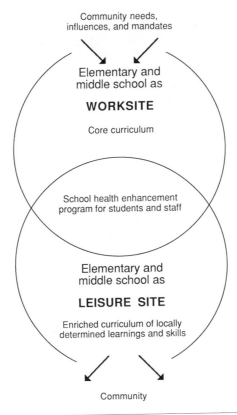

Figure 8.3 Link between the functions of elementary and middle school as worksite and leisure site.

Integrating the Core and Enriched Curricula

The school curriculum must accept responsibility for creating the circumstances necessary for learning. It should recognize that it is self-defeating not to create appropriate health levels conducive to learning. There is some evidence that physical education not only enhances wellness but also enhances academic performance. This causal relationship is not yet well understood, and is probably indirect, but the effects cannot be ignored (Seefeldt & Vogel, 1986). The school should also be responsible for the health enhancement of faculty and staff in order to optimize teaching and working. The people professionally engaged in health enhancement within the school have traditionally been home economists, health educators, and physical educators. These three occupational groups of teachers need to accept responsibility for creating two action programs: one for the development of the health conditions essential for the enhancement of mental and physical performance in students, and another for their colleagues and the other workers in their school.

Figures 8.2 and 8.3 demonstrate that where the core curriculum and the enriched curriculum overlap, formal concern exists for the skills, knowledge, and practices needed for wellness. The concern is for the healthy lifestyle management of both students and faculty, and covers all facets of life within the school as a worksite. This expanded responsibility at the core of the curriculum should be welcomed by the teachers in the disciplines involved. They will have to create an integrated curriculum with a clearly defined mandate for their students to develop healthy personal lifestyles.

The core curriculum offered by the consortium of home economists, health educators, and physical educators should address the cognitive and attitudinal bases for wise choices in the design of a healthy lifestyle. It should address the basic knowledge, communicate the appropriate skills, and involve the whole school in healthy practices over the long term so that correct attitudes are fostered. The criteria for the success of the integrated program will be the decisions made by the senior students as they plan and implement their own activity and leisure lifestyles.

The consortium of physical educators, health educators, and home economists will have to create worksite health enhancement programs for the entire school community as well. These health enhancement programs can be judged by the effects they have on the skills, knowledge, and practices of everyone in the school. If they are effective, the chances of maintaining a reasonable share of resources for physical education and health education will be improved. If these programs fail, then incompetent or ineffective physical and health educators will be more easily identified and removed from the system. Furthermore, the provision of health enhancing services to colleagues will move the school as worksite toward the center of the lives of all concerned.

The enriched curriculum is a critically important addition to the core curriculum. It should provide the multiplicity of courses, opportunities, and experiences necessary to create a menu of options for the students toward the end of their school careers. Community agencies should gradually be involved so that the senior high school students, in designing and practicing their lifestyles, are encouraged to develop a variety of interests that will blend well with the activities available in the community.

As suggested in Figure 8.4, the enriched curriculum should help the senior students clearly articulate a plan that involves activity in a private or public sector agency or club in the community. Being a member of a health spa, jogging group, sports club, or class at the local university or community center should be equally acceptable. In fact, such memberships may be more desirable because they precisely represent the transition to the community lifestyle at large. They will help increase the chances that the student will have devel-

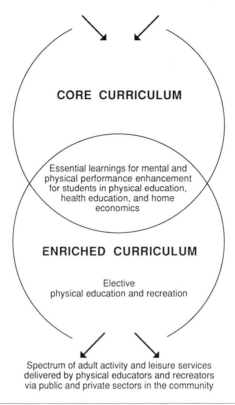

CORE CURRICULUM

Essential learnings for mental and
physical performance enhancement
for students in physical education,
health education, and home
economics

ENRICHED CURRICULUM

Elective
physical education and recreation

Spectrum of adult activity and leisure services
delivered by physical educators and recreators
via public and private sectors in the community

Figure 8.4 Professional involvement in the school curriculum and the enriched curriculum.

oped the skills, contacts, knowledge, and self-organization needed to continue a healthy lifestyle once in the adult community.

Conversely, physical educators should, via the enriched curriculum, actively seek the provision of community-based programs for their students both inside and outside the school. The programs should be designed to attract and recruit seniors into the community organizations. The penetration of the enriched curriculum by community agencies and affinity groups will provide at very low cost options in the community that are not usually incorporated into the school. Clubs and agencies should be actively encouraged to hold their introductory and developmental activities in the school itself. Such programs would be directed towards school-age youth, but others should not be precluded from participating. If the agencies providing the activity and leisure supply for the community can be brought into the school, the enriched curriculum will be even more securely linked to the activities available in the community.

To summarize, then, physical educators will need to reconceptualize their contributions to the core curriculum. Their curriculum should be conceived of as a health enhancement program offered cooperatively with home economics and health education teachers for both students and colleagues. Physical educators will also need to reconceptualize much of the current activity content of physical education in the enriched curriculum. The enriched curricular programs must build for students the basis for an enjoyable, healthy lifestyle and acculturation into the sports and leisure of the American society. The enriched curriculum will have to be built in concert with community recreators and the private citizens who create the activity and leisure supply in each community. Bridging the gap between school and community will require cooperation with community recreation workers. Creating an activity and leisure supply to support both the health enhancement and acculturation of students will bring physical educators into the community's mainstream.

Teacher Education in the Universities

The redesign of the school curriculum will also require new teacher education curricula in the universities. There will be need for a double major in physical education and health education, or a joint major in school health enhancement offered by the departments representing the two fields. The universities will return to the task of preparing people who are capable of delivering the essential learning skills in an integrated core curriculum, as was originally intended when the disciplines of health and physical education were initiated.

In addition, the management of the school leisure supply jointly with the existing leisure supply systems in the community will increase the importance of the community/school concept. Physical educators or school health enhancement specialists will need to be able to understand the processes of community development and create "down-reach" programs whereby community agencies and groups develop programs to serve their students. This will create a need for understanding the leisure service delivery system, the community development process, and the management of the multiple providers of enriched curricular services to the schools. Thus physical educators, by acting in concert with recreators to construct the enriched curriculum, and by integrating it with the core health enhancement curriculum, will also reunite these formerly closely allied fields.

Models for Community Physical Education

If the health revolutions are causing the rethinking of the services that physical educators offer to the school communities, then it surely is modifying our view of the avenues for service to the rest of society. Many new avenues for service are developing beyond the customary notion that physical education, in a content organized around competitive sports, is directed towards children and youth. A spectrum of concerns for physical education in the adult population is identified in Figure 8.5.

Physical educators can function all along this spectrum from the formal health care system at one end, to health enhancement in the center and the enjoyable development of leisure at the other. In Figure 8.5 the various functions are organized along a continuum. They run from *cure* at one end to *self-actualization* at the other.

Continuum of Goals for
Activity and Leisure in the Community

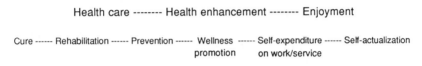

Health care -------- Health enhancement -------- Enjoyment

Cure ------ Rehabilitation ------ Prevention ------ Wellness ------ Self-expenditure ------ Self-actualization
                                                    promotion   on work/service

Figure 8.5 Continuum of professional goals for the activity and leisure industry in the community.

Cure, of course, involves the use of exercise technologists, adapted physical educators, and athletic trainers in the various functions that fall under the domain of physicians and other licensed medical practitioners. The goal is to cooperate with others to eliminate disease by using our knowledge of the role of exercise and movement. The next step, rehabilitation, involves similar specialties, but moves further into the restorative process where the original level of functioning is rebuilt.

Next, the continuum shifts to health enhancement. Here the goal is not to cure disease but to prevent disease from occurring and to achieve an optimal state of health. All facets of the field are concerned with the avoidance of accidents and/or the promotion of safety in order to avoid disease. Once safe existence is assured, then the professionals can turn their attention to achieving the enhancement of health, not merely the absence of disease. This text has focused heavily on this mission because creating a desire for a healthy lifestyle, as well as the means to develop one, are central concerns for all. But for physical education, the newly emerging, comprehensive fitness and lifestyle management curricula are preparing people to work with others in comprehensive health enhancement projects in the public and private sector.

When human beings are healthy, they then need a mission for themselves to bring a higher order of satisfaction to their existence. Mental health and satisfaction are achieved either through enjoyable and enriching work or through leisure. Order and a sense of contributing to the good order of the society comes from meaningful self-expenditure. When this is consistently possible, the person can achieve the highest state of health—self-actualization. At this level, physical educators work in their more traditional roles of facilitators, leaders, managers, and instructors in a variety of activity and leisure related programs.

Overlapping Professional Contributions

The involvement in the community of the three currently disparate disciplines of physical education, health education, and recreation is specified in Figure 8.6. Inspection of the matrix of concerns for the three disciplines reveals that each has specialties that overlap to a great extent. Thus this matrix represents an agenda for discussing how best to reconstruct the disciplines of physical education, health education, and recreation, each with their various specializations, in order to best serve the emerging social order.

Involvement of Physical Education, Health Education, and Recreation in the Community

	Health Care	Health Enhancement	Enjoyment	
Physical Education	Athletic training, weight control, adapted PE, cardiac rehab, and exercise scientist	Fitness and life-style management	Professional, part-time volunteer--coaching, instruction, leadership, program design, and management	Facilitation of affinity groups involved in sports, dance, play, exercise, and adventure
Health Education	Counseling and instruction, health administration, and community health specialist	Fitness and life-style management	Counseling, instruction management, community health development	
Recreation	Therapeutic recreation	Liesure counseling, mental health development	Management, leadership interpretation, instruction	As for PE above plus visual, performing, constructive, and social arts

Figure 8.6 Matrix of functions for physical education, health education, and recreation in the community.

Health Care

On the curative end of the spectrum, there is little competition among the disciplines of physical education, health education, and recreation. Several direct-client or patient-care specialties are concerned with cooperating with others in the curative health care business. At the curative end, adapted physical education specialists utilize their understanding of humans and of human movement to deliver a narrow and specific set of services, usually in face-to-face settings. They often work with clients in conjunction with other specialists and physicians. Health educators may be among the other specialists cooperating in the process to assist in the counseling and instruction concerning the disease processes; however, the contributions of the two specialties are separate. The physical educator usually works as an exercise scientist directly with the disease, condition, or disability; the health educator is usually concerned with the matrix of associated lifestyle processes and behaviors.

Community health education specialists also function at this point on the continuum as administrators of the health care system. The specialties of health education and physical education are relatively distinct and the two kinds of professionals, exercise scientists and community health specialists, operate not so much in competitive as in cooperative relationships.

Recreators seem to have only one avenue to service at the curative end of the continuum. Therapeutic recreation specialists are involved in the curative/rehabilitative process by bringing their understandings of the effects of leisure behavior to bear on the curative process. Clients' cognitive, affective, and motoric needs are not mysteriously suspended because they are diseased. Thus therapeutic recreators may be incorporated into the team at this point. However, they are most likely to be recruited to assist with chronic conditions that are limiting in some way, especially when that limitation may produce other diseases due to the degradation of the quality of life. Clearly, the functions of the adapted physical educator and the therapeutic recreator overlap substantially here.

Health Enhancement

In the center of the continuum in Figure 8.5 is "wellness promotion," or health enhancement. All three fields—physical education, health education, and recreation—have specializations that claim large interests in this area. Physical educators contribute to the clients' personal health enhancement program by their concern for the integrity of their clients' biology, or their fitness. The integrity of the clients is dramatically influenced by their activity patterns, their relative obesity, the interactions of their exercise with their stress management, and their diet, tobacco, and drug usage. Physical educators are also concerned with injury prevention and the acute and chronic management of exercise-related injuries and conditions.

Health educators find their principal contribution to adult client services in the community concentrated in health enhancement also. While health educators may be involved in a broader range of disease and wellness processes than the physical educator, their concerns also cover those claimed by the physical educator. There is very substantial overlap between health educators and physical educators; in fact, there may be no real functional difference between these professional fields at the actual point of delivery.

Both fields are concerned with the multiple facets of the health enhancement process as they affect the human being. One subset of concerns—fitness, for example—cannot be easily disassociated from the others.

It is most likely that at this point the two fields will be reunited by the pressures inherent to delivering high-quality and integrated services to the adult client in the community setting. Lifestyle management for wellness identifies the interests of the client, and these interests will eventually govern. Already there are joint degrees that link the two specialties at the master's level. It will not be long before the students, recognizing the benefits in acquiring an understanding of the entire wellness promotion/health enhancement process, will insist on further integration of the subject matter in order to enhance their employability.

Recreators' contributions to health enhancement must also be integrated into the health enhancement process. Leisure counseling specialists attempt to provide clients with the information and support necessary to create meaningful and enjoyable leisure lifestyles. If they are successful, they clearly affect the quality and the content of the client's lifestyles, and this reverberates, affecting the clients' wellness. Thus the process of leisure counseling should be incorporated into the health enhancement process. The techniques associated with it should simply be incorporated into lifestyle management curricula as part of the attempt to minimize stress and to improve mental health by creating a high-quality lifestyle.

It is extremely unlikely that leisure counseling will be able to survive as an independent specialty outside of the public sector. People will not pay enough for the referrals and the goals clarification that leisure counselors offer for the specialty to survive as an independent profession in the private sector. The nearest approximation to the leisure counselor is the travel counselor in the hospitality and tourist industry. But even here the principal source of support for the travel counselor comes from commissions for the sale of travel and tourism services and not from fees for advice. Travel and tourism counseling is not usually a viable primary occupation; leisure counseling is unlikely to be able to be marketed successfully either. Leisure counseling as a process may survive as part of a health service agency supported by tax dollars that manages the habilitation of disadvantaged or disabled individuals. Once again, the free market will determine whether leisure counseling can become a profession independent of lifestyle management.

Facilitating Enjoyment and Self-Actualization

At the right end of the continuum depicted in Figure 8.6 the processes involve personal enjoyment or enjoyment derived from the expenditure of time and energy in the service of others. Here, numerous volunteer coaches, instructors, and leaders offer their services via the affinity groups and clubs in any community. These efforts bring a sense of purpose to the volunteers and dramatically increase the leisure supply in the community. Of course, these services cannot be considered professional in the sense that they are delivered by people with professional preparation in the disciplines of physical education, health education, and recreation. For the volunteers, however, there is no delineation between the disciplines. They just get on with the job as they see it.

Even though some physical educators, health educators, and recreators volunteer their expertise, their efforts are small compared to the total efforts contributed by lay volunteers. The principal overlapping between professionals occurs between physical education and recreation specialists involved with community development through the facilitation of affinity groups, design of programs, creation of the management infrastructures for community programs, managing of sports programs, and development of volunteer systems and support groups. Employment opportunities in the public sector occur within departments of human services and/or departments of recreation within municipal and county governments. In the private sector, only limited opportunities occur within large and successful affinity groups. Here a few professionals are employed as managers, program designers, instructors, and so on to enhance the services provided by the membership of clubs and affinity groups to themselves.

Physical Education and Recreation

The leisure area of the industry exhibits a possible beneficial synergy between physical education and recreation. For this synergy to come about, we must first recognize that the provision of activity services such as sport, dance, exercise, and play requires expertise that is central to the skills and abilities of physical educators. Second, we must recognize that the leisure supply goes far beyond activity and must include concern for, and facilitation of, the visual, performing, and constructive arts. These are very broad areas that do not often involve physical educators except on an avocational basis. Clearly, the two fields would benefit from the recognition that they have complementary missions. A major motive for participation in activities sponsored by physical education and recreation is to visit with family and friends[1]. Forming and experiencing friendships is a need that links participants to their personal leisure supply and is a theme that runs through both professional groups' provisions for their clients.

It may be the role of the recreation profession to learn how to manage the leisure supply while employing specialists in any particular area. It is not the profession's mission to master a great deal of content that specialists are better

---

[1]In all surveys conducted by the author concerning leisure, the most popular answer to the question, "What would you like to do more of?" has always been, "Visit with family and friends."

qualified to handle in order to do all the face-to-face leadership. Those in the recreation profession should simply facilitate and manage the contributions of multiple experts who are able to advance the diverse interests of many clients. No one person can achieve a satisfactory level of competence in more than a few areas of interest, and this fact must be recognized by the recreation profession.

Challenges for the Universities

The models presented for the roles of physical education in the school and community show that physical education overlaps substantially with both health education and recreation. While these fields may be able to defend themselves as separate entities within the universities, businesses and agencies driven by clients' wishes will increasingly move toward integration. Departmental integration will present a substantial challenge to the organization of university departments, which for decades have been fostering disintegration by organizing themselves into separate entities. Some of the major issues for university departments of health education, physical education, and recreation are presented next.

Health Education, Physical Education, and Recreation

Health education, physical education, and recreation will have to face the fact that although their roots have been in service to youth, they will soon have to deal with adult clients and that those clients will be aging as the median age of the nation increases. Lifelong human development is the core of the mission of the three fields, and increasingly the clients will be seeking assistance with their health and life enhancement in a holistic way. The curriculum will have to be modified to ensure that new recruits to the professions learn how to deal with all ages and all types of clients. Youth and the school setting will remain important, but will be only one focus of attention. Despite this, many university classes remain organized around youth and the school, thereby restricting the utility of these classes because few of the students in them will actually be working with school-age youth.

A natural corollary of the assumption that the clients are young and are in schools is that the old prescriptive approach that exists at the core of youth programming will need to shift to a new role of listener, counselor, and friend. Classes in how to counsel, communicate with, listen to, and clarify values for youth and adults will be necessary.

While it is desirable that universities recruit students comfortable with and capable of leading adults, it is not critical from the clients' viewpoint that they do so. Market forces will soon cull professionals incapable of leading adults from the industry. However, it will be more humane and efficient if the universities can identify and advise students who are unlikely to be successful not to waste their time and the university's resources.

Historically, university programs serving the activity and leisure industry have exerted little selective pressure at point of entry or exit from their programs. Teacher education programs are almost incapable of eliminating people unlikely to be successful. There is a widespread belief that accurate denial of access is not possible technically and legally. Consequently, the notion of recruiting the likely candidates, rather than accepting all the applicants meeting the university's minima, is foreign to all three fields. However, the nation has been readied for the selection process by the plethora of demands for reform in teacher education and higher standards and accountability among teachers. The attitude that selection is not possible or desirable will be diminished by such reports; university departments will have to develop ways of selecting students likely to be successful teachers. Neither they nor their clients will be able to afford a five-year curriculum when there is little chance of success. Student selection will be required of departments preparing teachers, and the notion will spread to other career specialties. Universities will enter a period in which they will have to choose and be held accountable for the quality of the personnel they produce.

Finally, the services offered by professionals in the activity and leisure industry will increasingly be funded through the discretionary purchases of services made by adults. Accordingly much of the service delivered will occur in private business settings rather than tax-supported public sector agencies. The business of marketing, selling, quality control, and liability law will become fundamental topics for all three fields.

Preparation for Practice

The most significant challenge of all, however, will be the reintegration of the curriculum with the world of practice. Lawson (1985) is convincing when he argues that practitioners demand that the knowledge and information that they need for their work be not only true, but also relevant and useful. The problem for practitioners is that physical education has specialized to the point that it is not easy to derive relevant and useful guides for practice from the research findings of subspecialties. This specialization that has proceeded apace for nearly three decades began in response to challenges to the field in the early 1960s. The challenges caused Franklin Henry of Berkeley to lecture the profession on what was needed for physical education to become a university discipline (Henry, 1964). Often referred to as the important turning point in the recent development of university physical education, this lecture nudged the pendulum of the discipline's development away from professional concerns and toward the disciplinary concerns. It changed the course of research and scholarship in the field. Unfortunately, the lecture and the reforms it stimulated splintered the content of the field. The pendulum has swung far enough.

Now the need for the creation of fundamental understandings of the phenomena of human movement must be balanced with the need for more effective, reliable, and useful technologies in the world of practice. The next generation of professionals in the activity and leisure industry will not need a vast array of disconnected knowledge; instead they will need to know how to counsel and lead children *and* adults in lifestyle planning and implementation. All facets of health enhancement and human development will need to be integrated for effective delivery of services to clients. The current splintering of the discipline of human movement studies and the separation of physical education from health education and recreation prevents this from happening. Reintegration of knowledge and practice needs to take place in classes, complete departments, and especially in our scholarship.

New Blends of Knowledge/New Curricula

If departments cannot be reintegrated because of political power, then at least new curricular forms must be sought. New professionals should not have to choose a narrow subspecialty within the broad spectrum of human development, knowing that they will then necessarily be ill prepared for the market upon graduation.

The models for the delivery of service to the school and the community can be used as the basis for planning the integrated curricular themes that bring the university departments of health, physical education, and recreation together. Some suggestions derived from the professional functions presented earlier in Figure 8.6 follow.

Adapted Physical Education and Therapeutic Recreation. Adapted physical education and therapeutic recreation as subspecialties of the two fields overlap so substantially that in reality they are just one specialty. Where they exist side by side they should be merged for the sake of the clientele who have special needs.

Lifestyle Management. Next, health enhancement or lifestyle management should be a curriculum that merges some of the content of health education and physical education with recreation. Much of the health enhancement activity will occur in adult settings, usually in the private sector, and no single separate department can cover alone the broad spectrum of lifestyle management concerns. This is a critical growth area and cooperation will be rewarded by attracting the attention of students who seem to be better attuned to what is happening in the marketplace than their professors are.

Community Physical Education and Recreation. Community recreation and development offers another opportunity for cooperation. Increasingly, the activities of physical educators and recreators overlap in the process of augmenting the leisure supply and community development. Increasingly, too, physical educators work outside the schools and alongside recreators in the community. They work together in youth sport programs, adventure activities, private sector ventures, community centers, and with affinity groups. The activity and leisure industry needs physical educators with a broader understanding of community development and club and center management, and it needs recreators with better content skills.

It is impossible for any recreator to function in all facets of constructive, performing, written, visual, and activity arts. The breadth of the necessary leisure supply in American culture is so great that no one person can do more than be an expert in a very few activities and dabble in a few others. However, for the aficionados among the clients, dabbling does not permit effective leadership. The goal for recreators must be to facilitate the operation of all affinity groups that practice at the level desired in the community. There is little need for curricula in the content of American leisure at the undergraduate level. If undergraduates are preparing for face-to-face leadership roles, they will need to be experts in the areas already well established in the visual, constructive, and performing arts, and in crafts, museum management, hospitality operations, and so forth. They will also need to be experts in the content of sport and dance, or be blessed with a saleable set of skills derived from leisure participation outside the curriculum. Yet if these skills are generated in the university department of recreation there can be no doubt that quality will suffer and resources duplicating other content areas on campus will be wasted.

Leisure Service Management. Preparation for entry to the adult leisure industry should follow the model used for preparing teachers. In the education profession each would-be teacher acquires a set of skills, knowledge, and understandings from the experts in the content area. Would-be teachers then come together with students from other content areas to learn the common elements needed to function in the professional niche, in this case the school system. Undergraduate recreation departments should off-load all teaching in content areas to their expert colleagues in the primary content areas. They could then concentrate on socializing new recreation professionals who are about to offer content services on a face-to-face basis in the leisure industry. Education and recreation, as departments, should have analogous functions. The function for recreation is the professional preparation of people for the leisure industry after they have obtained their skills in the content areas elsewhere.

By the same process of determining the mission of the fields, physical education and health education should recognize the role that they each play in the process and send their students to the departments of recreation to be socialized into public and private sector adult leisure services.

At the graduate level, recreation departments should declare that they are preparing people for management functions in the public and private sectors of the activity and leisure industry. People with preparation and experience in a content area should return to receive higher education in leisure industry management. Physical education and health education should leave to the recreators the business of preparing managers for the activity and leisure industry.

If these recommendations were adopted, the mission of the recreation departments would come into focus. Duplication and competition for scarce resources would diminish, and the quality of the delivered service would improve. Capacity to improve quality steadily will be necessary as the professionals in the activity and leisure industry are driven by the rising expectations of the public for high-quality services.

Teacher Preparation in Health Education and Physical Education.   School health education and school physical education programs should be merged. If the reforms recommended by the Holmes group (Holmes Group, Inc., 1986) result in a redesign of the way teachers are prepared and a fifth year is added to the process, then it will be time to reintegrate the teaching of health education and physical education in the schools. The core curriculum, discussed above and in chapters 5 and 6, clearly requires the creation of a joint curriculum in which all facets of a healthy lifestyle are covered. The split between health education and physical education in preparing teachers for the school curriculum has been awkward from the beginning. The two teacher certifications should be reintegrated as a single certification for health enhancement educators, which would be to the advantage of the schoolchildren.

The community school notion and the enriched curriculum, if adopted, will occur at the boundaries of the school and the community at large. The best teacher preparation for this function will occur by combining the interests of physical education and community recreation.

The changes suggested here are simply some examples of redesigning the curricula around the occupational functions that will emerge as a result of the social changes surrounding physical education, recreation, and health education. They are suggested to prompt thought about what physical educators (and health educators and recreators) will actually do for their clients now and in the future. The adoption of any of these functional redesigns will be very costly to established departments and the status quo. However, it is time to review how new professionals are prepared for their missions, and to base that review on an analysis of what is going on around them. Changes will occur whether we like them or not. It is up to us in the universities to look forward objectively and plan wisely. We can be assured that other competing groups will be doing so.

Summary

This chapter has expanded the content of the previous chapters into models for the operation of the activity and leisure industry in its three major areas: the school, the community, and the university. The notions presented are the author's. Many other ideas are possible and probably desirable. What is important is that each member of the activity and leisure industry anticipate his or her functions and relate them to the changes that are occurring. Without a conscious effort to configure physical education to fit into the society that will be, physical education may not.

The Great Challenges Ahead

At the beginning of this book we discussed the multiple trends occurring in our society. Megatrends were combined into three great social trends that would influence physical education. We then examined in greater detail a series of subordinate influences that would work their effects on different aspects of physical education, and to a lesser extent, health education and recreation. Each represents a change to be accommodated to and each represents a major opportunity for the activity and leisure industry. In this final chapter all of this information is used to present guidelines for physical education—the great challenges ahead.

Changing Content for a Changing Client

The principal body of clients from which physical education will draw its support during the next thirty years or so will be adults. While school-age children will remain an important market in schools and youth sport programs, the center of gravity of the market will shift to older people. As the median age of the population grows, and as concern for health enhancement grows among the groups at risk—middle- and older-aged people—so the role of physical activity in the development of healthy lifestyles will also grow. The majority of adults can pay for the services they desire, and they will form the growing market. Delivering prized services to adults will present completely different challenges to the field. Unlike school-age children, the adult population is not aggregated by law into convenient groups and managed in facilities and programs supported by taxes. Adults will have to be recruited and maintained in the programs voluntarily. As a result, their wishes will be paramount, and we know they do not wish to participate in competitive team sports. Basketball, baseball, football, and the other major sports—the mainstays of physical education to date—will not be part of the content of adult physical education. Adults will demand to be treated as individuals seeking voluntarily to enhance their well-being, continue their personal growth and development, and improve their appearance while having fun with other like adults. Finding and developing a content suitable for the adult client will provide the field with a major challenge. This challenge will be met by further research into the motives behind adult participation and by retooling for a different market.

A corollary of this effect is the fact that new recruits into adult physical education will not simply be high school students entering university physical education departments. In earlier times, high school students selecting physical education for a career had experienced physical educators only as their teachers and coaches. Their ideas about what physical educators did professionally were in line with reality. Their views, however, are no longer necessarily valid. The world of adult physical education currently developing outside the school will not have been experienced yet by the freshman recruit. Consequently, a related challenge will be presented to the field to communicate the array of possibilities in the activity and leisure industry to its potential recruits. In turn, the nature of the recruits will change. Older people who have been in the working world will return to the university and transfer to the field as a result of their experiences. More frequently, the decision to enter physical education will be derived not from the desire to continue in the field because of outstanding ability in sport, but because of an appreciation of the possibilities the field has for lifelong human development.

Reintegrating the Disciplines

The time has come to address the problem of the splintering of the discipline of human development into minor professional fiefdoms. The splintering of physical education, health education, and recreation, and sometimes their further separation into narrow specialties, is harming the development of the activity and leisure industry. Clients cannot see that nutrition counseling nominally "belongs" to health education and that the role of exercise in the achievement of health and well-being "belongs" to physical education. A plethora of narrow specialties will not serve the client well. Thus, a major challenge for the activity and leisure industry will be to engineer the reintegration of health education, physical education, and recreation; we must now remember that adult clients will be signing the checks.

Achieving Professional Status

A further major challenge will be to create a profession of physical education. A source of debate for too long has been whether we are a profession or not, and if we are not, what shall we do to become one. The argument has raged as though we had complete control of the process and as though the answer mattered. The argument, however, has proceeded from the inside out. The question always came down to, How do we configure ourselves as a group of like-minded practitioners so that others consider us a profession? Presumably, the reason for achieving the status of a profession was to acquire respect and power.

Lawson (1985) has identified two major processes that must occur in tandem for any field to become a profession. The first involves a complex process of negotiation with the members of society to grant the field a monopoly of the functions and services defined by the field itself. Definitions of the problems to be solved must be constructed completely and convincingly. The process is long and drawn out and must be continually reinforced or policed in order to maintain the monopoly. The second process involves the creation of a body of specialized knowledge that reliably solves problems not easily and routinely managed by society. Lawson is pessimistic about the first requirement because the negotiations between the field of physical education and society have been largely ineffective so far. We have seen the development of credentialing (i.e., certification of teachers, athletic trainers, exercise technicians, lifeguards and water safety instructors), but presently no really effective system for creating and policing the monopoly exists. Unfortunately, in many specialties in the field past experience as an athlete or participant is considered enough qualification for a coach, health club worker, activity leader, and so on; in effect, there is no monopoly.

The second requirement involves particular knowledge, techniques, and understandings that enable the professional to work reliable effects at the behest of the client. In his analysis, Lawson (1985) argues that the body of knowledge used by practitioners in their daily work servicing clients is in fact influenced by their work. While practitioners are interested in scientifically validated knowledge, they generally require additional tests beyond scientific truth before they will incorporate it into their practice. The findings of scientists must be not only true, but relevant and useful. The practitioner is more likely to trust knowledge developed in the heat of daily usage, because that knowledge is validated in settings similar to those in which they themselves wish to use it. Scientists in physical education tend not to conduct research that relates to the world of the physical educator's work, but to build fragmented theory that often does not advantage the practitioners in their search for reliable effects in individual clients. Thus there is not yet an effective mechanism for developing the body of knowledge and transferring it to practitioners. Because the two conditions are not satisfied, Lawson doubts our professional status and fears the processes of deprofessionalization.

A more optimistic argument can be made. When surgeons gained the capacity to reliably alter the course of disease, and when their clients became confident that they could do so, the medical profession was born. At one time medical professionals provided the services of last resort. Before the nineteenth century one went to the hospital to die, or at least to engage in one last heroic effort to survive. Since then the process of professing to do medicine has acquired power and respect because it has delivered the effects desired by the people at large.

The field of physical education is beginning to demonstrate to more and more people that it has a set of goods it can deliver reliably. The beneficial effects of our field are fortunately multifaceted and thus there are numerous possible motivations for seeking our services. We can influence the development of the young, we can provide meaningful confrontations and tests for the adolescent, we can improve performance reliably, we can create settings in which people have fun, meet others, contribute to their health, and so on. To the extent that we can reliably accomplish these services at a price affordable to the members of our society, then we will gain influence and income. And as that situation accumulates and stabilizes over time, then respect for our contributions will be institutionalized into professional status. At that point, we will then be able to add the trappings desired by those who seek professional status.

A further positive development is occurring as litigation increasingly defines the standards of the profession (Kaiser, 1986). As the body of precedents build in liability law, so do the expectations for prudent professional practice. Thus in many lawsuits the qualifications of the defendant to make the judgment that the plaintiff questions comes under scrutiny. Increasingly, defendants argue that they were qualified to make a particular judgment because they had prepared carefully and had validated their preparation by passing an examination, in some cases had even satisfied a requirement to maintain their expertise (a Red Cross Water Safety Instructor, for example). In a sense, these are negotiations with society and as the body of precedents increases they empower the credentialing organizations. People want the defenses that come with their credential, and society will be disinclined to employ those that do not have the credential.

The status of profession, and the prestige and power that go with that cachet, is conferred—not declared. Declaring that we are a profession and configuring ourselves as though we are a profession will be only marginally and indirectly useful. The direct path to the status we seek proceeds through professional actions, not professional posturing.

The major question, then, should not be, How do we configure ourselves in order to be classified as a profession? Rather, it should be, How can we set out to produce beneficial and desired effects reliably and cheaply for large numbers of clients so that they cannot do without us? We should start from the perceptions of the clients we serve. In other words, we must be perceived as behaving professionally by our clients before we can expect them to ascribe professional status to us.

Developing a Code of Ethics

Our clients' perceptions of whether or not we behave professionally will come from our transactions with them. They want to be treated fairly and honestly with their own best interests of paramount importance. They need to feel that if they voluntarily place themselves under our influence, they will not be taken advantage of. There must be conviction that physical educators can be trusted (U.S. Department of Health and Human Services, 1984).

All physical educators must behave at all times in a trustworthy manner. Trustworthiness comes from each individual's code of beliefs and ethics. However, we must publicly declare that we seek to be trusted; and to assist each physical educator in doing so, we need a code of professional ethics. Such a code will be immensely helpful in setting standards and showing our public what can be expected.

A code of ethics will foster two immediate purposes. The first is that, when followed, it will lead to repeat business. Brand loyalty is a major feature of marketing strategies. Creating the perception that physical educators practice first in the interests of their client brings confidence, trust, and loyalty. This is simply good business. Second, a code of ethics will influence the way in which litigation exerts its pressures on the field and will thus permit us to police our own ranks more effectively.

Reliable Production of Beneficial Effects

In addition to behaving ethically in the interests of our clients, we must also be able to produce effects reliably. In other words, we have to be able to do what we claim. Accordingly, we need theories, technologies, and continuing education. In other words, we need (a) a body of reliable knowledge about the effects of sport, dance, exercise, and play on human development; (b) the application of that knowledge to produce beneficial effects for our clients on demand; and (c) systems for communicating theories and technologies quickly to new and existing practitioners.

When we are trusted by our clients to produce beneficial effects we will be rewarded. The efforts currently spent trying to create the structural conditions of a profession would be better spent on ensuring a vast number of satisfied clients. In their book *In Search of Excellence* Peters and Waterman (1984) reported that one of the characteristics of the best-run companies in the U.S. was that they concentrated on the fundamentals of their business. The good companies "stuck to the knitting"; they knew what they were supposed to do and they made sure they did it well.

As physical educators, we must never forget that we are in the business of delivering high-quality, reliable, and beneficial physical activity services to all people. Our field will become a profession when our clients know that they can achieve their personal goals more readily and reliably with our help. If we collectively stick to our knitting, then rewards in terms of status, influence, and income will inevitably result.

Shifting Power to Individuals

At the root of most of the changes influencing physical education is a fundamental shifting of power in the activity and leisure industries from physical educators to their clients. This shifting of power has influenced every corner of physical education, and the process is just beginning. While it has unnerved some established leaders in the field and modified long-standing programs, the shake-up presents many opportunities for the field to reshape itself and grow in influence in American society.

Deeply held beliefs about the role of government and the desired shape of the American capitalistic economic system have altered fundamental attitudes towards government-provided social services. People increasingly accept the idea that government should play a limited role, defining only the basic structures and rules, interfering with the economy as little as necessary. The healthier the economy the better for all eventually. Deregulation of business, withdrawal from state and local affairs, reduction of subsidies and the enervation of welfare systems, increased rewards for effectiveness, reduced inflation, and higher unemployment have all resulted from such ideology. Many people believe that more taxes simply give more power to government at whatever level. The goal of diminishing the role of government and increasing the effectiveness of the free market economy has been growing in popularity and has drastically shaped attitudes, legislation, and policy (Greenwald, 1986). These forces have drastically influenced the activity and leisure industry.

The back to basics tax revolt occurred because of a general disenchantment with the efficacy of government programs to resolve social ills. People came to have more faith in the capacity of the free market and the energy of individuals motivated by reward to solve problems. People in the private sector seemed to be able to accomplish more for less than the government could.

Of course not all people shifted their opinions, but enough of them did to alter the balance of thinking and power. In general, the system is now biased to reduce the role of government and increase the spheres of influence exerted by individuals in the private sector to change the shape of America.

This fundamental change affects the basic structure of physical education. The shift in thinking has occurred at precisely the time when the baby-boomers grew up and when it became obvious that the graying of America was in full flood. Prior to the shift in opinion, the role of physical education was to design programs to meet the needs of the various cohorts and sell them to the politicians. Large efforts, sometimes involving the electorate, to influence annual and biennial budgets were required. Once the annual emergency of the budget process was resolved, the problem became a matter of spending the money wisely. The whole industry was attuned to convincing those in the political system (in one way or another) that physical education and activity was good for some fraction of the population and should be funded.

Arguments rationalizing the "good" of physical education were made by the few, to the few, for the many. School physical education, community recreation, and university physical education budgets originated mainly from taxes; but the picture has changed dramatically. Shrinking tax dollars, and an increasing belief in the importance of individuals as controllers of the services they desire has increased the tendency to demand that users pay. Furthermore, government has resisted involvement in new social service ventures precisely when interest in adult health enhancement has boomed. Arguments now have to be made by the few directly to the many consumers.

Physical educators have been forced to find nongovernmental sources for the money they need to do their jobs. Old sources have dried up, and old alliances have ceased to be useful. New strategies and vocabularies have emerged. While school physical education continues to exist, a new system of activity and leisure services in the private sector has begun to grow. Physical educators are increasingly realizing that they are in a business rather than in a tax-supported social service.

As the fraction of the field that depends on the direct sale of activity and leisure services to clients increases, the importance of marketing, sales, and managerial skills will rise. As the transition takes place, entrepreneurs will redefine the field and its limits. The process will be unnerving to those who eschewed possible wealth for the security of a public sector occupation. Physical educators driven by a sense of vocation will rue the change because receipts and profits will become central concerns, rather than the more ethereal and idealistic concerns for the good of the people involved.

The worst fears about the demise of physical education as a social service will materialize. However, there is a positive side in this new atmosphere of accountability and client power. With a share of the available tax dollars, physical educators had too much power in that they were not accountable for the production of the effects they claimed. The shift of power to the clients holds the physical educator directly accountable for providing satisfactory service. This will result in an activity and leisure industry that pays close attention to the wishes of the clients. As the sophistication of the clients increases and as the field becomes increasingly accountable, then market forces will drive the field to new levels of efficiency and imagination.

The activity and leisure industry will be more volatile as a result, but the long-term trend will be towards greater participation, improved health, and better service. Volatility and the turbulence of fad, fashion, and whimsy may be irritating, but they are evidence that the field and its clients are creatively pushing and pulling to find new ways to realize a high-quality existence. The long-term future of physical education as part of the activity and leisure industry looks good. The time between now and the first decade of the next century, however, will be a little frightening—and a lot of fun. It will be a good time to be a physical educator because the field has the potential of substantial growth.

Inside Out/Outside In

The ideas presented in this book and the projections for the future of physical education may well be irritating to many professionals in the field. Physical educators have been used to deriving their arguments for doing or changing things from some basic philosophy related to their view of the best of all worlds. The idealists struggle to construct their prescriptions from the inside out. This book has consistently viewed the field from the basis of what is or what is presumed to be shortly. It makes its prescriptions from the outside in. Thus the conjectures and prescriptions found herein were woven from political, economic, and demographic threads. The process was essentially one of looking at the influences of the "real world" on the field as it evolves, and it proceeded from the outside in, rather than from logical extensions of fundamental beliefs about what ought to be.

In that sense a net of economic, demographic, and political factors has been cast over the field. These features will exist independently of our beliefs and will determine the extent to which we are able to achieve our goals. They will sometimes thwart us, and sometimes accelerate us towards our goals even faster than we had planned. For example, the fitness bubble did not burst because it became embedded in the stronger force for health enhancement. Health enhancement came about only partially because it was a good idea. Its major impetus came from the need for cost containment in the health care industry and because of the aging of the baby-boomers. So although professionals have constructed arguments for lifelong activity as long as the field has existed, it was only when major economic and political forces aligned themselves correctly that the notions of health enhancement and disease prevention nudged into the consciousness of most people. Thus we ride the crest of a new wave only partly created by our own efforts.

Other examples of an outside force accelerating our development as a field can be explained by the effect of the baby boom in the late forties and fifties. That boom first created a massive need for teachers and then a need to expand the universities. Since physical education was schoolchild oriented at that time, it was forced to expand. Professional preparation of teachers became the primary focus of the field. For some, it became the exclusive focus.

Then came the arrival of the baby-boomers to the universities. Their arrival coincided with a period of wealth, political stability, and post-Sputnik fever. Expanding the universities became a national priority. The expansion came at just the right time for physical education, because it coincided with the need to respond to the attacks from the outside on the credibility of physical education. Those in the field had an opportunity to expand their horizons and recruit an enormous number of new physical educators selected for their ability to contribute to the scholarship of the field. Had the Soviets not launched Sputnik and had Conant not launched his by now famous attack on the academic content of physical education at the same time universities were expanding, physical education would be very different today. Forces outside the field were enormously influential and were quite removed from our desires as physical educators. The same will be true in the future.

Close attention to the political, economic, and demographic realities of the emerging society in which we live is as important as deciding what ought to be. We can realize our highest ideals for the field only to the extent that they are possible. What is achieved is, to a great extent, determined by the larger forces. Physical education needs a dose of economic, demographic, and political realism; this book has tried to provide exactly that.

Epilogue

New specialties will emerge in response to pressures from outside the three fields of health education, physical education, and recreation. While we discuss and weave and feint, the economy will demand that the energetic among us reconfigure ourselves. The rewards will be great enough that some of us will do it. Students will force a restructuring of the curricula in the universities so that they are better able to function in the schools and in the adult communities when they graduate. The strong pressures for health enhancement nationwide and the commercialization of the health care sector will add fuel to the fire. The pressures from the community and the federal government to improve the quality of the schools will mount. Across the board, the pressures for accountability and tangible contributions in exchange for the billions of dollars spent on both school and community physical education programs will be inexorable. And they will work to the benefit of client and professional alike.

Furthermore, these pressures of the market will shape the field anew in its efforts to meet the demands of the adult society, and will actually present physical education with multiple opportunities. The next career cycle, the next thirty years, will be a time of great growth in opportunity for the physical educators who can respond flexibly and rapidly to the turbulence of our rapidly changing society. Our time has come—let us enjoy it.

*The Nature of Prediction*_____

The nature of prediction presented in this appendix is a simple model of the predictive process. Although this model is not necessary for understanding the materials that form the focus of this book, it is included here for readers interested in a more detailed explanation of the way the future is predicted.

Projection, Prediction, and Prognosis

The future state of any phenomenon is determined by several factors that come together. The way these forces come together is demonstrated in Figure A.1. The first element in the model represents the current situation. This current value or status represents the basic datum that is transformed by the action of the other elements in the model. Thus the assessment of futures must always start with some notion of the present.

The next item on the path to the future is inertia. The size of the element to be changed affects its rate of change. The larger the system, the more inertia it has and the more resistant it is to change. In other words, the larger the system, the stronger the force for the change needed to change it. It is often

$$\left(\begin{matrix}\text{Current} \\ \text{state}\end{matrix} \times \text{Inertia}\right) + \left(\begin{matrix}\text{Existing} \\ \text{trends}\end{matrix} \times \text{Potency}\right) + \left(\begin{matrix}\text{New} \\ \text{trends}\end{matrix} \times \text{Potency}\right) +$$

$$\left(\text{Interventions} \times \text{Potency}\right) + \frac{\text{Inexplicable}}{\text{events}} = \text{Future}$$

Figure A.1 Forces affecting the future.

hard to change an individual's mind or habit, and it is massively harder to change the course of groups or societies. So large systems or aggregates, by virtue of inertia, tend either to continue as they are or to continue to change along the same trajectory. They are easier to predict.

An example of differing inertias is the time and effort necessary to change the policies and behaviors of the NCAA versus a comparable policy change in the New Games Foundation. The former is a massive organization with well-established operations and is desperately in need of reform. The New Games Foundation is much smaller, newer, and more flexible. The NCAA has much more inertia, and so it will respond to the need for change much more slowly and with difficulty. The New Games Foundation will be much more agile. People making predictions about the likely future of such organizations must consider the inertia of the system in question.

Returning to Figure A.1, if we know where we presently are, the scale of the phenomena of concern, and the potency of the existing forces that are currently inducing change, we can extrapolate into the future. Simple extrapolation makes the assumption, however, that no new forces will enter into the equation to upset existing trends. Some new forces can be recognized, though, and can be used to alter the extrapolations to make predictions about what is likely to happen.

The next item in the model indicates that predictions for the future must also address what will be done in response to the changes. Society will not just sit idly by and allow change to occur; people will respond and attempt to intervene in the process. A beautiful example has been the revival of New England. Firmly locked into the old "Rustbelt" of a declining manufacturing economy, the people had the choice of accepting the decline, or doing something about it. A massive and spirited intervention by the New Englanders has replaced the older industries with new ones and rescued the region.

The possibility for intervention to alter an outcome is the most important ingredient for predicting the future. It passes to those in the present the possibility of influencing their own futures. It is the central notion that sustains the concept of the modifiable future. The remaining set of new forces are those that are inexplicable or unpredictable and nothing can be done about them specifically other than to expect them and allow enough flexibility to deal with them.

The model shows that futurology has its own structure depending on the elements in the equation that are used. If only the first two elements are used, the futurist defines the status quo, identifies the current forces for change, and, weighing their inertia and potency, forms a *prediction*. The prediction involves the extrapolation of the time line of old data into the future. This is the most common form of futurism. It works well for the short-term future—say five years or so. The inertia of the existing system can easily resist the perturbing effects of a weak new trend. Thus, until a trend picks up steam, its potency is usually insufficient to invalidate the prediction.

If futurists attempt to identify future forces, weigh their potency, and extrapolate the old data with corrections, then *projections* are formed. Projections are contingent on the assumptions made about the nature and potency of the new trends identified by the futurists. Projections are rarer than predictions for obvious reasons. They attempt to reach farther into the future and they include the use of new developments that are at the time poorly understood. Projections are usually used to attempt to understand perhaps up to twenty years into the future. Even if they are inaccurate, projections are useful because they serve to alert the people involved to the possibilities (if not the probabilities).

The last element in the futures equation involves assessing the impact of one-time events—provided the future event can be accurately predicted. These events are usually unpredictable, yet may have substantial effects. For example, stock market trends that have been marching steadily in a given direction can be upset by the news of an assassination in the Middle East. No futurologists can possibly be held responsible for foreseeing these events, yet they may well invalidate their predictions.

Finally, if futurists, after considering the predictions and projections available, go on to offer informed opinions about the nature of the future, then they are making *prognoses*. Depending on the nature of the informed opinion, a prognosis can be valuable because it can codify the problems and focus attention on developing events. Much of this book uses prognoses.

The problems for futurologists now become clear. We must define the present situation and quantify trends currently at work to change it. Projecting corrected data is the next step. Once a projection is made, allowances must then be made for possible error. Of course, the new forces and the likely nature of the errors cannot be determined. The futurologist must make estimates, or simply guess, what will disturb the projections. At this point, futurologists hedge their bets and prepare different *scenarios* with estimated probabilities of the outcomes.

Forces for Change

Forces inducing changes in our situations do not always act in a straight line. Some forces tend to accelerate a change for a time, and then set up conditions that cause a deceleration; the trend line describing these processes is an "S-shaped" curve. Let me give you a simple example that ran its course during a period of a few years at the University of Oregon. The university physical education department occupied a very old building and had built a weight training room in the old boxing room. This weight training room represented the state of the art of the 1950s, and was adequate for the population of the university at that time. It functioned for thirty years unchanged without supervision, with the least possible maintenance and equipment replacement, and was used on an average of a few hundred times per week. Then came two unpredictable events: A large room twice the size became vacant at the same time a benefactor agreed to fund a redevelopment of the space. The weight room was dramatically enlarged and improved.

The pattern of usage responded. Those who habitually used the room came more often and stayed longer. Persons repelled by the poor facilities in the preceding years were now attracted to the new ones. They began to use them and the word went out. Use of the room began to snowball exponentially as more people told more and more people about the new facility and its services. Within a year, the frequency of usage began to number in the thousands per week. Soon, however, a new force began to influence the situation. As thousands crowded into the facility, it became less comfortable; costs in inconvenience began to rise. As this happened, some marginal users gave up, spent less time, or came less often, and the rate of increase in users slowed down. One year later growth ceased, and the usage rate stabilized at a new and much higher level.

The new level can be expected to continue until a new force develops to alter it. Of course, we can predict that if the carpets wear out, the supervision slips, the hours are reduced, the equipment is not maintained, and so forth, the costs of participation will rise against the benefits, and usage will further decrease. We can be certain that these effects will occur since we have experienced such effects in like facilities in the past; wear and tear are familiar effects. Of course, what cannot be predicted is whether the current fashion for men and women of all ages to engage in all forms of weight training will continue. So if we maintain the facility at its current level as a plush, efficient, and well-managed facility, we can predict that the pattern of current usage will continue. The critical question becomes one of projecting whether new fads, fashions, or technologies will disturb the current pattern. In physical education we are influenced significantly by the size of our clientele; thus we should watch for signs of change in our usage statistics and in the world around us. When these are detected, we can intervene by changing the things that we can change to maintain as high a level of service to as many people as possible.

The weight room usage curve has changed along an S-shape. It first accelerated away from its baseline as a result of new circumstances. After a while, growth itself introduced impediments to further growth, and the rate of growth decelerated. Finally, the curve settled at a new level. This curve is commonplace and expresses a life cycle of a force for change. The new force appears after a while to be producing a linear effect. Other things being equal, this could theoretically continue forever. However, the effects of the first force eventually induce other forces that limit its potency, and change eventually ceases. In the weight training room example, without the interventions necessary to maintain the facility, usage itself will debilitate the setting, and the usage curve can be projected to turn downward again toward zero as the resource is exhausted.

The forces inducing trends in the usage rate can be defined. The first force, the enlargement and refurbishing of the room, was self-reinforcing. It induced accelerating change. However, later in the cycle it became self-limiting because it induced a second force—overcrowding. The new effect prevented the continued growth induced by the first force. In making predictions and projections, one must take into account whether the forces being dealt with are self-reinforcing or self-limiting. In fact, given the prevailing conception of the world as a finite resource, it can be assumed that eventually self-limiting conditions will be reached in every prediction and projection.

Projecting and Predicting for Activity and Leisure

The example concerning attendance at a weight training facility represents a situation of very limited importance. Providing predictions and projections for physical education as part of the leisure market is relatively easy if one is interested in massive processes like the percentage of the gross national product that is spent on leisure services and products. The predicted statistics are the result of underlying forces manifesting themselves in the purchasing decisions of over 200 million people. The inertia of the process is considerable, and the trends can be projected forward with confidence. The percentage has not shifted much and as the GNP and discretionary income have grown, the amount of money spent on leisure products and services has grown also. Leisure is important to people and captures an important slice of their discretionary income.

While we as individuals or organizations may be reassured that our industry, as a whole, will grow, the critical question for each of us is whether *our part* of the industry will grow. Immediately we are faced with the problem of necessarily projecting and predicting about a tiny fragment of the activity and leisure industry. By definition, that part of interest to us will have little inertia. It will be upset by weak forces, local one-time events, and rapidly acting fads and fashions.

A recent and dramatic example of inexplicable influences on a segment of a market was the remarkable rise and fall of the video game market. For two years, the video game market rose spectacularly, and then plummeted equally spectacularly. As Valentine has described,

Industry growth seemed limitless in mid-1982 and video games were expected to penetrate 50% of all households in short order. Yet twelve months later companies in that sector reported losses totalling hundreds of millions of dollars. In the third quarter of this year (1984), retail sales of video game hardware and software fell 63%. It appears that video games will soon be little more than a footnote in the history of the leisure time industry. (1984, p. L13)

People soon discarded their video games, additional games did not sell, and the number of new customers simply did not materialize. The easiest way to think about this phenomenon is that video games were a fad or fashion. The trend ignited, burned intensely, and then sputtered out. Those banking on orderly growth in video games were disappointed, but they were not wrong. The size of the market and the percentage of growth over two years suggested the trend had inertia and could thus be projected. It was the result of an inexplicable falling from grace by the product.

The lesson for us in the activity and leisure industry is that it is very difficult to protect ourselves from the influences of fads and fashions. We should be suspicious of all trends. Just as we gear up to take advantage of them, they may sputter and die. Extrapolation is dangerous, and wise operators try to create an organization that can respond quickly to changes in fashion. The most useful stance is always to retain flexibility. Flexibility should be built into programming, facilities, and personnel. Without flexibility, we cannot respond easily, and with organizational agility, to those sudden shifts that catch us unaware.

Because projecting is difficult and fraught with error does not mean that physical educators should avoid trying. Wise physical educators will develop scenarios or prognoses for their futures in an attempt to manage the futures of their organizations and the experiences of their clients. The prognoses should always contain several answers to the question, In what ways can the prognosis be wrong, and what should be done if they are? And finally, physical educators should also be prepared for the possibility that they are correct.

References_____

Advisory Committee on Intergovernmental Relations. (1984). *Significant features of fiscal federalism: 1984 Edition*. Washington, DC: U.S. Government Printing Office.

Akin J.N. (1985). *Teacher supply/demand 1985: A report based on an opinion survey of teacher placement officers*. Madison, WI: Association for School, College and University Staffing.

Boyer, R. (1985). *Places rated almanac*. Chicago: Rand McNally.

Brooks, C. (1985). *Baseline data for physical activity participation of American adults*. Internal report, University of Michigan, Division of Physical Education, Ann Arbor.

Carnegie Council on Policy Studies in Higher Education. (1981). *Three thousand futures*. San Francisco: Jossey Bass.

Carter, D. (1985, August 26). The boom turns gray. *Seattle Post-Intelligencer*, pp. C5, C8.

Christie, W.D. (1979). *The influence of position and occasion on college football injuries*. Unpublished master's thesis, University of Oregon, Eugene.

Cohn, V. (1985, April 3). Medicine, Inc. *Washington Post Weekly Journal of Medicine, Fitness and Psychology*, pp. 11-15.

Conant, J.B. (1963). *The education of American teachers*. New York: McGraw-Hill.

Congressional Clearing House for the Future. (1985). *Tomorrow's Elderly: Issues for Congress*. Washington, DC: U.S. Government Printing Office.

DeMott, J.S. (1985, February 4). Here come the intrapreneurs. *Time*, pp. 36-37.

Dror, Y. (1975). Some fundamental philosophical, psychological and intellectual assumptions of future studies. *The Future as an Academic Discipline. CIBA Foundation Symposium 36 (new series)*, **36**, 148-155.

Drowatsky, J.N., & Armstrong, C.W. (1984). *Career perspectives and professional foundations*. Englewood Cliffs, NJ: Prentice-Hall.

Duncan, V. (1985). *Essential learning skills* (OR 97310-0290). Salem, OR: Oregon Department of Education.

Dunnett, F. (1984, October). Swimming pools: Development, programming, and marketing. *Club Business*, p. 31.

Ehrlich, H. (1985, April 12). Education's high price. *USA Today*, p. 1.

Ellis, M.J. (1987). The business of physical education. In J. Massengale (Ed.), *Trends and futures in physical education* (pp. 69-84). Champaign, IL: Human Kinetics.

Ellis, M.J., Edginton, C.A., & Howard, D. (1985, October). *Health enhancement in leisure services*. Paper presented to the American Academy of Leisure Sciences, Dallas, TX.

Ellis, M.J., & Ulrich, C.U. (1983). The Oregon story. *Journal of Physical Education, Recreation and Dance*, **54**, 14-17.

Farquhar, J.W., & King, A.C. (1984). Health promotion in health care settings. *Proceedings of Prospects for a healthier America: Achieving the Nation's Health Promotion Objectives* (pp. 21-39). Washington, DC: U.S. Department of Health and Human Services.

Fowles, D.G. (1985). *A profile of older Americans: 1984*. Washington, DC: American Association of Retired Persons.

Frankel, M.M., & Gerald, D.E. (1982). *Projections of educational statistics to 1991, Vol. 1—Analytical report*. Washington, DC: National Center for Education Statistics.

Godbey, G. (1976). Time deepening and the future of leisure. *Journal of Physical Education and Recreation*, **47**, 40-42.

Greenwald, J. (1986, July 28). A new age of capitalism. *Time*, pp. 28-39.

Hawkins, D., & Verhoven, P. (1968). *Educating tomorrow's leaders*. Washington, DC: National Recreation and Park Association.

Henry, F.M. (1964). Physical education: An academic discipline. *Journal of Health, Physical Education and Recreation*, **35**, 32, 33, 69.

Holmes Group, Inc. (1986). *Tomorrow's teachers: A report of the Holmes Group*. East Lansing, MI: Author.

Houston, P., Schiller, Z., Atchison, S.D., Crawford, M., Norman, J.R., & Ryser, J. (1984, December 17). The death of mining. *Business Week*, p. 84.

Jevons, F.R. (1975). A dragon or a pussy cat? Two views of human knowledge. In *The Future as an Academic Discipline. Ciba Foundation Symposium 36 (new series)*, **36**, 66.

Kaiser, R.A. (1986). *Liability and law in recreation, parks and sports*. Englewood Cliffs, NJ: Prentice-Hall.

Kantrowitz, B., & Joseph, N. (1986, May 26). Building baby biceps. *Newsweek*, p. 79.

Kiefhaber, A.K., & Goldbeck, W.B. (1984). Worksite wellness. *Proceedings of Prospects for a Healthier America: Achieving the Nation's Health Promotion Objectives* (pp. 41-56). Washington, DC: U.S. Department of Health and Human Services.

Kilman, L. (1985, September 17). Americans aware of fitness: Most people make time to exercise. *Eugene OR Register-Guard*, p. C1.

Klint, K.A. (1985). *Participation motives and self-perceptions of current and former athletes in youth gymnastics.* Unpublished master's thesis, University of Oregon, Eugene.

Kolbe, L.J., & Gilbert, G.G. (1984). Involving the schools in the national strategy to improve the health of Americans. *Proceedings of Prospects for a healthier America: Achieving the Nation's Health Promotion Objectives* (pp. 57-70). Washington, DC: U.S. Department of Health and Human Services.

Kraus, R. (1984). *Recreation and leisure in modern society* (3rd ed.). Glenview, IL: Scott, Foresman and Company.

Kuntzleman, C.T. (1978). *Rating the exercises.* New York: Morrow.

Lawhorn, J.B., et al. (1970). The child and leisure time. *The Report to the President of the White House Conference on Children.* Washington, DC: U.S. Government Printing Office.

Lawson, H.A. (1984). Problem-setting for physical education and sport. *Quest*, **36**, 48-60.

Lawson, H.A. (1985). Knowledge for work in the physical education profession. *Sociology of Sport Journal*, **2**, 9-24.

Leo, J. (1984, July 23). The eleventh megatrend. *Time*, pp. 104-105.

Levine, A., Wells, S., & Kopf, C. (1986, August 11). New rules of exercise. *U.S. News and World Report*, pp. 52-56.

Linder, S.B. (1970). *The harried leisure class.* New York: Columbia University Press.

Martens, R. (1975). *Social psychology and physical activity.* New York: Harper and Row.

Meadows, D.H., Meadows, D.L., Randers, J., & Behrens III, W.W. (1972). *The limits to growth: A report from the Club of Rome's Project on the Predicament of Mankind.* New York: Universe Books.

Melville, D.S., & Maddalozzo, J.G.F. (1986). *The effects a physical educator's appearance of body fatness has on communicating exercise concepts to high school students.* Paper presented at the Northwest District Alliance for Health, Physical Education, Recreation and Dance Conference, Vancouver, WA.

Miller, L. (1984). Estimates of the population of the United States by age, sex and race. In *Population Estimates and Projections—Series p. 25 #949.* Washington, DC: U.S. Government Printing Office.

Naisbitt, J. (1983). *Megatrends: Ten new directions transforming our lives.* New York: Warner Books.

National Professional School Health Education Organization. (1984). The National Professional School Health Education Organization's "Comprehensive school health education." *Health Education, 15*(6), 4-7.

O'Donnel, M.P., & Ainsworth, T.H. (1984). *Health promotion in the workplace.* New York: John Wiley.

Orlick, T., & Botterill, C. (1975). *Every child can win.* Chicago: Nelson-Hall.

Peters, T.J., & Waterman, R.H., Jr. (1984). *In search of excellence: Lessons from America's best-run companies.* New York: Warner Books.

Platt, J.R. (1975). Discussion comments on a paper by Dror, Y. *The Future as an Academic Discipline. CIBA Foundation Symposium 36 (new series), 36,* 155-156.

Reiff, G. (1986). *Fitness for Youth.* (Explanatory materials prepared with Blue Cross/Blue Shield of Michigan.) Ann Arbor: University of Michigan, Division of Physical Education.

Richmond, J.B. (1979). *Healthy people: The surgeon general's report on health promotion and disease prevention* (DHEW [PHS] Publication No. 79-55071). Washington, DC: U.S. Government Printing Office.

Richmond, J.B. (1980). *Promoting health, preventing disease: Objectives for the nation.* Washington, DC: U.S. Government Printing Office.

Rudolph, B., Leavitt, B.R., & McCarrol, T. (1985, November 18). Tobacco takes a new road. *Time,* p. 71.

Russell, G. (1986, April 28). A maddening labor mismatch. *Time,* pp. 48-49.

Seefeldt, V., & Vogel, P. (1986). *The value of physical activity.* Unpublished report of the National Association for Sport and Physical Education, Reston, VA.

Seidentop, D. (1972). *Physical education: Introductory analysis.* Dubuque, IA: William C. Brown.

Sessoms, H.D. (1986). *Education for recreation and park professionals: A paper prepared for the President's Commission on American's Outdoors.* Unpublished manuscript.

Sisley, B.L., & Capel, S.A. (1985). *Oregon coaches background survey: Background of coaches in Oregon high schools 1984-1985.* Unpublished manuscript, University of Oregon, Department of Physical Education and Human Movement Studies, Eugene.

Solomon, J. (1986, April 21). Working at relaxation: A special report on the business of leisure. *The Wall Street Journal,* pp. 19D-25D.

Spencer, G. (1984). Projections of the population of the United States by age, sex and race: 1983 to 2080. In *Population Estimates and Projections—Series P-25 #952.* Washington, DC: U.S. Government Printing Office.

Starr, P. (1982). *The social transformation of American medicine*. New York: Basic Books.

Stephenson, W. (1967). *The play theory of mass communication*. Chicago: University of Chicago Press.

Swanson, W. (1985, April). The fall of doctors. *TWA Ambassador*, pp. 60-64.

Thorpe, R.D., Bunker, D.J., & Almond, L. (1986). A change in focus for the teaching of games. In M. Pieron & G. Graham (Eds.), *Sport Pedagogy. Proceedings of the Olympic Scientific Congress, 1984* (pp. 163-169).

Toffler, A. (1980). *The third wave*. New York: Bantam.

Toufexis, A. (1986, July 21). Putting on the ritz at the Y. *Time*, p. 65.

United Press International. (1984, April 25). Fitness movement enters work-sites. *Eugene Oregon Register-Guard*.

Upward with the arts. (1985, January 14). *Forbes Magazine*, p. 12.

U.S. Department of Commerce. (1985). *Statistical Abstract of the United States, 1985. Edition 105*. Washington, DC: U.S. Department of Commerce.

U.S. Department of Health and Human Services. (1984). *Proceedings of Prospects for a Healthier America: Achieving the nation's health promotion objectives*. Washington, DC: U.S. Government Printing Office.

U.S. Travel Data Center, U.S. Department of Labor. (1985). *1983-84 economic review of travel in America*. Washington, DC: U.S. Government Printing Office.

Valentine, P. (1984, November). Leisure time. *Standard and Poors Industry Surveys*, pp. L13-33.

Van Huss, W. (1985, April). *Vital research questions: Present and future.* Alliance Scholar Address presented at the American Alliance for Health, Physical Education, Recreation and Dance Annual Convention, Atlanta, GA.

Veal, A.J. (1982). *Recreation in 1980: Participation patterns in England and Wales*. London: Polytechnic of North London.

Wetrogran, S.I. (1983). Provisional projections of the population of states, by age and sex: 1980 to 2000. *Population Estimates and Projections, Series P-25, #937*. Washington, DC: U.S. Government Printing Office.

Williams, F. (1984, October 3). Who wins the bread now. *The Daily Telegraph* (London), p. 18.

Wilmore, J.H. (1982). Objectives of the nation—physical fitness and exercise. *Journal of Physical Education, Recreation and Dance*, **53**, 41-43.

Wolf, P.M. (1974). *The future of the city. New directions in urban planning*. New York: Watson Guptill.

Author Index_____

Subject Index

A

Abortion, 90
Absenteeism, 90
Accessibility of activity and leisure programs, 101
Accident prevention, 83
Accidents, 82, 84, 92
Acculturation, 110-111, 141-142
Activity and leisure
  basic needs preemptive, 7
  consumptive, 8
  productive, 8
  "prosumption," 8
  retailing, 32, 132
  social diversity, 35
Activity and leisure industry, 5, 7, 19, 183, 189, 195
  ban on smoking, 91
  cost shifting, 62
  defined, 4-6
  economic surpluses, 9
  entry qualifications, 13
  health enhancement, 80, 100-103, 131-141
  health objectives, 89-103
  health, physical education, and recreation, 51
  in-migration, 5
  inelasticity of demand, 10
  management, 185-186
  market size, 39, 69-70
  mission, 7, 74, 90, 176-182, 194
  population diversity, 24
  population effects, 43
  population shift, 51-55
  prediction, projection, and prognosis, 203-204
  secondary, 7-8
  service industry, 39
  sex roles, 24
  sport, 153-158
  subsidy, 150
  support source, 9, 66-68
  U.S. health objectives, 90-103
  work and leisure shifts, 61
Activity and leisure personnel, lifestyle role models, 100-103
Activity and leisure programs, 69, 176, 180-182
  access, 101
  access as a moral problem, 101-103
  adolescents, 82-83
  adults, 84-86, 116-128
  alcohol use, 92-93
  children, 82, 106-114, 167-176
  handicapped and disabled, 88-89
  healthy foods, 94
  infants, 80-81
  maldistribution, 101
  older adults, 87-89
  smoking, 91
  stress, 99-100
  young adults, 82-84, 114-116, 167-176
Activity and leisure retailing, 7, 32
Activity choice, 36
Activity industry, 12
Adapted physical education, 92-94, 177, 179, 184
Adolescents, 82-83
Adult health care market, 85
Adult health enhancement, 84-87, 194
Adult health enhancement programs, 86
Adult market, 117, 149, 158, 165, 182, 189
Adult motives for participation, 116, 161, 198
Adult participation rates, 117-126